Everything You Wanted To Know About Freelance Writing

How to Develop Article Ideas and Sell Them to Newspapers and Magazines

&

How to Find, Price and Manage Corporate Writing Assignments

Paul Lima

Published by
Paul Lima
www.paullima.com

Everything You Wanted to Know about Freelance Writing
Copyright © 2010 by Paul Lima

Cover design, Paul Lima
Copyright © 2010

Published by Paul Lima
www.paullima.com/books

Manufactured in the U.S.A.
Published in Canada

All rights reserved. No part of this publication may be reproduced, stored in or introduced into a retrieval system, or transmitted in any form or by any means (electronic, mechanical, photocopying, recording or otherwise), without the prior written permission of both the copyright owner(s) and the above publisher of the book.

Second Edition 2010

Library & Archives Canada/Bibliothèque & Archives Canada Data Main entry under title:
Everything You Wanted to Know about Freelance Writing
Lima, Paul

ISBN 978-0-9865630-9-6

1. Title

Preface

Welcome to *Everything You Wanted to Know About Freelance Writing*, a workshop-in-a-book that combines two popular books on freelance writing: *Business of Freelance Writing: How to Develop Article Ideas and Sell Them to Newspapers and Magazines* and *The Six-Figure Freelancer: How to Find, Price and Manage Corporate Writing Assignments*.

The first part of this book is devoted to an overview of the freelance writing business, including what you need to get started, time management, and the twin fears that hold most writers back.

The second part of this book is devoted to developing article ideas and pitching them to periodical (newspaper and magazine) editors. It also covers how to conduct interviews and write article leads.

The third part of this book is devoted to freelance writing for the corporate market (large enterprises, small and medium businesses, and non-profits) and focuses on how to find, price, and manage corporate writing assignments.

Unlike many other books on writing, this one makes no outlandish promises of instant riches or mega-success. Freelance writing can be a lucrative business or it can produce a decent, steady income. Sometimes it can be frustrating. It can also be personally rewarding. That is the nature of freelancing: it ebbs and flows. You need a plan to minimize the ebbs and maximize the flows. In many ways, that is what this book is about: creating the plan that will help you become a successful freelance writer.

When it comes to the business of freelance writing, this book is meant to point you in the right direction, get you started, and help you avoid common mistakes many beginners (and some veterans) make. Through the advice, hints, and tips in this book, I hope to inspire you, give you options to pursue, and help you create a solid foundation upon which to build as you launch or boost your freelance business. Beyond that, it is up to you to do the work required to succeed—on your terms. But this book can help you do it.

As Gord Graham, freelance writer (www.thatwhitepaperguy.com) and past-president of the Professional Writers Association of Canada, writes:

"The Six-Figure Freelancer delivers an exciting message: freelance writers can make a good living! I urge any freelancer struggling to make ends meet to get Paul Lima's down-to-earth book, study it, and do what it says. You will look back and realize this was a turning point in your writing life."

Paul Lima
www.paullima.com

Contents

Part One: Getting Started

Chapter 1: What Freelancers Do 1
Chapter 2: Reality Check 5
Chapter 3: Time Management 12
Chapter 4: The Twin Fears 20

Part Two: How to Develop Article Ideas and Sell Them to Newspapers and Magazines

Chapter 5: Know Your Editor and Audience 26
Chapter 6: Do the Math 34
Chapter 7: Clustering Introduction 37
Chapter 8: Ideas: Developing Your Own 41
Chapter 9: Discovering More Article Ideas 49
Chapter 10: Building Your Portfolio 54
Chapter 11: Querying Editors: Overview 58
Chapter 12: Sample Query Letters 65
Chapter 13: More Sample Query Letters 73
Chapter 14: 20 Rules for Query Letters 79
Chapter 15: Multiple Submissions/Follow Up 82
Chapter 16: Writing Article Leads 86
Chapter 17: Soft and Feature Article Leads 99
Chapter 18: Finding Markets 111
Chapter 19: Idea Acceptance: Now What? 115
Chapter 20: Research and Interviews 121

Chapter 21: Copyright and Business Issues 134
Chapter 22: Additional Query Letters 140

Part Three: How to Find, Price and Manage Corporate Writing Assignments

Chapter 23: Business Vision 150
Chapter 24: Do the Math, Again 158
Chapter 25: Corporate Market Services 163
Chapter 26: All About You 173
Chapter 27: Target Corporate Sectors 182
Chapter 28: Business Plan 188
Chapter 29: Five Marketing Arrows 198
Chapter 30: Generating Repeat Business 200
Chapter 31: Networking Success 210
Chapter 32: Advertising and Promotion 220
Chapter 33: Cold Calling and Direct Mail 228
Chapter 34: Cold Calling 235
Chapter 35: Sample Pitch Letters 242
Chapter 36: Online Strategies 246
Chapter 37: Marketing Plan: Big Picture 255
Chapter 38: How Much to Charge? 262
Chapter 39: Accurately Pricing Services 270
Chapter 40: Managing the Process 284
Chapter 41: Cold Call Tips; Final Notes 292
About the Author 294

Everything You Wanted to Know About Freelance Writing

Part One:

Getting Started

Chapter 1: What Freelancers Do

So, you want to be a freelance writer. *Why?*

   I presume you have asked yourself this question. I hope your answers included some of, or even all of, the following:
- I enjoy learning.
- I like to conduct research.
- I like to interview people (even though I consider myself shy).
- I don't mind having to bug people about getting back to me.
- I like to talk on the phone, use e-mail, surf the Web.
- I love to write; I live to write!
- I like to edit.
- I'm okay with having someone else edit my work (or I'm not okay with it, but can accept it if it means I get paid to write).
- I'd like to use what I like to do to earn an income, albeit one that may be rather modest in the beginning.
- I want to run my own business.
- I work well on my own.
- I am disciplined—or can be when I have to be.
- I thrive under the pressure of deadlines.

Does that sound like you? If not, now is a good time to pause and think about what it means to be a freelance writer, especially one who focuses on writing for newspapers and magazines or for corporate markets. Most of your work is done from home, on the phone or by e-mail, although you may meet interviewees in coffee shops, at their homes or at their places of business.

   If you are a travel writer, you will travel—but you will be working as you move from place to place, which can actually interfere with the pleasure of travel. Also, the money isn't the greatest, especially when you first start out. As with any business, it can take you a year or more to build up your network of contacts and generate repeat business. (But I will have more, much more, to say about money later in the book).

But if that does sound like you, *bravo*! Let's get started.

What do freelance writers do?

When it comes to acquiring and publishing articles, periodicals (newspapers and magazines and some websites) are voracious beasts. Although most newspapers have full-time staff, they also hire freelancers to fill in the reporting gaps and to write articles for special sections. In fact, editors at an incredible number of newspapers, magazines, trade publications, and news, lifestyle and information websites hire freelance writers to write scores of articles daily.

Corporations are also voracious beasts in terms of consuming internal and external communications. Corporations communicate with staff, customers, vendors and suppliers, shareholders, and other stakeholders on a regular basis using e-mail, letters, brochures, and flyers; booklets and other publications; media releases; case studies; website content; videos; podcasts; and by other means.

With that in mind, you can run a full-time or part-time freelance writing business if you possess the following skills and abilities:

- Solid research and writing skills
- The ability to communicate effectively (by phone, e-mail and face-to-face)
- Basic business skills (which most people have, even if they think they do not)

For the most part, freelancers work on projects they have sold to editors, on articles that editors have assigned to them, or on corporate writing projects. Sometimes, they work from the client's office. But generally, other than meetings or interviews, they work from home—or telecommute, as it is called. On occasion, freelancers work for publications or corporations on short-term contracts or assignments.

I believe freelance writers—freelance journalists (news stories, feature articles, how-to, and other articles) or freelance corporate writers (ad copy, press releases, reports, manuals, public relations, and so on)—are in business: the business of writing. Writing, however, is only one aspect of running a freelance writing business.

As the proprietor of your own business, you are responsible for most of the following most of the time:

- Identifying your product (what you want to write about or the type of writing you want to do)
- Developing article ideas or responding to requests to write articles or documents on particular topics
- Identifying your market (editors, publishers, companies, government agencies, PR agencies, and so on) that might be inclined to buy your services/ideas
- Pitching or marketing your services to your target market
- Following up on your pitches
- Negotiating a fee for service (at times this may be fixed by the publication or client)
- Producing the goods (once you land the job)
- Invoicing for services and, on occasion, collecting overdue accounts

Does that sound a lot like work? It is. Freelance writing is a business. To be a successful freelancer, you have to work at developing your business so you can do what you want to do—write. And, of course, get paid for your writing.

Running any business involves work

There is a difference between business winners and business failures. Business winners do the work that the business failures don't even know they should do, or are—for whatever reason—unwilling to do. By the end of this book, you will know what work you have to do to get the work you want to do.

Here's a quick caveat: Most businesses fail because the owners underestimate the amount of work required to get the business off the ground and overestimate the revenue they will make in the first year or two. In addition, many businesses fail because the owners do not clearly define their services and identify their target market(s).

> "What does defining services and identifying target markets have to do with writing?" you may ask.

You are not alone in asking that question. Most freelance writers, before they became successful, would have asked the same thing.

Let me ask you this: What are you going to write about? What types of articles or documents are you going to write? What markets will you target? How will you identify the person who can hire you?

If you say you are willing to write anything for anybody, then you will find yourself writing nothing for nobody. I am not sure if that sentence is grammatically correct, but I hope the point has been made: You need to identify your services (the topics you want to write about, the types of articles or documents you want to write) and your market (the publications that are in a position to purchase your articles and/or the sectors for which you intend to write) before you start to market yourself as a freelance writer. In short, allow me to drop the F-bomb: You need *focus*.

That doesn't mean you can never write about other topics, do other types of writing, or write for other publications or sectors. It simply means focusing your article-pitching and writing-marketing efforts on what makes sense to you, given your knowledge and experience, while staying open to other opportunities.

Also, as you gain more experience, you will find that you can broaden your focus. On the other hand, some writers narrow their focus as they gain more experience and become specialists writing about niche topics or producing niche documents for niche markets. Either way is fine, as long as you are focused on what makes sense to you and your freelance business. But I am getting ahead of myself. I will have you do a lot of work on finding your focus before I get you pitching and promoting. So don't sweat the F-word for now.

One last thing. Freelance writers need to have a thick skin. It can take time to break into the writing business. Many editors and corporations have favourite writers or look for writers who have credentials in a particular area. But, as I mentioned earlier, periodicals and corporations are voracious beasts. They need to be fed daily.

There are ample opportunities to make a decent, solid, or even lucrative living as a freelance writer, as long as you are methodical and business-like in your approach to this business. And that's what this book spells out: the business-like methodology you need to adopt to become a successful freelance writer.

Chapter 2: Reality Check

Before we get into the business of developing story ideas and pitching editors or finding corporate clients, I would suggest a little reality check is in order.

If you are getting started as a freelance writer, you need to be realistic. It takes time to develop contacts and generate repeat business. So, with that in mind, ask yourself:

- Can I afford to start slow and grow?
- Can I live without a pension plan and various benefits (unless you are covered by another person's plan or until you can afford your own)?
- Can I work productively from home making cold calls, talking on the phone, sending and receiving e-mail, conducting research on the Web?
- Do I have experience writing for periodicals?

Did you answer yes to those questions? If so, carry on. If you answered "absolutely not" to any of the above, carry on as well. Obviously, you want to become a freelance writer—and the good news is you don't have to give up your day job to become one. You can freelance part-time and adjust to the business realities of freelancing before you take the plunge as a full-time freelance writer. If you are looking at freelance writing as a quick way to earn a load of cash, however, see the first bullet in the above list.

What if you have no experience?

Just as you would not hire a plumber, electrician, or auto mechanic who had no plumbing, electrical, or auto-mechanic experience, most editors or corporate clients (not all, but most) will not hire writers who have no writing experience.

When pitching editors or marketing your services to corporate clients, you have to demonstrate your writing ability, as we will see when we look at query letters and sales pitches. By demonstrating your ability to write, you make your lack of writing experience much less of a liability. However, that means you have to be able to write. If you have little or no experience writing news articles, profiles and features, media releases, case studies, website content, and so on, consider taking workshops and courses at your local community college or university or online to hone your writing skills.

Editors and clients will often want to see some samples of your work or a portfolio before assigning a story or a writing job. But everybody has to start somewhere. It's up to you find—or make—your starting place and grow from there. But we will discuss ways of developing and showcasing your writing ability and your portfolio.

Family ties

If you are getting started in this business and have a family, it is important that they understand what you have to do to make this business work, how you have to apply yourself even when (especially when) you are not generating revenue. Take an evening and discuss with your family what it is you want to achieve and the work it will take to realize your goals. Get the family onside early to avoid misunderstandings, conflicts, and resentment later. This can happen, especially if you work from home.

Having said that, you don't have to become a time ogre to make this business work. Freelancing has a degree of flexibility. Although most interviews and meetings take place on weekdays during business hours, a great deal of the getting-started research and marketing can be done evenings and weekends. Sometimes you may be able to give up a few hours during the day to a child, spouse, or partner. But, if appropriate, let that person know you will be researching or writing in the evening or on the weekend.

For instance, the day I wrote this, I conducted a 45-minute interview at 9:00 a.m. I worked on this book while scheduling other interviews by e-mail until 11:00 a.m. I took my daughter to pick up a friend for a play date. I did a bit of writing when we got back and then fed the kids lunch. They then played in the backyard with the understanding that they should not interrupt me unless there was an emergency (or if they were in desperate need of lemonade). Other than that, "Daddy is working!"

I'm not saying do it my way. Your circumstances may be entirely different. However, find a way to do it, because you need to be working at getting work until you have work. It is up to you and yours to make it work.

Getting started

Some businesses require a lot of cash to get started. Although you could spend a lot of money on equipment, office space, stationery, business attire, and so on, freelance writing does not need to be a capital-intensive business. In fact, you may already have what you need to get started.

Computer

It goes without saying, but I'll say it: You need a computer. It can be a Windows-based PC or a Mac. The important thing is you must be able to communicate (transfer files, e-mail, and so on) with editors, interview subjects, public relations companies, and corporate clients who mostly use Windows-based PCs and Microsoft Office. I am not saying you need a PC to be in business. If you use a Mac, you will be okay as long as you can deliver files editors and clients can read and edit.

Laptop computer

It's nice to have a laptop if you are away from the office or home office a lot, and great if you want to work while at the airport, on vacation, or hanging out in the backyard by the pool. (Yes, some freelancers have pools!)

Also, with wireless hot spots becoming more prevalent, you can use your laptop (and many other portable computing devices) to access e-mail from almost any room in your house or while at the local café enjoying a latte. However, don't break into your piggy bank to buy a laptop if you are just getting started. Buy one only if you want to use a laptop exclusively (in other words, you don't need a desktop) or can justify it as a business expense that will make you more productive or help you earn more money.

Contact management and scheduling software

The former lets you create contact lists, including names, e-mail addresses, phone numbers, and other information. The latter lets you schedule appointments.

You can set up the scheduling software to remind you of meetings, phone calls, or tasks; you can schedule reminders minutes, hours, or even days before the item is due.

The full version of Microsoft Outlook (not Outlook Express) includes a contact management application and Tasks and Calendar, two applications that let you schedule tasks and calendar entries. I find it is all I need; however, I know some writers who use more sophisticated contact and scheduling applications. Find something that works for you so you can keep tabs on your contacts and your schedule.

Internet connection

E-mail makes the world go 'round. You should be able to send and receive attached files and access the Web (where you may find yourself doing considerable research). Cable and DSL Internet connections let you connect to the Internet at high speeds and keep your phone line free. Smart phones, like the Blackberry or iPhone let you send and receive e-mail and text messages and surf the Web. If you are getting started, however, they may be overkill. Again, think about your budget and the technology you need to be productive.

Telephone

A phone is useful. A speakerphone lets you keep your hands free (to type or take notes), but the voice quality can be annoying. A headset phone keeps your hands free and the voice quality tends to be good to excellent. Without a speakerphone or headset phone, you might find business puts a kink in your neck. Literally.

Call Management

Unless you live in a remote area, you most likely have high-speed Internet access. If you have dial-up Internet access, consider a second phone line for voice calls (and faxes, although they are pretty much passé). If you cannot afford or don't want a second line, make sure you have Call Answer (voice mail). Call Answer takes messages when you are on the phone or away from your office.

Call Waiting is another option. It notifies you of an incoming call when you are on the phone. I find Call Waiting irritating, but many small-business owners use Call Waiting, often in conjunction with Call Display, to determine if they should take incoming calls when they are on the phone.

Cell phone

Consider a cell phone. It is not absolutely necessary, not if you are working from home most of the time. But if it makes you more productive or helps you generate revenue, get one. Personally, I would not rely exclusively on a cell phone. Even with the advances in technology, the voice quality can be less than stellar, compared to the voice quality of land lines. And batteries still die.

Fax machine

E-mail has all but killed the fax machine. Some editors or clients, however, may need to fax you information, so you may want fax software on your computer. You can receive and send faxes on your computer using fax software, but you may have to consider a dedicated fax machine or an all-in-one unit if you need to fax hard copy back to clients.

Before you buy

Before you buy a computer or any office equipment, shop around. Although I have had my share of fun with Microsoft applications, I recommend them because they are primarily what the business world uses. But I know many freelancers who work on Macs and do just fine in this business, especially now that Mac and PCs are more compatible than ever.

For computer or office equipment, find a local dealer you trust or a national chain with reliable warranties and return policies in case you have problems. If you buy from an independent dealer, ask for referrals and check references before you buy!

Office space

Unless you are holding meetings, all you need is space for your equipment, a small desk, and a filing cabinet. The space should be a relatively comfortable working environment that affords you privacy—away from the TV, kids' play area, and from other potential distractions, like the fridge.

If you need to meet with clients or editors or interview subjects (most work is done over the phone, by e-mail, or in the subject's office), it may be possible to do so in a kitchen or living room (depends on your relationship with the client and your family), or you might rent boardroom space for a couple of hours.

Business cards and websites

These days, business cards and websites are essential business tools. Hand out your business cards when meeting editors or potential clients for the first time and at any networking opportunity.

As for a website? A domain name (website address) is almost as important as a business card. If you are targeting corporate clients, the website might be more important than a business card.

On paullima.com, I post samples of my periodical writing (many corporate clients like to review work written for newspapers and magazines), samples of my corporate work, and my list of writing and training services. While editors will not often find you online (we will look at how you have to pitch them), I have had many clients call and ask for a quote on a job because they had been to my website and liked what they saw. I now generate about 50 to 70 per cent of my *new* business through my website.

You do not have to spend a lot of money to set up a website. If you have an e-mail account, you may even have free Web space. But you may also have an ugly Web name, like the one I used to have: http://www3.sympatico.ca/plima/plc. I suggest you register your name, or your company name, as you website address. (There is more about websites and search-engine optimization later in the book.)

Health Insurance, Pensions, and Taxes

Unless they obtain coverage, or are covered by an insurance plan of a spouse, partner, or other family member, freelancers do not have health or dental insurance. Also, unless they contribute to retirement plans, they do not have a pension plan.

As a one-person operation you are vulnerable to business disruptions due to illness. If you are the sole provider of a family, you might want to keep that in mind. Ask yourself if you can afford to work without medical or dental coverage. If you feel that you need coverage, you can look into private medical and dental plans, or into group coverage offered by some writers' organizations or other associations that cater to independent practitioners. Sometimes, you can also find replacement income plans that kick in should you become ill. These plans tend to be a tad expensive, so they can be tough to pay for if you are just starting out.

I am not saying you have to bite the bullet and pay for coverage; I am saying, depending on your situation, it is something you should think about. For instance, when I was single, I did not have life insurance. Now that I am married and have a daughter, I have life insurance.

As for a pension plan? If you just staring out, you probably don't want to think about retirement yet. It doesn't hurt, however, to speak to a financial planner to find out about your retirement plan options. It could be as simple as investing 10% of your revenue in a registered retirement plan. Also, if you are going to speak to a financial planner or accountant, ask about how much you should put aside for taxes.

I still recall the day my accountant said, "I have good news and bad news." I asked what the bad news was. She told me I owed the government a gob-smacking amount in taxes. What's the good news?" I asked. "You have had your best year ever," she said, and then we worked on a plan to put aside some money each month so that the gob-smacking amount I'd owe the government next year would not sting, as much. Also, I started to pay my taxes on a quarterly basis so that I would not have to take a chunk of change to pay the government in one shot. (In some instances, quarterly payments may be mandatory.)

If any of this seems scary, seek advice from experts and make decisions that will help you minimize any potential pain.

Chapter 3: Time Management

I find a degree of organization helps me effectively deal with editors and clients. Sometimes, for instance, an editor or client will shout, "Catch!" and throw an assignment, or several assignments, at me or ask if I can meet a particularly tight deadline. If I can quickly focus and set up interviews, do any required research, and get the work in on time (meet the deadline), I end up looking organized and professional. And it is my experience that clients and editors like to work with organized, professional people.

When I was starting out as a freelancer, I connected with the editor of *Toronto Computes*, a Toronto-based computer publication. I pitched a few article ideas and he bought one, which I wrote and filed. Then I a pitched a few more ideas. He bought a couple, which I wrote and filed. Then he started calling me with assignments.

After he did this a few times, I told him I appreciated the work and asked him why he was calling me. (I wanted to motivate other editors to do the same thing as I stated to expand my business.) I'll never forget what he said. "Lima, you're a good writer. But you get your articles in on time and meet the assigned word count. In my books, that makes you a great writer."

Deliver insightful, clean copy, on time, and meet your word count, and you are more likely to generate repeat business. Editors will be more open to your ideas. They may even call you and offer you assignments. But to get to that point, you have to be organized and you have to manage your time efficiently and effectively.

Resistance is natural

If you feel yourself resisting—thinking there is not enough time in the day to do what you want to do, or chiding yourself for being a born procrastinator—then you should understand that such resistance is natural. However, it is your job to overcome resistance by managing your time effectively. Otherwise, you will have difficulty developing your business and meeting deadlines.

I know time management can be a complex issue for some people; however, managing your time effectively can also be as simple as knowing what to do with your time, and scheduling how you will use your time based on your business priorities.

Three Ds

Let's examine time management in more detail. To start, I want to discuss the three D's.

To succeed as a freelance writer, you need the three D's: Desire, Dedication, and Discipline. This holds true whether you are new to writing or you are a veteran who wants to boost your business or take it in a different direction.

Let's look at the three D's in practical terms. The fact you are reading this book demonstrates that you have desire. However, it is tough to move forward without applying yourself to the business of freelance writing. That takes dedicating time in a disciplined manner every business day (and sometimes evenings and weekends) to get your writing business off the ground.

In short, you need to dedicate a certain amount of time each day to your business, whether you are making money or not.

Let's say you want to work 20 (or more) billable hours per week (billable hours are hours when you are on assignment, not the hours you are issuing invoices, writing query letters, marketing your services, or sorting files). And let's say you are currently working zero to 10 billable hours a week. What do you do?

I recommend you dedicate the difference (at minimum) between the number of billable hours you are working and the number of billable hours you want to work to the task of marketing your business. In other words, invest your time conducting market research (to find periodicals and editors or corporate clients), developing ideas and pitching them (query letters) or marketing your writing service, and following up—all of which is covered in detail in this book.

There is no point in dedicating yourself to this business unless you are going to be disciplined about it. Discipline means you work at becoming a successful freelance writer every weekday and every week of the year (unless you are on vacation). Therefore, every week you should either work your desired number of billable hours or dedicate those hours in a disciplined manner (which is why this book shows you how to build a marketing plan) to tasks that will help you expand your business.

Take the "Timesheet Test"

Before you can start to manage your time, it helps if you know how you are using your time. With that in mind, I want you to take the Timesheet Test. For the next four weeks, keep a detailed timesheet that outlines how you spend your day. Be ruthless in what you record. You can set up a timesheet in your word processor, spreadsheet, or even a paper-based journal.

A typical timesheet starts at your waking time (or post-coffee time) and goes to six or seven in the evening (or later if you are a night owl). You may even want to include weekends in your timesheet.

What you are doing is trying to turn desire into dedication and dedication into discipline. It is far too easy to say you are working at your business when, in fact, you are not. The timesheet is your reality check. Look at it at the end of each week (or even at the end of each day) and see whether you have invested time in marketing, promoting, and developing your business.

By reviewing your timesheet, you can find and plug time leaks that may be keeping you from succeeding. For instance, if you watch TV during typical business hours, I would suggest you have a time leak. If you live in a city like Toronto that has four major daily newspapers and you read each one cover to cover each day, I would again suggest you have a time leak. (You might say you are conducting market research, but if you read each one each day, you have a time leak.)

See timesheet example on the next page.

Sample timesheet

Time	Monday	Tuesday	Wednesday	Thursday	Friday
8:00 - 8:30					
8:30 - 9:00					
9:00 - 9:30					
9:30 - 10:00					
10:30 - 11:00					
11:30 - 12:00					
12:00 - 12:30					
12:30 - 1:00					
1:00 - 1:30					
1:30 - 2:00					
2:30 - 3:00					
3:00 - 3:30					
3:30 - 4:00					
4:00 - 4:30					
4:30 - 5:00					
5:00 - 5:30					

While I am asking you to keep a timesheet for the next four weeks, I hope you will continue to record your activities beyond that time. You have to know how you are spending your time so you can use it as productively as possible. Also, if you do any corporate writing or editing, you will often bill on a per hour basis and submit a timesheet with your invoice. So, get used to recording your daily activities on a timesheet now, while you have time!

Is the Internet eating your precious time?

Before we move on, I want you to examine your relationship with one of the greatest productivity tools ever created. And I want you to examine your relationship with one of the greatest time wasters ever created. Ironically, the productivity tool and the time waster are one and the same: the Internet.

How do you start your business day?

If you are like many writers I know, you turn on your computer and spend an hour or more reading and replying to e-mail. You may also visit your Facebook page, check tweets on Twitter, write a blog entry, read online newsletters and newspapers, and surf the Web.

Does that sound like you?

If not, congratulations. The Internet is not eating your precious time. You do not have an Internet time leak to plug. If all the e-mail you read and all the Web-surfing you do is directly related to conducting your business, then, once again, congratulations. You are managing your time well. (If you are not making the money you want to be making, you might not be managing it as productively as you can be managing it, but at least you are not wasting it.)

If, however, you start your business day with lengthy personal or non-business-related e-mail and Web-surfing sessions (such as spending social time interacting with friends on Facebook and followers on Twitter), allow me to ask you a simple question: Why are you allowing other people to set your agenda and steal your time?

If you have assignments, requests for quotes, research material, feedback on first drafts, and other business-related information landing in your in-box daily, then you should start your day reviewing work-related e-mail that generates billable hours. If, however, you are launching your freelance business, or if you are attempting to boost your freelance income, time spent reading personal e-mail and surfing the Web is, in short, time wasted.

How should you start your day if you are not working the money-making hours you want to work? You should start your day conducting marketing tasks (that will be outlined in this book) that will generate billable hours.

Why do so many freelance writers (website designers, graphic artists, consultants, and other independent practitioners and small-business owners) start their day wasting time? Many think their problem is one of poor time management. If you think that, then you have bought into the time-management myth: "You are a born procrastinator who must exercise supernatural will to overcome this insidious malaise."

Frankly, most writers (and other independent practitioners) waste time because *they do not know how they should spend their time.* They may have some vague idea of what they aspire to do, but they do not have a road map to lead them to that destination. They do not have a business vision. They have no goals. They do not have a marketing plan.

Such people fritter away valuable hours hoping that work will find them—that assignments will fall like manna from heaven. If you have been a freelance writer for a number of years, occasionally a former editor or client may call. But can you afford to sit back and wait for that to happen as you read newspapers, watch TV, play computer games, surf the Web, or read personal e-mail messages?

Which leads me to ask, how many e-mails are in your in-box right now?

Keep your in-box empty

Believe it or not, your goal should be an empty in-box at the end of each day. Can you achieve this? Yes, you can. I am living proof. I empty my in-box by the end of each business day. However, if you need further proof that you can, and should, keep your in-box empty, read these e-mails I received from someone who took *The Six-Figure Freelancer* workshop, based on the first edition of this book.

> **July 4**: After taking your Six-Figure Freelancer workshop, I was sceptical about the importance of emptying your in-box every day. Then I found a book that also recommends emptying your in-box every day. It reinforced all you said. I am going to try it. Only 3,589 more e-mail messages to go!

August 1: I did it! I cleaned out my in-box and now I'm keeping it that way! Take that, 3,589 e-mails! I can't believe it! I feel like this gigantic weight has been lifted from my shoulders.

Focus on work-related tasks

E-mail messages in your in-box can move your focus off the tasks you are supposed to do to develop your business. They can also lead to an overwhelming and overpowering sensation that you have so much to do and no time to do it.

How do you overcome the problem, and the associated feelings? When you receive e-mail, do one of the following:

- Read and delete.
- Read, reply, and delete.
- Read and file (in an appropriate folder).
- Read, reply, and file (in an appropriate folder).

In Microsoft Outlook, as well as many other e-mail applications, you can create folders for personal e-mail and each publication or corporate assignment you are working on, and you can move relevant e-mail into appropriate folders. In Outlook (the Office version, not Outlook Express) you can also move e-mail into Tasks and Calendar.

> **Tasks** allows you to schedule tasks (like replying to the e-mail you moved into Tasks). A reminder can be set to pop up when the task is due.
>
> **Calendar** allows you to block time for meetings, interviews, cold calls, and so on. A reminder can be set to pop up days, hours, or minutes before the scheduled event. Say you have to shower and dress before you travel for 30 minutes to get to a meeting. Set your reminder to pop up two hours before the meeting so you have time to do all that.

I am suggesting that you can use Calendar and Tasks (or equivalent applications in your scheduling software) to keep your in-box empty and to schedule your time more effectively.

The use of these applications—or a paper-based to-do list and calendar—also comes into play as you land assignments. You will have to set deadlines, schedule interviews, and book time to conduct research. Plus, as you will see, you can use these tools to schedule your marketing tasks.

But I'm busy working!

Perhaps your time is already filled with paid writing tasks. That's cool. But are those writing assignments generating the kind of work you desire or the revenue you want? If not, ask yourself this: How much time do I spend looking for better-paying assignments or clients who value my writing and pay me appropriately?

If you are not writing as many articles as you want to write, doing the volume of corporate writing you would like to do, writing for markets you would like to break into, or writing for markets or clients who pay a decent rate, then you should start your day engaged in tasks that will generate the work you want to do.

Whether you are looking for a lot more or a little more work, different types of work, or better paying gigs, look at how you spend your time now and, as you go through this book, look at the ways you should be spending your time if you want to make a go of it as a freelance writer. In other words, set your priorities based on what you want to do, and dedicate your time in a disciplined manner so you can turn your writing business desire into your writing business reality.

Chapter 4: The Twin Fears

As discussed in the previous chapter, marketing is what you do with the gap between the billable hours you want to work and the billable hours you are working. It's what you do in a systematic manner with your non-billable hours so you can generate billable hours.

Writers like to write. They don't like to sell. I find that ironic because many writers write sales and marketing material. Why is it we can so easily do for others that which we don't do for ourselves? The answer is simple. Many writers, even those who write for the corporate market, don't understand that they are in business. They fail to apply basic business principles to their writing businesses.

Once you know, or accept, that you are in business, it's easier to apply business tools, business marketing tools in particular, to your freelance writing business. For instance, if you wanted to do nothing more than write for periodicals, you would follow the ten-step periodical marketing approach outlined here:

1. Make a list of the ideas about which you want to write.
2. Select the publications for which you want to write.
3. Develop a series of query letters based on your ideas and targeted to the publications you've selected.
4. Send queries to editors at the right publications.
5. Follow up.
6. Repeat as often as required—generally five to ten pitches per week—until you are busy writing.
7. Generate repeat business with the editors who were most open to your ideas.
8. Monitor your deadlines and repeat steps one to five as required to ensure a steady flow of work.
9. Search for new, interesting, and better-paying markets.
10. Repeat steps one to nine—in a planned and systematic manner.

Marketing numbers game

Almost all freelance writers who want to write for newspapers and magazines understand that the 10 steps above represent the marketing process that should be followed. But most do not follow the process, or they do not follow it in a dedicated and disciplined manner.

Most writers pitch queries intermittently and wonder why work is intermittent. Or they get busy writing and stop pitching altogether. Then, when they meet a deadline, they wonder why they have no other deadlines. Or—and this is my favourite—they freak out over the concept of sending out five to ten pitches per week.

"What if editors accept all my pitches? I won't be able to write all those articles!"

That, my friends, is what I call a *good problem*. But one that most likely will not occur. Why won't it occur? That fear—*I will be too busy*—feels real, but it's irrational. How many editors are going to buy your ideas? How many are going to buy them at the same time and have the same deadline? Besides, you can negotiate deadlines. And, if need be, you can even say "no" to an assignment.

But isn't it possible you could be given two or three assignments due around the same time? Yes. It's possible. And the problem is...?

If and when that happens, rejoice! You are in business. Pull back on the marketing throttle and work like the dickens to meet your deadlines. Same with writing for the corporate market. Too many writers are hit and miss with their marketing. They fear that they will generate too much business and, ironically, do not generate enough.

In short, unless you have editors or corporate clients calling you constantly, you have to be constantly marketing. You see, marketing is, in many ways, a numbers game. And you have to play the numbers. Yes, your marketing material (which we will look at) has to sell you and your services effectively. But there is no point in putting together brilliant marketing material and then sitting on it because you are afraid you are going to be *too* busy.

Twin fears

But let me address that fear—*the fear of success*—as well as one other fear—*the fear of failure*—for a moment. The twin fears hold so many writers (and others) back.

Fear of failure is easy to define. It's the fear that you will do something, like market your writing services, and fail at it. Because you have that fear, you don't market your writing services. And guess what? You fail at your business.

Or you try—perhaps feebly, or even with a lot of vigour—and things don't work out immediately. What do you do when that happens? "Woe is me," you moan. "I pitched 10 potential corporate clients last month and got no work. I am such a failure. Nobody loves me; everyone rejects me." Then you stop marketing because you fear continued failure and, of course, your writing business fails.

When people don't buy your services, they are not rejecting you. They don't need, or have not been convinced that they need, your services. You can take it personally and quit. Or you can understand that that is the nature of business—it's a numbers game—and you can keep knocking on doors.

Fear of success is more complex because it often involves elements of the fear of failure. It can, however, be as simple as fearing that you will be successful and that you don't deserve success. So, you don't do what you have to do to be successful, and you fail.

Fear of success, when co-mingled with fear of failure, goes something like this: you fear that you will be successful at your marketing, and that your marketing success will then lead to failure. In other words, you will land writing assignments, but you will suck at producing them: you will fail to please your client.

This is what the voice inside your head might sound like, if you could tap into your sub-consciousness: "What if I market my writing services and land clients? Then what? I might fail to deliver the goods. Oh my!" With that in mind, or with that in your sub-conscious mind, you don't market your services, or you do so only half-heartedly. I mean, what's the point? If you are going to succeed at landing work, and then fail to deliver it, you might as well quit now.

But that is not you. *You* are going to move forward.

But just in case it is you in some small way, allow me to tell you this: You are not alone in having those fears. Every writer has them. Most of us have both of them. I know I do. When I launch a new marketing effort, I think about all the time, energy, and money I am putting into my marketing, and I think it's all for naught. "This is stupid. Nobody is going to respond to this."

Then the phone rings or an e-mail lands in my in-basket from a new prospect. Someone has responded to my marketing effort. I should be elated, no? But instead, I think, I don't know this person or this company. I'll never be able to figure out what he needs. I can't do this. Who the hell am I to think I could be a writer?

I swear to God, it's almost debilitating. And the fears, both of them, are always there. You would think they would take a vacation or something. But no! They are always there. So, what's a person to do? Short of going into long-term psychotherapy to get over my fears, I figure I have five choices:

1. Allow my fears to defeat me.
2. Deny them.
3. Ignore them.
4. Work through them.
5. Harness the fears.

If I allow them to defeat me, I will have to go find a job. Look at my business vision, my *Why*. I don't want to find a job. Look at my *Where*. I want to work mostly from home. Look at my *When*. I want flexibility in my life. So, allowing my fears to defeat me means sacrificing my vision.

If I deny them, they will still be there, sabotaging me. Only I won't be conscious of why I am failing. I will just blame myself. But I am not in denial. The fears are there; they are difficult to ignore. It's like trying to ignore a bully shooting spit-balls at you. You can ignore him, but you still get hit with spit-balls.

You can work through your fears, which is what I used to do. That's like trying to run with a stitch in your side or a cramp in your leg. You can run, but it hurts like crazy. Still, you are moving forward, and that's a good thing.

Instead, I harness my fears. I use that negative energy like fuel, and I let it propel me into motion. Allow me to give you an analogy: Harnessing the fears is like jumping from a plane, scared out of your wits, and shouting, "*Geronimo!*" as you fall through space. It's exhilarating. Scary, but exhilarating.

For example, the first time I was asked to write a white paper—in this instance, a 20-page, research-intensive paper on Customer Relationship Management (CRM) for a major research firm—I could have let my fear goad me into declining the offer. And I was intimidated. At the time, I had read many white papers, but had never written any. I had, however, written feature articles for newspapers.

I thought about how I felt the first time I was asked to write a 2,500-word feature for a newspaper. Frightened, is how I felt. I had never written anything longer than 900 words. But I said yes—*Geronimo*!—and did all right. Sure, the editor came back to me with a few questions and had some comments on structure, but he seemed quite pleased with the first draft. Over the next seven years, I wrote a feature every month or two for that same editor. All because I harnessed my fear and agreed to take on the job.

I also thought about the time I was asked to write training curriculum for courses that were to be offered to workers in the threads and fibres manufacturing industry. I have an adult education background and had previously written training material, but I knew nothing about the threads and fibres manufacturing industry. Still, I thought for a moment and said yes—*Geronimo*!—and fell flat on my big fat face! I just could not wrap my head around the mechanics of writing training curriculum on a topic about which I knew nothing. After a couple of drafts, the client and I agreed to go our separate ways. But you know what? That was a decade ago. I survived. I learned that it is all right to say yes and flop on occasion.

Sure, the ego was bruised, but I got back up and carried on. I learned how to ask more questions, look at more samples, and check my gut before saying yes to a job that seemed, initially, out of my league. And I certainly didn't let that failure keep me from taking risks and stretching my writing wings when opportunities felt right.

So I said, "*Geronimo*!" to the research firm and wrote the white paper. It wasn't painless—took me 25 percent longer to write than I thought it would (more on estimating time later in the book)—but the job got done and, with a couple of revisions, everybody was happy. Shortly after that, I was asked to write a number of articles on CRM for a newspaper supplement. With the white paper CRM experience under my belt, that was (almost) a piece of cake.

Just as I have found my way of dealing with my fears, you have to find your way to deal with yours. Otherwise, they will hold you back. And based on my experience and the experiences of many other writers I know, there is no reason for that to happen.

Geronimo!

Everything You Wanted to Know About Freelance Writing

Part Two:

How to Develop Article Ideas and Sell Them to Newspapers and Magazines

Chapter 5: Know Your Editor and Audience

Ask any newspaper or magazine editor what they are looking for in a freelance writer and their Top 10 list might look something like this:

1. Develop great ideas appropriate to my audience
2. Pitch me using clear, concise, focused query letters
3. Follow up once, and then leave me alone
4. Be open to negotiating the article's slant
5. Conduct great research
6. Conduct stellar interviews
7. Deliver solid, focused, clean copy
8. Meet your deadline
9. Meet your word count
10. Be open to discussing edits and revisions

Artistic creativity for articles in newspapers and magazines is limited, especially when compared to fiction or poetry magazines, as writing for periodicals tends to go through several phases:

- the story you propose (query letter)
- the story the editor negotiates with you
- the story you write and submit
- the story that comes out of the editing process

If you are not able to work with your editor, you might want to consider another line of work because there is a degree—sometimes a great degree—of collaboration required when writing for newspapers and, in particular, magazines. Magazine editors will often send your work back, asking for revisions or additional information.

However, daily-newspaper editors, who do not have the luxury of time to ask for revisions, will often make changes on the fly. It's part of the nature of the work and your relationship with editors. They are the gatekeepers, standing between you and their readers. (For what it's worth, contacts in the corporate market can be even more demanding—or picky—than periodical editors.)

If you are not flexible, adaptable, and open-minded, you may find yourself in conflict with editors. This means you will not generate repeat business, which means you will spend considerable energy marketing—looking for clients.

While you can discuss your point of view, the editor, for the most part, has the final word about anything you create for their publication. You can always remove your byline from an article but, if you study the tone and writing style of the publication and discuss and define the assignment in detail up front (as this book shows you), you can minimize changes. Still, you have to expect them. But this is not a book on editing, so let's figure out where to begin if you want to make a go of it in this business.

Plethora of opportunities

When it comes to writing for the periodical market, the problem is not a dearth of opportunities but a plethora of opportunities—in terms of number of newspapers and magazines (and corporate contacts) out there and the types of articles they require. But it doesn't always feel that way because there are many freelance writers and aspiring freelancers out there too, and they are all pitching story ideas. You have to stand out in the crowd, which is why we will spend time on what you have to do to focus your ideas, to find contacts, and to best communicate with the contacts you have selected.

Before you begin to sell your ideas, you have to know your editor and audience. As a freelance writer, you are writing primarily for an audience of one—the editor. Editors hold the key to the gate through which you want to pass. If you can impress editors, they will open the gate to a much wider audience (readers) for you. Your job is to impress one editor before you can communicate with readers.

To help you send the right article idea to and editor, read the publication. Pay attention to leads (also spelled "ledes")—the first paragraph, or first few paragraphs, of the article. Do the leads start with hard news, people, situations, settings, anecdotes, clichés, research results? Do they start in the past, present or future?

By reading and analyzing the leads, you will discover what your potential editor is curious about and how he or she likes articles to begin. This information should shape how you write your query letter because the lead of your query letter, as we shall see, should mimic the lead of an article. That's how you capture the editor's attention and demonstrate your writing ability.

With that in mind, two of the most important questions you can ask before you embark on life as a freelance writer (beyond, "Will editors return my calls?" or "Will I be able to pay the rent?") are:

- Why do people read?
- Who are the readers of (publication X)?

Primarily, most people read because they want to be entertained or informed. Entertaining writing can be informative and informative writing can be entertaining. Whether you are writing to inform or to entertain depends to a large degree on:

- The publication
- The subject matter (topic) of the article
- The slant (angle) you are taking on the subject
- The primary purpose of the article: inform, educate, entertain, teach, warn, solve, persuade, and so on.

Readers are not homogeneous

Readers are not a homogeneous mass. They come in a variety of shapes, sizes, genders, colors, abilities, and ages. They have a variety of needs and a variety of opinions. Readers of a particular magazine or newspaper, however, frequently share common demographics, political or religious beliefs, social attitudes, interests, concerns, or hobbies. How can you tell what their similarities are? By what they read.

Do you read *Snowboarding Magazine*? If you do, you probably snowboard—just like the thousands of others who read it. And if you read it, you are probably (not necessarily, but most likely) male, 18 to 35, university-educated, with an above-average income. Suddenly the readers of Snowboarding start to look like a homogeneous mass—particularly to those companies that advertise in the magazine.

If you can prove to the editor of *Snowboarding Magazine* that you can meet the expectations of the readers—write in the tone and style (the language or lingo) of the readers—then you will enhance your chances of writing for the magazine.

So what are you going to write about and how are you going to meet readers' expectations? You determine what their interests and expectations are by reading the publication and looking at the advertisements. That determination will help you tailor your article pitch or query letter. (Much more on query letters later in the book.)

Repeat business

If your article meets the expectations of your editor (content, tone, style, word count, deadline) and the readers, then you have written a successful article, and the editor is more likely to use you again—be open to your pitches or even offer you assignments. If you generate repeat business with several editors, you are well on your way to generating a steady income and a successful freelance-writing career. You can then spend more time writing and less time marketing.

So how do you figure out what these expectations are?

Journal set up

Occasionally, I will present exercises meant to help you apply the material in this book. I suggest you do these exercises in a journal or a specific file on your computer. Or not. It's up to you to organize your life! I find a degree of organization helps me effectively deal with editors and assignments. Sometimes editors will shout, "Catch!" and throw an assignment at you. If you can respond in an organized and efficient manner, you will appear to be professional and that will help you generate repeat business. At least that is my experience. (Also, some editors are quite disorganized—they are busy people—so it helps if you are organized.)

Journal exercise: Analytical reading

When Margaret Atwood was asked what advice she would give to any aspiring fiction writer, she said, "Read." Admittedly, Atwood is a novelist and poet (although she has written a great deal of non-fiction). However, I would suggest her advice is also true for aspiring non-fiction freelance writers. As you read articles, ask yourself how the writing is influenced by the publication (business, consumer, lifestyle, political, industry-specific), the reader, the subject, the slant or angle, and the purpose of the article. Develop critical reading skills, become an analytical reader. Doing so will make you a better writer and will help you pitch query letters that are much more interesting and better targeted to the publication.

Before moving onto the next chapter, select a news article and a feature article from newspapers, magazines, or sites on the Web. Do some analytical reading. Use your writer's journal to make notes.

You should read each article at least three times. Read it the first time for interest or pleasure. Read it the second time for understanding. After reading it the second time, write a synopsis of the article. Keep your synopsis to about 75 words.

As you read it the third time, answer the following questions:

- What type of article is it? A personal essay, opinion piece, editorial, hard news (current story), backgrounder to the news, a profile, how-to, in-depth analysis, investigative feature, something else?
- What is the subject matter or topic?
- What is the focus/slant/angle? (The writer's take on the topic.)
- What is the purpose of the article? Are you learning how to do something? Are you gathering useful information? Are you being entertained? Are you laughing or crying?
- Did you enjoy the writing? If so, what made it enjoyable? If not, why not?
- Was there conflict? If so, what is the main issue in conflict? Who is on what side of the issue? Is the issue resolved? If so, how? If not, why not?
- What captures your attention and what holds your interest—the conflict, the overall writing style or tone, the purpose, or all of the above?

Also, examine the writing structure of each article you analyze:

- How does the article start (the lead)?
- What does the writer do in the lead to draw you in? (The lead is generally the first paragraph or two of news articles; feature article leads are usually longer; more on leads later in the book.)
- If you were successfully drawn in, exactly how was it accomplished? What captured your attention?
- How does the writer keep you moving through the article? How does the writer keep you interested?
- How does the article end? Is it a satisfactory ending? Why or why not?

- Where in time and space does the story begin? Where does it end?
- How does the ending relate to the beginning, if at all?
- If the writer uses quotes or paraphrases, when, where and why does he do this?

This analytical reading exercise should be done a couple of times a week as you make your way through this book. You will learn a great deal about how to write and structure articles from this process. If this feels like work, good. It is work—work that will make you a better writer. It is also part of the work you must do if you want to target particular publications. Otherwise, you will end up like many freelancers: sending inappropriate queries to inappropriate publications, and experiencing appropriate rejection.

If you are resisting this exercise because it seems like too much work, remember this: writing is work. Analytical reading will make you a stronger, more informed, more polished writer—one who is more likely to get published.

Even if you do your analytical reading and target your query letters, you will still experience rejection. Rejection is part of the business. Don't take it personally. Editors only have so much space and they receive many article ideas. So, instead of taking so-called rejection personally, you are going to use it to your advantage. How? We will discuss how you can leverage rejection to your advantage in a subsequent chapter when we discuss following up on your queries.

What do writers write?

So what do freelance writers write for the periodical market? (We'll look at what they write for the corporate market in Part Three of the book.) They write a variety of articles for a variety of periodicals: newspapers—including daily, weekly and community papers—and magazines—including consumer, general interest, business, sports, niche and specialty, and trade magazines. In addition, they write for websites that cater to executives, business owners, and consumers.

Articles that freelancers write include:

- Hard news (politics, education, health and safety, murder and mayhem, social issues, and so on)
- Investigative features (in-depth look at many of the above topics)

- Business news (profiles of businesses and/or business leaders, financial reporting)
- Sports and entertainment
- Lifestyle news and features
- Product, movie, theatre, book reviews
- Service and/or how-to articles (Service articles are articles that are of service to businesses or consumers. They inform the reader of trends and issues and tell the reader what to do, why to do it, and how to do it. How-to articles are one of the largest service categories.)
- Columns, editorials, opinion pieces
- Industry-specific news for specific industry publications (trade magazines)
- Personality and business profiles

Let's look at news storied and features in more detail here. Later in the book, we will look at writing leads for both.

News stories

News stories are often written in what is known as inverted pyramid style. Draw a one-dimensional pyramid (okay, a triangle). Now draw one upside down. Notice when you draw a triangle upside down the 'top' is much wider than the bottom. In a news article, the writer packs as much pertinent information into the first few sentences—the lead—usually answering the story's W5 questions: Who, What, Where, When and Why. The lead also sometimes answers 'How'. (More on leads later in the book.)

News stories present the facts with little, or limited, embellishment. The paragraphs are short—sometimes only one or two sentences. The stories do not build to a climax or end with a grand flourish. Old-style news editors feel they should be able to cut off a news story anywhere after about the third paragraph and run it. If you consider yourself a creative writer, that might make you say, "Ouch!" However, newspapers are often tight for space—it's those darn ads—and editors have to edit quickly.

I mentioned old-style news editors, but the fact is news stories have evolved. Once you get off the front page of the first section or the business section, you will find articles that read like magazine features. They are more story-like, with a beginning, middle and end.

Ironically, as newspapers include more features, many magazines are moving to shorter news and service (how-to or information-specific) articles. So, it helps if you are able to master both news and feature styles. (Do your analytical reading to help you find out how!)

Feature articles

Just as newspapers used to be the primary domain of news stories, magazines were once the primary domain of feature articles. As I said, almost every major newspaper now runs feature articles and traditional news stories. And most magazines run feature articles as well as short, breezy, newsy articles. Some magazines (*Maclean's*, *Time*, *Newsweek*) are more like newspapers than traditional magazines and some sections of newspapers are more like magazines.

Rather than having a newsy W5 lead, the feature-article lead is meant to spark readers' interest and draw them into a long, leisurely look at a subject, person, or event. The lead may focus on a scenario, a person, or a detailed retelling of an event. It may pose questions. It may be blunt. It may seem, at first blush, to be obscure. If you see yourself writing feature articles, you owe it to yourself to read features analytically: see how they start, what effect the leads have on you, how they pull you into (or fail to pull you into) the story.

Because feature articles examine subjects or topics in detail, they usually involve a great deal of background research and a number of interviews. They are structured to keep the reader interested, often juxtaposing apparently contradictory details that draw the reader through to the conclusion of the feature. Editors will often work with you on the structure of a feature article. And they will never just lop off the end.

In between news and feature articles are "soft" articles. They can be found in newspapers and magazines and are generally short—250 to maybe 900 words. Typically, they focus on one topic (a new trend, a personal or business profile, a preview or review, and so on). Such articles tend to start with non-news leads that are shorter than feature leads. We will look at these types of articles in the leads section of the book.

Chapter 6: Do the Math

Before we look at developing article ideas and pitching them to editors, we should talk money.

I have been a freelance writer for almost two decades. People often ask me if one can make a living freelancing for newspapers and magazines. So what do I say when people ask me, "Can I earn a living as a freelance writer?"

"Define living."

I know some writers who make a healthy living freelancing for newspapers and magazines. And I know others who could not afford to continue as freelancers. You can say that about all sorts of people who run their own businesses. Some are successful; some are not. If you are the primary breadwinner of a family and want to own a house and car and take elaborate vacations each year, you might find it difficult to make what you define as "a living" freelancing, especially in the getting-started phase. However, that is the case with any small business. It takes time to get the business off the ground.

If, on the other hand, you live a frugal life, freelancing for newspapers and magazines beats a job that has you saying, "Would you like fries with that?"

Financially successful writers take a business-like approach to freelancing. They develop numerous article ideas, pitch the right ideas to the right editors at the right publications, and follow up. They control the amount of time they spend conducting interviews and research and writing, and they invoice for their services. If payment does not arrive promptly, they follow up.

But even the most successful freelancers hit a financial ceiling—the limit to how much they can earn freelancing for periodicals. Say, for instance, you write 50 articles in a year. That's one a week (with two weeks off for good behaviour). I actually wrote 100 articles one year, so 50 is more than manageable, even if it does not seem like it initially. (You get faster—and better—with experience.)

Articles can range in length from 200 words to 2,500 words, although you can write the occasional longer feature. Let's take an average length of 1,000 words.

Now we do the math:

50 articles times 1,000 words equals 50,000 words

But how much can you earn per word?

Community papers pay anywhere from zero to 10 or 15 cents per word. Most large urban daily newspapers pay anywhere from 35 to 60 cents per word. Occasionally they pay more for special supplements or glossy magazines they publish. And they sometimes pay more if they want a particular writer to cover a particular topic, but that's more of an exception than the rule.

Industry trade magazines pay 25 to 60 cents per word; some high-end trades pay a dollar per word. Glossy consumer magazines you find on newsstands pay 50 cents to one dollar per word. A few have cracked the one-dollar barrier, paying $1.50 or $2 per word. That, too, is the exception, not the rule.

So let's say you average 75 cents per word. Let's do the math:

50,000 words times 75-cents per word equals $37,500

If you average $1 per word, here's what you would earn:

50,000 words times $1 per word equals $50,000

Of course, if you write more articles or longer articles, or earn more per word, then your gross incomes goes up. Fewer articles, shorter articles, or earning less per word puts a dent in your income. Also, from your annual gross income, you deduct taxes, pension-plan contributions, and business expenses.

Does that add up to a living to you? Will it let you pay for rent, food, clothing, and entertainment? If so, you can make a living as a freelancer.

The fact is, many writers earn more; many earn less. Those who earn more write more articles and longer articles and/or they write only for one dollar-plus per word publications. Some writers who earn more combine periodical work with higher-paying corporate writing gigs.

Where you fit into the spectrum will depend on how many articles you can write each year, the average length of the articles, the per-word rate of pay, and if you choose to also write for the corporate market.

We will talk about money again when we look at how to discuss your rate, how to invoice, and how to follow up on invoices when you have to. But first, let's develop some article ideas.

Chapter 7: Clustering Introduction

So now you know you might have to write 50 or more articles per year if you want to earn a decent living as a freelance writer. While editors might send you the occasional gig once they get to know you, if you want to make a living as a freelancer, it is up to you to develop article ideas and pitch them to editors.

To help you with that, I'd like to introduce you to a right-brain technique I use to help me develop ideas: Clustering. I first read about clustering in *Writing the Natural Way*, a book by Dr. Gabriele Rico (www.gabrielerico.com). Clustering is a word-association exercise that will be introduced here and that you will use later to help you develop article ideas. It is also an exercise you might use after you have conducted interviews and research, but before you start writing your article, as shall be explained.

Clustering involves jotting down notes on all you know about, and associate with, a topic before you write about it. It helps you get your knowledge down on paper and lets you focus on writing by reducing the time you have to spend pondering your subject, leafing through notes, or scratching your head.

You will find a picture of a cluster below, but allow me to describe the process here. To cluster, you do the following:

1. Write a keyword or phrase in the middle of a page
2. Draw a circle around and underline the keyword or phrase
3. Draw a dash from the circle
4. Write the first word or phrase you associate with the keyword
5. Circle the new word or phrase
6. Draw a dash from that new word or phrase
7. Write down the next word or phrase that comes to mind
8. Circle that new word or phrase
9. Repeat

When you run out of word associations, return to the keyword, draw a line from it, write down the next word or phrase that comes to mind, and continue the process. When the next word-association string runs dry, go back to your keyword, draw another line and write down the next word or phrase that comes to mind. Continue with this process. Work quickly. Do not censor yourself. Put down everything and anything that comes up until you finally run completely dry.

Why draw the lines and circles? They are meant to get your brain firing on all synapses and spark the creative side of your brain. As you continue your cluster, you will soon have on your page something that looks like a messy spider's web. You may have three word-association strings; you may have a dozen or more strings. What is important is you work rapidly and do not censor yourself.

Picture is worth a thousand words

Above is a cluster using the keyword *clustering*. Doing the cluster helped me write down everything I might want to write about clustering, and then some. As you should see, it is not censored!

Clustering exercise

Before you cluster, read over the above instructions. Also, before you begin, loosen up on a scrap of paper by quickly drawing circles and dashes and circles and dashes. All you are doing here is loosening up! Once you are ready, cluster the keyword below.

If you are ready, write down the keyword and cluster. If you are not ready to cluster, take a break. But once you are ready...

Keyword to cluster:

Apple

> **When you have completed your cluster, continue reading the chapter.**

Why cluster here?

Later, you will do more clustering and use the results to help focus your article idea creation efforts. At this point, I just want you to play with the technique and get a little practice.

Clustering can be fun and practical. If you have not tried it, go back and cluster! If you have clustered, try another one. Are you writing about anything right now? Is there something you are particularly interested in? Pick a keyword and cluster. See where it takes you. Or, if you want additional words to cluster, try any of these keywords:

- *money, time, help, work, education*
- *passion, hobbies/interests, weather, Christmas*
- *home, mother, father, health, dinner*
- *favourite actor, music group, movie, book...*

Or come up with other words to cluster. The point is to try a few more cluster exercises before you read on.

Journal exercise: Writing

Turn that cluster into writing! That instruction might seem vague, as all you have is a web of words and phrases. But take a look at your cluster and let it inspire you to write (without conducting any other research) a page or two on one of the topics you clustered. Choose any slant or angle, any tone or style you want. You should find something buried in your cluster that will get you started. If not, try some other clustering exercises and see what they inspire.

Have fun with it. Because, if this is not fun—you pick the topic, conduct internal research, and write freely—then you have to ask yourself if you really want to write. So, go ahead. Before you read on, take some time to cluster and write.

Practical clustering application

Clustering can be applied to any writing. If you research a topic, you can cluster a key phrase associated with it before you write. Examine your cluster and you might find a natural outline. Organize the outline and fill in the blanks, so to speak, before you write a first draft.

I once had to write a report about establishing a continuing-education computer-training department for a college. After a great deal of research and several meetings where many opinions were expressed, I sat down to write... and found myself blank. I was on information overload and could not think straight. So I clustered:

Computer Education Centre

Clustering helped me put on paper all issues, costs, benefits, and challenges that had been discussed in various meetings and other reports. The cluster allowed me to create an outline with sub-points under each heading. Then, all I had to do was fill in the blanks.

Four hours later, the first draft of the report was complete. Yes, I had to go back to some of the research I had done to get prices, projections, and other details, but I knew where in the report this information was to go.

Whether your are writing articles for periodicals or documents for corporate clients, clustering can help you work faster, more efficiently and even more creatively. It's what you are paid the big bucks to do.

Try it. You might be amazed at how well it works.

Chapter 8: Ideas: Developing Your Own

Now that we know how to cluster, let's apply it and develop article ideas. But first: have you done your analytical-reading exercise? If you still require motivation:

> "When you find a story in which you absolutely loved a character, re-read it 10 more times for business: analyze every line to learn how that author made you laugh or cry. When you learn the secret, use it in your next story."
> — W. P. Kinsella

Although Kinsella (author of *Shoeless Joe*, which was made into the movie *Field of Dreams*) is primarily a novelist, what he is advocating here is appropriate for freelance writers. By the way, when he says "use" what you've learned, he is not advocating plagiarism. He is talking about modeling or applying techniques used by others to your writing. It's worth stating again: you can learn a great deal about writing by reading and by analyzing what you read.

Finding ideas

I am an advocate of conducting internal research to discover ideas for articles. Allow me to start with a few words from Gabriele Rico, the author of the critically acclaimed *Writing The Natural Way*: "What the writer often lacks is not ideas but a means of getting in touch with them."

Developing ideas is essential if you are to develop your freelance-writing business. Many people who want to write feel they lack ideas for articles. Conducting internal research is one of the best ways to find ideas for your writing; clustering is one of the best ways to conduct internal research. It helps you find ideas and helps you put flesh on the bones of your ideas.

What comes first?

Some aspiring writers buy writers' directories, look up addresses of publications, and pitch dozens of query letters helter-skelter to publications in the directory. The question I pose is this: "What comes first, the chicken or the egg? The article idea or finding publications?"

I say the idea comes first. Of course, I've been wrong before, but stick with me here for a moment.

Writers' directories can be intimidating. They list hundreds of newspapers and magazines in dozens of categories. Looking through writers' directories (or websites that list periodicals) will have you running all over the place trying to find ideas that fit the publications in the directory. What I suggest you do it this: develop a number of ideas and then go looking for the appropriate markets. That seems a more focused way of working. Ultimately, you have to decide if you want the chicken or the egg to come first. And, if you do the opposite of what I say and it works for you, then keep on doing it.

Sometimes, I confess, I go magazine shopping to see if looking at a variety of magazines can inspire me. But not often. Am I going to write for hundreds of publications? I think not. I've written for fewer than 35 publications and I've been making my living, successfully, as a freelance writer for almost two decades.

Why might you write for only a few publications? The secret to successful freelance-writing is focus, coupled with repeat business. To become focused, you have to develop excellent ideas and pitch them to selected publications. If editors like your ideas and you do your job well (deliver clean copy on time to the assigned word count), editors will be more open to new queries from you, and might even toss you assignments. That equals repeat business. Once you are writing for half a dozen or so publications on a regular basis, you spend less time pitching queries and more time writing for pay.

By developing focus—expertise in the areas about which you write—you will reduce your per article workload and be able to recycle ideas and reuse research material. That means you will be able to write more articles more quickly, and increase your income. Ah, but talk, talk, talk... When do we develop article ideas?

Clustering revisited

As I'm sure you recall, clustering is a form of word association that helps you conduct what I've referred to as "internal research." As you cluster, your mind makes associations it would not have otherwise produced. Clustering gets your knowledge out in the open and can be used to spark article ideas.

Once you have written down what you know about a topic, you review it and formulate article ideas (as I will show you). Then you search writers' directory or online periodical directories and look for publications to which you can pitch your ideas. All will be explained. Let's start with clustering.

Journal exercise: Clustering

The focus here is on word association. (If you need to, reread the instructions on how to cluster, presented in the previous chapter.) Once you are ready, start to cluster the word below.

Keyword to cluster:

Writing

> **When you have completed your cluster, continue with the chapter.**

Your internal source of ideas

By reviewing your cluster, you should be able to see all associate with writing. If you wonder how that will help you develop ideas, well, it might and it might not. It depends on how creatively you look at your cluster. (We will work on looking at it creatively later in this chapter.)

The exercise above was, however, meant to help you loosen up and get you flexing the muscles on the creative side of your brain—and to get you thinking about your relationship with writing. It's okay to have a love-hate relationship with writing, but if it's all hate all the time, I'd suggest you might want to consider pursuing a vocation other than freelance writer!

Before you cluster the next word, one we are going to use to develop article ideas, let me tell you a bit about Stevie Cameron, an award-winning investigative journalist and author. For years she worked full-time for *The Globe and Mail* and wrote *On The Take*, a controversial book about Brian Mulroney's years as prime minister of Canada.

Can you guess what her first article was, the one that got her started in the writing business? Written for *Chatelaine* (a monthly magazine for Canadian women), it was "Cookies you can bake and give away at Christmas." Do you know what Stevie Cameron did before she became a journalist? She worked as a chef. Her first article started close to home, you might say.

With that in mind, here is our next exercise.

Journal exercise: Clustering

Make sure you have a fresh piece of paper, maybe two, for this exercise and cluster the new keyword below.

Keyword to cluster:

ME

That's *me*, as in *you*, not me (the book author). Cluster *me* as comprehensively as possible.

> **When you have completed your cluster, continue with the chapter.**

What to do with *Me*

What do you do with the information you have gathered through clustering ME? You mine it—hunt for writer's gold or raw article ideas. You then forge the raw ideas into article ideas you can package or pitch to editors.

One writing student, a schoolteacher, pulled the following threads from her ME cluster:

Children, mess, clean up
Education, teachers, kids, chaos, frustration

She mined the cluster threads by asking questions:

Why do kids enjoy making a mess? Why do they hate cleaning up? Can clean up time be fun time? Are there techniques teachers can use to motivate children to clean up?

Why did she ask questions? Most articles answer questions—in particular they answer *who, what, where, when, why* and sometimes *how*. Therefore, asking questions is a good place to start when developing article ideas.

Here's proof. Below is a query I sent to an editor with the *National Post*. (I had worked with this editor extensively and felt comfortable with a fairly informal query; you will see a number of examples of formal queries later in this book.)

> We hear so much about skilled immigrants who lack "Canadian" experience and/or credentials and cannot find jobs in Canada—doctors, engineers, (heard a story today about a global communications consultant, experienced with multinational firms, who has been in Canada and out of work for three years).
>
> Would you be interested in an article that looks at small and medium businesses that have hired skilled immigrants? Where do they find the employees? How do the employees stack up and fit in? What shape would the company be in without the immigrant workers? How did the immigrants overcome barriers to employment? How are they doing? (I'm not talking working at fast-food restaurants here, but skilled immigrants in positions related to their education and work experience.)
>
> At this point, I have no contacts, but if you are interested, I'd research this further. (I will not use Information Technology workers as they are kind of cliché.)

My editor replied in 48 hours with, "I like it. When can I have the story?" Again, I had been writing for the editor for several years and felt free to tell her I had no contacts. She knew me and trusted me to deliver. While I am getting ahead of myself here, I wanted to show you how asking questions, and promising to answer them, got the editor interested in my article idea. (Let's wait until the chapters on query letters for more on using query letters to pitch ideas.)

So what did the schoolteacher do with her questions? She forged an article idea by creating a short, simple benefit statement:

> Techniques teachers could use to motivate children to clean up after play would save teachers time, diminish their frustration levels, and get kids working together.

Is your article idea light going on? Can you see what she might write about? Can you start to imagine the research and interviews she would have to do before writing an article on *"How to motivate children to work co-operatively together to clean up after play time?"* Can you see the publications, or types of publications, that might buy such an article?

With that in mind, look at your *ME* cluster again to see where your cluster threads will take you. If your answer is nowhere, look harder or cluster *ME* again—spend a little more time at it. Or you might cluster some other keywords—*education, work experience, hobby, interest, passion*. Or, pick your own words.

Find ideas. That's your job. Without them, there are no articles.

Clustering in action

Allow me to share a personal mining/forging example with you. When I looked at a clustering exercise I completed when I first started freelancing, I found the following thread:

Computers – DOS – Windows – frustration – courses – productive

You might be able to tell from this that I found using computers to be a frustrating experience until I took several courses. In addition, as you may recall, I was involved with a computer education centre for a while. So it is no surprise a computer thread would be part of my *me*. Building on the thread, I asked questions such as:

To be productive computer users, should individuals take computer courses? If so, should they take them before they buy their computer? After? How long after? Should they take courses to help them buy the right computer? Should they take classes or hire private trainers? Or does it depend on what they want to do? Who benefits more from training: consumers or business people? Or does it depend? Should companies set up training internally or contract it out? If contract it out, how do you hire the right trainer and measure training results?

Can you imagine the type of benefit statements I might have created? Can you see the articles—notice the plural here; there is more than one article I could write—that might be written here? Can you imagine the publications that might publish them?

For the record, I have written numerous articles that focused on learning how to use computers and how to benefit from computer training for a variety of publications—and they were not all computer publications. One publication was geared towards parents, two towards seniors. One was a community newspaper, several were major daily newspapers, one was a small-business publication, one was a computer publication aimed at consumers, and a couple were computer trade publications aimed at businesses.

Also, for a year, I wrote a monthly column on training and education for a national computer magazine. Why did the editor pick me? I pitched him and he could see from my clips (sample articles) that I was a computer-training writing expert. Notice the word *writing* in that phrase. I was not a computer trainer but I had written about computer training from a number of angles and perspectives. Can you see how my focus on training helped me reduce my per article workload by recycling ideas and reusing research material?

I cluster ME whenever I need a kick in the pants as far as finding article ideas are concerned. It is something you too can do on a regular basis—several times a year, at least, and more often when you are getting started in this business. Invariably, something different comes up. It's up to you to see it and to figure out how you can use it.

Now go look at your *ME* cluster. See what you can find. Don't be concerned if you come up empty or with only a few nuggets. You didn't know what we were going to do with ME. So now that you know how you are going to use the cluster, you might want to try clustering ME again. Also, try some of the other words I've suggested previously, such as *hobbies, interests, passion, work experience, education* and so on.

Journal exercise

We all know more than we think we know. If you are saying, "I don't know anything" or "I don't know much," then you are creating barriers to your success.

You have the raw material for article ideas in you. You don't need hundreds of ideas to get started but you should be able to find five or more solid ideas to get you started.

Once you have clustered ME (and any of the other words I have suggested), do the following:

- review your clusters
- pull two or three threads from each of them (feel free to remove words that don't belong or to add words/phrases that come to mind)
- mine the raw material
- forge benefit statements

This process should help illuminate your article idea light bulb, help you see what your article would be about, and help you imagine some of the research you would do and the interviews you would conduct before writing any of the articles.

Once you have developed ideas for articles, look for the types of publications that might publish your article. Search your writers' directory (you can find writers' directories online at Amazon.com, Amazon.ca, Chapters.ca, and in most bookstores) for suitable publications. Also, search the magazine stacks in your local library or search the Web using the Google, Bing, or Yahoo! search engines. But don't pitch any queries just yet!

Beyond clustering

Clustering is not the only way you can develop article ideas. I have developed a number of ideas while walking my dog. I sold four of the dog walking-inspired ideas, and then sold an article, "Ideas, Inspiration and Dogs," on how I develop ideas while walking my dog. You can read that article online at www.paullima.com/articles. After reading it, you will understand why my motto is "ABC—Always Be Curious!"

In the next chapter, we will look at other ways to discover and develop article ideas, as well as how to build your portfolio. However, if you have a dog, go walk it and look for article ideas! Or, take yourself for a walk and look for them. Be curious about the world around you. That is part of your job!

Chapter 9: Discovering More Article Ideas

While you can generate scores of article ideas through clustering, it is good to look at external sources for article idea inspiration as well. Doing so will broaden your perspective and open your mind to other possibilities.

I was fortunate enough to write a bi-weekly communications column for *Fast Forward*, the former technology section of the *Toronto Star*, for seven years. I say "fortunate" because a regular gig means regular income. The downside? (There's always a downside.) Twice a month I had to come up with ideas relating to technology and communications from a consumer or small-business perspective. In other words, twice a month I had to work, whether I wanted to or not.

Okay, so it was a good problem to have.

Coming up with ideas was not as difficult after the first year or so. The research I did over the years meant I had more ideas than I could use. In addition, PR agencies were always sending me press releases with material I could build on. In the beginning, however there were weeks when my communications-column idea file was empty.

Let your fingers do the walking

One day, while looking up the name of a company in the *Yellow Pages*, I stumbled across the heading: *COMMUNICATIONS*. Thumbing through the companies listed under communications, I came across an ad for a company in Mississauga (near Toronto). The ad claimed the company had the "World's Largest Fax Machine as listed in the Guinness Book of Records." Tah-dah! Did my article idea light bulb burn brightly? It was like finding an instant article. Okay, not quite an instant article. As I have said, freelance writing is a business that involves more than writing.

Here's what I had to do to write my 'instant' article:

- Call the company; find out who the media contact was.

- Contact that person; tell him I wanted to write about their BIG fax.
- Schedule the interview.
- Do background research on fax machines.
- Develop questions to ask during the interview.
- Conduct the interview.
- Arrange for pictures of the fax machine to be sent to my editor.
- Write and submit the article.

Even if you do not have a regular column to write, the *Yellow Pages* (print or online versions) can be a great place to find article ideas. Take some time, let your fingers do the walking and see if you can be inspired by category headings and individual listings. Look at your *ME* cluster and see if you can find *Yellow Pages* headings that relate to any of your *ME* cluster threads.

By way of an aside, surfing through the *Yellow Pages* can also help you find potential markets. If you don't live in a big city, try to find the *Yellow Pages* for large urban areas at your local library, community college, city hall, or chamber of commerce. Look up NEWSPAPERS, MAGAZINES, and PERIODICALS.

Also, take a more creative look at the *Yellow Pages*. Look for headings that have hundreds of listings. Think about it. If there are hundreds of lawyers, doctors, pizza parlours, hair stylists and beauty salons, architects, accountants, jewellers, and so on, then there are publications (trade magazines) that cater to these businesses. Because of the critical mass working in these (and other) fields, advertisers want to reach them. Placing ads in trade magazines (magazines targeted at people working in specific sectors) is a good way to reach target audiences.

If there are publications that cater to these people, there must be editors of those publications looking for articles. Can you find the publications? Can you develop ideas to pitch to the editors of these publications? If you like to conduct research, you now have a business-related research challenge!

Other external sources of ideas

There are many other external sources for article ideas beyond clustering and the *Yellow Pages*.

National and international publications (or television news) are a great source of ideas. How so? If you want to write for a local or community newspaper, learn how to analyze national and international news from a local angle, one that would appeal to readers in your backyard.

Consider these two headlines:

> War in Eastern Europe
>
> Famine in Ethiopia

Are there people who have moved into your city or neighbourhood from these areas? Might a local human-interest story, one that focuses on their upheavals, adjustments, and accomplishments of these people be of interest to the editor of the local paper?

When a ski lift collapsed in British Columbia, it made the national news. Are there ski resorts in your area? What safety precautions have the owners taken to ensure the same thing can't happen there?

Several years ago, housing construction starts were down across the country. But in Barrie, Ontario (about 60 miles north of Toronto), housing starts were up. Why? (This answer might make for a local story or it might even make for a local story that has national interest.) How does your area compare with national trends? I'm not just talking about housing trends. Think in terms of housing, crime, other social or cultural issues, immigration, economic issues, legal or political issues, and so on. If your area is leading in a trend or bucking a trend, you have a local story—and you might even have a local story of national or international interest.

Now that you've seen a few examples, find several article ideas of your own by analyzing the national and international news from a local perspective.

More ways to find article ideas

You can also find article ideas by reading magazines, reference books, the want ads, and famous quotations. For example: Does a 'stitch in time' really 'save nine'? If so, how? Does this apply to sewing? Does it apply to preventative maintenance for cars, appliances, your health, retirement savings...? Can you see other article ideas in this or other clichés?

You can find ideas by talking to people—social workers, teachers, students, business people, taxi drivers, and so on. You can find them by eavesdropping on conversations in restaurants or grocery stores, by listening to the radio, and in many other places. But you have to be open to them or you will not see them. In short, it is your job to ABC—*always be curious*. So take a creative approach to thinking about article ideas.

When we got a new dog, people, total strangers, would come up to as I walked him and ask me questions about him. These people would normally not even look at me (nor I at them) on the street. But once I had the dog, it was as if we were old friends. *Ping*. On went my article idea light bulb. Shortly thereafter, out went my query (which you can read in the query letter chapter). And, 48 hours later, in came my assignment.

I met a novelist in a writers' group. During a conversation, she told me that for a long time she thought she was never going to finish her "damn novel." I asked why and she described the adversity she had to overcome to write it. Her story went beyond the typical struggling artist story. *Ping*. On went my idea light. (The query is included in the book; you can read the article, "Dreaming of Fat City," online at www.paullima.com/articles.)

As I said, it is our job to be curious. Beyond that, it is our job to translate our curiosity into article ideas, write query letters, and pitch them to the right editors at the right publications. And then, when the idea is accepted, it is our job to write and file the article.

Idea file

If you are going to find all these ideas, what are you supposed to do with them? A freelance writer should always be prepared. You should always have a pen and your journal or a small writing pad (or a personal digital assistant, smart phone, or laptop) with you. That way, if you stumble across an idea, you can write it down before you lose it. Trust me, if you don't write it down you will lose it. I've been there, done that, bought the T-shirt!

Once you have an idea written down, expand on it. Use clustering to help you get down all you know about the topic, to see where information gaps might exist, and to help you focus your research. Ask questions, write out benefit statements, jot down the type of publications—or the names of publications—that might be interested in the idea.

If you are not going to use the idea right away, file it in a properly labelled file folder you can keep in a filing cabinet or in a digital idea folder on your computer. If there is something in particular you want to write about, set up a topic folder and gather information by clipping related newspaper and magazine stories or by bookmarking articles on the Web. You don't have to print out all you find on the Web to file it. You can bookmark website addresses in your browser. When stuck for ideas, or if you have some spare time, rummage through your idea files for topics worthy of query letters.

But enough about lofty ideas. It's time for a journal exercise!

Journal exercises: Developing ideas

Remember this: no ideas equals no articles. The techniques below can help you find article ideas, but you should also find your own way to always be curious!

Read, watch, or listen to the national news. In your journal, jot down several major stories. How you organize this next part is up to you, but I'd suggest you jot down each major story on a separate sheet of paper or in a separate data file. Below the major story, write out possible local angles. How is this major story playing out in your community? Are you part of the trend or bucking the trend? Make a list of sources—people you would interview if you were to pursue this story. Jot down questions you would ask these people.

Use the *Yellow Pages*, a reference book, or the want ads to find possible article ideas. Once you find a topic that intrigues you, cluster the a keyword based on the topic to discover what you know about it. Treat your cluster the way you treated threads from the ME cluster: take a thread or two, ask questions, write out benefit statements, and jot down the type of publications (or names of publications) to which you might pitch the idea.

Search the classified ads of a major newspaper over several days. Don't stop until you find idea inspiration in the classifieds. There are dozens of ideas there, just waiting for someone like you to always be curious. Ask questions about the topic, write out a benefit statement, and jot down the type of publications (or names of publications) to which you might pitch the idea.

Chapter 10: Building Your Portfolio

It's great to have ideas and great to pitch them (as we will do in the Query Letter Chapter) but if you have not done any writing or have only done a little, how do you let editors know you are the right person for the job? Most (not all) editors want to see writing samples (clips) before they will hire you. There are several ways to build your portfolio. If you don't have a portfolio, I suggest you try some of these ideas. If you have one, you might want to skim quickly through this chapter and move on. Having said all that, a brilliant query letter can go a long way to convincing an editor to give you a shot.

If you have no articles (or only a few) published, you may have to do some writing for free to build your portfolio. Some writers might disagree with this approach. They say you should never give anything away. I suggest you never give away your work to publications that normally pay writers. Instead, carefully target publications close to you that can use your writing services. *You* is who you are, what you do, the organizations you belong to and so on.

Check your *ME* cluster. Do you belong to a church, school, community or business organization, hobby or non-profit organization, company or agency, union or association? Does it publish a newsletter, magazine, or some other in-house publication or website? Often in-house publications or websites are edited by overworked volunteers. Find out if you can contribute to a *you* publication or website (one that is close to who you are and what you do). They are great places to get a few articles published under your name (known as a byline). If you land a gig, be professional in your dealing with the editor: deliver solid copy, meet your assigned word count, and file your copy on time (meet your deadline).

While many local church, community, school, and business organizations produce local newsletters, they are often part of a provincial, state, or national organization. And the provincial, state, or national organization may produce a glossier publication. Can you contribute local news to it? Or write on bigger issues for it? Find out.

Some associations produce professional newsletters. Many of these publications have editors on staff and pay for contributions. If you are a member of an association that produces a professional publication, find out how you can contribute articles to it. Instead of submitting a formal query, e-mail or phone the editor and ask if he or she can send you the writers' guidelines (information or guidelines on what types of articles the publication is looking for, how to query the editor, and how to submit articles if your query is accepted).

Also, as you successfully complete freelance freebies, ask the people you've worked for if they will act as references, give you testimonials (for your website), or refer you to others who might be able to pay you to write. Having said all of that, a brilliant query letter can go a long way to convincing a editors to give you a shot. But it does not hurt, and it can help, to build your portfolio.

Other ways to generate clips

Consider writing letters to the editor. While most community newspapers or newspapers in small towns print every letter they receive, newspapers in larger cities and national magazines select letters. Read the letters published in several major publications for style, tone, and content. Read several articles in the publication and select one to respond to. Write your letter and mail, fax or e-mail it to the editor. Instructions for submitting letters are included on the letters page or as part of the publication's masthead (the area in the paper where you can find the editor's name, the publication address, and so on), or on the publication's website.

If you live in a small town or a defined community in a larger urban area, there may be a local newspaper or a community newspaper in your neighbourhood. The paper might have an open space where columns from community members are published. If not, the editor may be open to accepting article or column proposals. The editor may even pay a small honorarium for published work. Call or e-mail and ask for details.

Perhaps your local or community paper publishes book and movie reviews. They may even pay for the articles, or at least for the book or the movie ticket. If you have never written a review before but are interested in doing so, read and analyze reviews in other publications first. Then write up a few sample reviews to show the editor. This may replace formal clippings and land you a gig.

Most large city newspapers have an op-ed page, the page near, before, after, or just opposite the editorials, where they publish freelance work pertaining to national, local, political, social, or personal issues. They may also have open space pages. For instance, *The Globe and Mail* publishes a personal essay each day on its Facts and Arguments page. Check out the op-ed pages or open space pages of several papers and submit articles. Such articles are generally submitted on spec: you write and submit the article without sending a query letter. If the editor likes it or finds it topical or appropriate, he publishes it and sends you a cheque for a small amount.

Submitting on spec

When you submit on spec (speculation), you write the article, submit it, and hope the editor will run it and pay you for it. While submitting on spec to the op-ed page is one way to try to get published, some freelancers never query and only submit articles on spec. However, not all publications accept articles on spec. Check the masthead or writers' guidelines (which may be online or available by e-mail).

Those who write on spec tend to write about topics they know well, so they do very little background research and conduct few, if any, interviews. I have written on spec on occasion but stay away from it now, as do most freelancers. I do not advocate submitting on spec beyond the getting started phase because when you submit on spec, you do the work with no guarantee of publication or payment.

Again, writing on spec might be a way to get a byline or two, but it's not how you make a living as a freelance writer. Also, most editors do not like on spec submissions. They'd rather review article ideas (query letters) and discuss the idea, word count, due date and other details with the writer. Your on-spec article might be too long, too short, or not well focused. This essentially means you went to a lot of work to write the article when you could have sent in a query and then gotten paid for writing the article the publication was actually looking for. So query first. But don't fall in love with your query ideas. Editors might accept your basic query but ask you to alter the focus somewhat. In other words, if you have a thin skin, work on thickening it so you can work with, not against, your editors.

My give-aways

Have I ever given my writing away?

For the record, I got my first byline by writing for my high school newspaper. I also wrote several free articles for my university (York University) newspaper and college student magazine. I also worked as the editor of an in-house employee newsmagazine and wrote articles for the publication.

Outside of school and work, my first article was a review for a community paper. It was about musicians who had played at a local coffee house. I made no money for the review but it didn't bother me because the coffee house (which I supported) benefited from the publicity.

When I launched my freelance business, I wrote an article on changes in the education system for a community newspaper. The paper didn't pay for the article, but it agreed to cover my transportation expenses to and from the event. After filing my article, I submitted an invoice for $4 to cover bus fare. Seeing the $4 figure on the invoice must have made the editor feel as if she was exploiting me because she sent me a cheque for $10. Somehow, I felt I had arrived and I have been paid for my words ever since.

So do what you need to do to get your first couple of articles published. Then it's time to get paid for your writing!

Chapter 11: Querying Editors: Overview

At this point in the book, you should have some sense of the following:
- what freelance writers do
- what editors expect
- how to develop ideas
- how to build your portfolio

All of this is important background. But, let's face it, you can do all that (and I encourage you to do it; it is vital), but that doesn't make you a freelance writer. You become a freelance writer when you start selling ideas to editors who pay you. To sell your ideas to editors, you need to pitch them using the query letter.

If you ran a business manufacturing widgets and wanted Sears to buy your widgets, you would pitch the benefits of your product to an appropriate product buyer at Sears. If you baked pies and wanted to sell them to consumers, you would open a storefront and promote your pie business. The query letter pitch and the follow-up are your sales and marketing tools. Without using them, you will be hard-pressed to become a freelance writer.

Many freelance writers have difficulty with the idea of sales and marketing. Perhaps because they see writing as a creative or artistic process, they feel marketing sullies the art. Although I see writing as a creative process, I see freelance writing as a business—one that involves sales and marketing—as well as the creative process.

Almost anybody so inclined can write without selling. I have written many short stories and poems that I have not sold. (I have also sold a number of them—not for much money, I confess.) I do not confuse writing short stories and poetry with my freelance-writing business. Simply put, if I didn't market my writing services and sell my ideas, I would not earn a living as a writer. I want to earn my living as a writer, so I market my services and sell my ideas. Full stop.

Target market

When pitching ideas, I target my markets. It is better to send a few queries tailored to publications you know publish articles like the ones you are proposing, than to send a generic 'are you looking for writers?' query to 20 or more magazines in the hope one might bite.

There are two basic approaches to marketing your work—submitting unsolicited manuscripts (on spec), which we have touched on, and querying (pitching ideas) by mail or e-mail.

You can also pitch article ideas by phone. I don't recommend it, but I know a few writers who have been successful at it. The fact is, editors are busy people. If they are on deadline, trying to get their publication out to the printer, and you call with an idea, they are likely to quickly say no and you will get shot down before you get to take your best shot.

It is better to send an e-mail query letter and let the editor review it when he or she has time. It is also easier to follow-up on a query by phone than it is to pitch an idea by phone, but more on follow-up later. Overall, I favour the e-mail (or mail) query for three reasons:

1. It is what most editors expect from freelance writers.
2. Many editors will not look at unsolicited manuscripts—a query is shorter, easier to read, and demonstrates the writer's knowledge of the topic and their ability to write.
3. It takes work to write a query letter but it takes more work to write an article; I want to know that I will be paid to write an article before I do the work.

New writers are often concerned that editors may not buy their ideas because they have limited or no writing experience. By submitting the full article, the writer hopes the editor will like and buy it. More often than not, however, the article is too long, too short, not focused enough, or not focused on what the editor would have wanted. Or simply does not get read.

Why would you research and write an article, and then submit it not knowing if the editor wants it? The query letter, on the other hand, is your calling card. It is proof you have done some thinking and research and can write. It gives you the chance to sell your idea and yourself. It is where the business of freelance writing starts.

Editors expect to receive query letters. They know writers who submit or pitch their article ideas using query letters understand how the business of freelance writing works. In short, freelance writing is a business and query letters are your primary sales and marketing tool, especially when you are getting started.

Query: *Pitch*-er perfect

Again, query letters are the classic way of pitching ideas to editors and demonstrating your ability to write articles based on your ideas. When you think of your query as your basic marketing tool—a sales letter customized to solicit business from a very targeted market (one editor)—it all begins to make sense.

Your query letter must be focused on the idea and flawless—no spelling or grammatical errors—in execution, reflecting the detailed care you will give your article. For newspaper or magazine articles, a query letter addressed to the editor will outline the following:

- Your article idea—the focus of the article or what the article is all about.
- The sources, or potential sources, of information.
- Why readers (of the target publication) would want to read the article (demonstrating your knowledge of the magazine's readership).
- Why the article should be written now.
- Why you should be the one to write the article, i.e., a paragraph about you (which your *ME* cluster should help you write).

Your writing must be impressive—tight and creative, but not far-out and wacky (unless you are writing for a far-out and wacky publication). Even then, you want to be professional. You want to intrigue the editor and tickle his or her curiosity.

Also, your central idea must seem like something the publication's readers would be interested in or benefit from, and it must be credible. If you propose to profile or interview the president or prime minister, for example, and you have no political experience or no obvious access to that person, the idea will not appear to be credible. It will appear to be beyond your reach, unless you explain exactly how you will accomplish what you propose to do.

Query opening example

Allow me to show you an example of a query subject line and lead (opening) I consider about as close to perfect as you can get.

> **Subject**: Article Query: Show your true love
>
> Dear <Editor's Name>:
>
> The same bunch of roses that says "I love you" to a mother or "I'm sorry" to a lover could mean long-term illness in communities where they were grown. Doctors studying the issue in Ecuador have revealed the thorny side of the cut-rose industry as they work toward a fairer flower.
>
> The predominantly young workers who toil in the cut-flower industry do not always notice they have medical problems, which tend to manifest later in life. Others, like one young mother I met while attending a community clinic held by the Centre for Studies and Consultation in Health (CSCH), cannot hold a pen straight and exhibits other disorders. But she continues working with cut flowers to make ends meet.
>
> Dr. Jaime Breilh of the CSCH says they first thought poisoning through acute pesticide exposure was making cut-flower workers ill. As they studied the issue, however, they learned low-dose chronic exposure to pesticides caused the problems.

Of course the query goes on from there, as you will see from other examples in the book. But what I want you to do here is imagine this query with the above subject line landing in the editor's in-box before Mother's Day or Valentine's Day. The editor might think it is a query for another typical "love" article but would open it to check it out because, after all, the editor is looking to run love-oriented articles around Mother's Day or Valentine's Day. He just hopes they go beyond the usual clichés and perhaps offer a bit of fresh insight.

Imagine, now, as the editor gets to the end of the first paragraph: suddenly, everything Mother's Day or Valentine's Day stands for has been stood on its head. The flowers we send to show our love could be making people sick? If this is something the editor did not know, then this information captures the attention of the editor and causes the editor to read on.

As the editor reads on, he sees a well-written, well-structured query letter. He learns that the author, having been to Ecuador, has first-hand knowledge of the situation and has sources she can contact when writing the article, which means this is a credible issue.

In short, the editor is interested and intrigued and experiences an attitude adjustment. Expecting another "show your love" query, the editor discovers a powerful story.

That is what you have to do in your queries: capture the attention of the editor, hold the editor's interest, and influence attitude. If you can do that, you will dramatically increase your chances of closing the sale. Again, there will be much more on writing queries. But I wanted to set the stage for you here.

Channel of choice

You can query by mail, fax, or e-mail. Most publications accept e-mail pitches, but a few do not. Check out the writer's guidelines, usually available on the publication's website. (Some information may also be available in the masthead—the credit section—of the publication.) If guidelines are not available online, call and ask or send an e-mail. You can also send a self-addressed, stamped envelope (SASE) to the publication and request the guidelines.

Submitting by e-mail

When e-mailing your query, use proper format (full block, single-spaced with a double space between paragraphs; see query examples in this book). Make sure your phone number and e-mail address are included below your name at the bottom of the e-mail.

Address your e-mail to a specific person (the editor). Use his/her name and correct title. Try to keep your letter to the equivalent of one page (400 to 600 words). Include a brief biography or paragraph about yourself at the end of the query. (Examples of query letters follow in the next chapter, with additional examples in the last chapter of this section, so you'll get to see what I mean.)

Do not send your query as an attached Word or PDF file. Instead, embed your query in the body of the e-mail message. Many editors, fearing computer viruses, will not open unsolicited attachments. If the guidelines request attached files, however, then send attached files.

There are a couple of ways to send clips when you cannot send attached files:

- Ask the editor if he or she would like to receive clippings by mail, fax, or by e-mail as attached Word files or by e-mail as embedded text. Follow the editor's instructions.
- Direct the editor to samples of your writing on your website, if you have one. In my case, I send them to www.paullima.com/articles, or to specific URLs (specific Web pages) of the articles I want the editor to read.

Keep your e-query out of the trash folder

Most editors accept e-mail queries because it's a convenient way to communicate. Some editors, however, do not like e-mail queries because they feel e-mail has made it too easy for writers to submit queries. The e-queries are often sloppy. Or, if the editor rejects one idea, the writer submits another a few minutes later. "It's like writers don't pause to think anymore," one editor told me.

Beyond submitting thoughtful, well-written queries, there are three rules you can follow to improve your electronic communications with editors and to help keep your e-queries out of the trash folder:

1. **This-isn't-tennis rule**: If an editor rejects an idea, don't fire back another one minutes later. The editor may think you're going to be a pest. Allowing at least a few days between queries gives the editor the impression you've been thinking about why the first idea didn't work and that you've been trying to come up with a better idea.

2. **Editors-aren't-elephants rule**: Just because you listed your credentials in your first e-mail query, don't assume the editor remembers who you are. Include your credits in subsequent queries, at least until the editor accepts several ideas.

3. **One-at-a-time rule**: Queries containing multiple ideas work better on paper than in e-mail. Editors who don't like your first idea may not scroll down to read more. If you're determined to send more than one idea at a time, send no more than three, number them, and alert the editor up top. For example: "Here are three ideas I think will be right for your magazine's readers."

Submitting by fax or mail

Almost every publication accepts e-mail queries. But you might find a few that do not.

Whether sending by fax or mail, use proper format (full block with one-inch margins on each side is recommended). Single-space your text; double-spaced between paragraphs. (Again, sample query letters in this book will make this clear.) If you need to submit by mail, print your query letter on quality paper, but do not used coloured paper.

Make sure your phone number, address, and e-mail address are on the query and address it to a specific person (the editor). Use his/her name and correct title. Keep your query letter to one or 1.5 pages. Include a brief biography and samples of your writing. Do not apologize for inexperience.

About *you*

An important part of the query letter is *you*: why should you be the one to write the article? You tell the editor about you in a brief paragraph towards the end of your query. As you pitch different publications or companies in different sectors (for corporate work), adjust your bio to reflect your strengths in relation to the article idea, the type of publication, or the company you are pitching.

Journal exercise: About you

I suggest you look at my bio at the end of this book (About the Author) and write a full bio for yourself.

After reading about me, look at your *ME* cluster. It should contain a great deal of information about you. Use that information to help you write a detailed bio. As you sell new articles to new publications, add the information to your bio. When you send out a query, boil your long bio into one paragraph about you that includes information pertinent to the query and publication that you are pitching.

Chapter 12: Sample Query Letters

Let's review a query letter template and a few examples of query letters. Several of the sample letters below are set up as if sent by mail. If you are sending by e-mail, drop the name, address, and date. Get right to the pitch.

First, let's start with a query letter template.

Person's Name
Position (usually Editor)
Publication Name
Address

Dear Mr./Ms. Last Name:

Opening Paragraph. Make it read as if it might be the lead of the article. Or pose an intriguing question. Or outline a startling new trend.

Support Paragraph. Build on the introduction of the central idea and put your opening paragraph in context. Maybe include some statistics or trend information. Or discuss the economic, political, legal, environmental, or social/cultural reasons behind, or implications of, the person/subject/concept you are proposing to write about. Also, demonstrate a reason why the article would be of interest to the readers of the publication.

Source Paragraph. Demonstrate you have done some research and have access to sources that can comment on, or otherwise contribute to, your article. The higher placed the sources are, the more convincing you have to be about your ability to reach the appropriate sources.

Ask For The Order Paragraph. Literally, ask if the editor is interested in the article. If it is a time-sensitive topic, give a deadline.

About You Paragraph. This is where you add something about you and why you are the right person to write such an article. Be sure to include your contact information: phone, e-mail, and website (if you have one).

Sincerely,
Your Signature
Your Typed Name
Encl.: Clippings

With that in mind, when it comes to writing query letters, your goal is to:

- Capture the editor's attention and demonstrate your ability to write.
- Introduce the editor to a central idea, person, place, concept, or situation.
- Demonstrate that the topic is of interest to the publication's readers.
- Demonstrate that you are the writer for the job.

Query letter for style

This query letter that I concocted is presented for style only. Having said that, since creating this query, I've seen several articles addressing the theme of "an apple a day" and the impact that fresh fruits and vegetables have on health. So you never know what you can turn into an article.

> Dear <Name>:
>
> Is there any truth to the expression 'an apple a day keeps the Doctor away'? Yes, and here's the proof.
>
> According to the Nutritional Institute of Canada, one apple a day contains the daily-recommended dose of vitamins X, Y, and Z. Apples are also an excellent source of roughage, contain no fat and very few calories. Apples make great snacks for kids. Baked or turned into applesauce, they can be used as a side dish for main meals or as scrumptious dessert.

> The readers of (Magazine Name) are health-conscious individuals who are concerned about nutrition and diet. Would you be interested in a feature story on the healthy habit of eating an apple a day?
>
> Along with verified health and nutritional facts about apples, my article will include an interview with the noted apple authority, Johnny Appleseed. I can also provide several of his favourite apple recipes.
>
> I spent three years working in an apple orchard and have written short articles on apples for my community newspaper and church newsletter. Samples of my writing are enclosed. If this article is of interest, please feel free to contact me at (xxx) xxx-xxxx or email@mydomain.com.
>
> Sincerely,
> Your Signature
> Your Typed Name
> Encl.: Clippings

Your last paragraphs for an e-mail query might read something like this:

> I spent three years working in an apple orchard and have written short articles on apples for my community newspaper and church newsletter. If this article is of interest, please feel free to contact me at (xxx) xxx-xxxx or email@mydomain.com.
>
> Sample articles are available at www.mydomain.com. If you would prefer that I e-mail you samples of my writing, please let me know. I can send Microsoft Word files or embed two or three samples in an e-mail message.

Query that worked

The query letter below was targeted at a business trade magazine. Trade magazines are the bread and butter of many freelance writers. The query is a very workman-like letter that hits on all the elements. However, if you want to write more scintillating articles, you have to spice up your query letters and target publications that are open to publishing more interesting, controversial, personal, or creative works of non-fiction.

We'll look at different kinds of query letters in the book, but let's start with the one below.

> A recent study by Peat Marwick concluded that computers are not a panacea for office productivity problems. Office automation often leads to frustrated employees, a loss of productivity and a poor return on investment. Why?
>
> Because of a lack of training.
>
> An article focusing on what organizations can do to profit from automation by taking a planned approach to training would appeal to the human resources managers who read your magazine, as many of them are responsible for training programs.
>
> Such an article would include an overview of the Peat Marwick study and advice from training consultants to show your readers how to determine training needs, establish objectives, choose training programs, select trainers, and ensure objectives have been met.
>
> Are you interested in the article I have outlined? If so, please call me at (xxx) xxx-xxxx.
>
> I have had news and feature articles published in the *Toronto Star, Toronto Computes, Computer Dealer News*, and several other computer and business publications. I have also taught business courses at George Brown College and have conducted several management-training programs.

Another query that worked

The query letter below might seem like writing on spec. After all, the query became the first half of the article, but it was not on spec. I still had work to do after pitching the query.

My goal, not having ever written an article quite like the one proposed here, was to impress the editor with my ability to place tongue slightly in cheek while delivering informative writing. It was a risk. But the *National Post* (the publication I was targeting) often runs irreverent articles, so it was a risk I was willing to take.

The query was targeted at the Toronto section of a national publication, which makes sense, I think you will agree.

Subject: Query: Is Toronto a friendly town?

Toronto is known as a city where you cast your eyes down when you pass a stranger on the street. Not only is this acceptable behaviour, it is expected. I've lived in Toronto all my life and never thought anything of it. It's part of the culture of this city and, quite frankly, I rather enjoyed the urban isolation—finding solitude in a crowd.

Then we got a dog.

In the last four months, since the Giant Schnauzer puppy arrived in our home, I have spoken to more strangers on streets and in parks than I have in the 45 years in which I have lived in Toronto. Individuals, couples, entire families—stop me on the street, greet me like an old friend and ask me dozens of questions, all of which I am expected to answer patiently while our dog sniffs them, their children, their grocery bags, their dog(s).

At first, I was taken aback by the sudden familiarity. It felt like an invasion of privacy. I even told my wife I was going to create an FAQ, a sheet with answers to frequently asked questions:

- Kohl - Spelled k-o-h-l
- Giant Schnauzer
- Cross between Standard Schnauzer and Great Dane
- 4 months old
- 27-inches and 100-pounds, when he's full grown...

I am getting used to what feels like celebrity status, even if the dog is the centre of attention. It's as if I've discovered a whole new city, and I kind of like it. I find myself looking strangers in the eye, watching to see if they are looking at Kohl, if they might want to ask me the frequently asked questions. If they are looking at Kohl, I slow down. My body language becomes more inviting.

Recently, I caught myself smiling—actually encouraging strangers to talk to me. While most people are content to talk about the dog and move on, some (shocked that they have actually initiated a conversion with a stranger) start in on other topics beyond the dog.

> I did not know this could happen in Toronto. But if I had talked to other dog owners, I would have discovered it is a common phenomenon. And if I had talked to <Dr. Name>, a professor of psychology at the University of Toronto, I would have discovered why.
>
> Would you be interested in an article on my recent dog-walking experiences in Toronto and the reasons behind why such an aloof town can suddenly seem so friendly?
>
> [Concluded with my *About Me* information blurb.]

The pitch was so perfect that 72 hours later, the editor asked me to write the article, to simply pick up from where the query left off. All I had to do was talk to another dog walker and the psychologist who could explain the phenomenon. (We will look in detail at what you discuss with an editor when he or she says *yes* to your query.)

Another query that worked

This query was submitted to *More* magazine by freelance writer Carla Maria Lucchetta. It led to an almost immediate positive response. Carla introduces her proposal first, indicating the sections of the magazine for which it might be suitable (and demonstrating that she is familiar with the magazine).

She then gives the editor links to her clips and produces a suggested headline. Then she pitches her idea using writing that is so stellar that it, like my Giant Schnauzer query above, became the lead of her feature article. Notice also how Carla nudges the editor to get back to her sooner rather than later. In short, if she doesn't hear back in about two weeks, she can follow up or simply send the query on to another editor.

> **Subject**: Query: Matchmaker, make me a match…
>
> It's a Wednesday night at the height of summer, a beautiful time of year to embark on a new venture, or so I like to tell myself. As I fuss and fumble with the curling iron, my carefully applied makeup is sweating off with the effort to get my hair just the right type of curl—feminine but not sexy.
>
> I've chosen to wear a new green floral halter dress, bought for another occasion but not yet worn. It seems ideal for my first ever match-maker date.

I pull on my flats to finish the look. I've never seen the man who's arriving in mere minutes to whisk me off to an undisclosed location for dinner, so I can't be sure if he's taller than my 5 feet 8 inches.

I've spoken to the gentleman on the phone but once. He seems nice—polite, respectful, engaging, interested. But to be honest, I'm feeling a bit nervous about a few pointed questions he's already asked me. It's his prerogative, since he's paying for the time-honoured matchmaking process, and this date, but I still feel uneasy. How is my relationship with my father, he wanted to know. When and why did my last relationship break up? And, my favourite by far, why have I never married?

All loaded questions, all surprising to have to answer before I've even cast my eyes on the man. Not to mention, my life-long fear of dating is grounded in not having just the right answers to questions like these. In fact, I usually do anything to avoid dating, finding it an extremely contrived form of socializing with a too obvious a purpose. I've always just met men and hung out with them, and soon enough you're hanging out a lot more, or not at all. I guess that only works when you're under at least 35.

So, why exactly am I, a middle-aged, never-married woman, travelling down this awkward road in an attempt to find the man of my dreams?

The rest of the story I am proposing for More magazine will follow the matchmaker date as it happens, punctuated by insights on the experience and what I learned in the process—about myself and my willingness to embark on such a practice, and where it leaves me at the end of it all.

I am a never-married woman, at the tender age of 47. People in my life believe that dating is something I'm well versed in. Actually, it's the opposite.

What I hope to show in the piece is that no matter if you are re-entering the dating world, or have basically never left it, there are adjustments you have to make to accommodate the reality of age, availability of men/partners, and how the way you feel about yourself changes over the years, mostly for the good.

I am a freelance feature writer. You can see my writing clips at www.herkind.squarespace.com/my-recent-articles. My writing style is best portrayed here: http://thetyee.ca/Life/2006/02/16/EssentialRaunch.

More query letters may be found in the next chapter; but first, here is a journal exercise for you.

Journal exercise

By now you should have some ideas for query letters. You may even have some publication(s) you want to pitch. Before you go forth and write your query, determine if you have to gather any information other than what you know. It could be you have to look at research studies to find some facts and figures. Maybe you have to pre-interview someone you would like to quote so you can include some flavour of what that person might say (and demonstrate to the editor that you have access to him or her). If you need to gather information, do so. And then write your query. If you don't need to gather any additional information, write away.

Your goal is to get one or two query letters written so you can soon start pitching. Again, seldom does one simply sit down and dash off a query. The query letter reflects thought and work. It contains more than a simple "I'd like to write an article about …"

You have to augment your initial idea through thought and research, list some sources, and demonstrate an understanding of the publication and its readers. Of course, your query should also demonstrate that you can write and that you have what it takes to move from idea to article.

So, what are you waiting for? Go for it!

Before you read the other query samples, write your first draft of at least one query letter.

Chapter 13: More Sample Query Letters

The query letter below was written by prolific freelance writer and writing instructor Paul McLaughlin (www.paulmclaughlin.ca) and was submitted to *Saturday Night* magazine. Notice how Paul does not say much about himself. He's written for this editor before. However, also notice how well the query is crafted. Just because he knows the editor does not mean he is going cut short the details of his query.

> Dr. David Gotlib of Toronto is one of the few mental-health professionals in North America, probably the only one in Canada, willing to treat people who believe they've been abducted by aliens, a number that runs into the thousands worldwide. A serious and shy person, he believes "abductees" deserve treatment for their experiences—which, he says, can be incredibly traumatic and disturbing, whether real or not. Although he doesn't think aliens are literally traveling to Earth, he says the vast majority of abductees aren't crazy or imagining things. He suggests there's a far more complex explanation.
>
> Next month, Gotlib will spend five days at a UFO abduction conference at MIT, where he will lead a movement to protect abductees from amateur UFO investigators, many of whom misuse hypnosis to help abductees remember their experiences. The conference promises to be a fascinating event.
>
> I propose a feature that will focus on Gotlib and his crusade to establish ethical guidelines within the bizarre UFO community. The article will take readers beyond the headlines of UFO stories and present an informed study of the abductees, what they experience, whether their experiences have any substance or meaning to society, and the dangers the abductees face from false memories induced through hypnosis.

> I think your readers will find it compelling and original reading, as this angle is rarely, if ever, explored from a serious approach.
>
> As you know, I have extensive experience as a freelance writer and feel more than confident I could produce a layered piece on this fascinating subject. If you like the idea, please contact me at your earliest convenience (the UFO conference is in three weeks) to discuss the details.

Many readers say they find themselves chuckling at the opening of this query. But by time they get to the end of it, they want to know more about the phenomenon and Dr. Gotlib. As McLaughlin writes, "The article will take readers beyond the headlines of UFO stories and present an informed study of the abductees…" In other words, he promises to take a fresh and original (and serious) look at a subject that is often the butt of ridicule in the tabloids. That's what editors want: fresh, original ideas, which is why this effective query led to an immediate sale.

Another query that worked

This query is by a freelancer who asked to remain nameless.

> Moments after lowering your bikes from the car, you glide along the banks of the lazy Connecticut River under a pine-scented canopy. Next, you are pedaling slowly past The Elms, Marble House, and Beachwoood—Newport's palatial "cottages"—on your way to sapphire waters, salty air and the sandy crescent of Gooseberry Beach.
>
> "By Car and Cycle Along New England's Spectacular Coast," the suggested article, takes readers on six short, fascinating rides to savour scenery and history and break up an otherwise tiring car trip.
>
> A non-challenging way to introduce the family to the joys of bicycle touring, the invigorating rides also explore quaint, Victorian Block Island, white-sailed Marblehead, historic Salem, and unspoiled Gloster, Rockport and Annasquam.
>
> Three weeks after I receive your okay, I can deliver 2,000 words on the pleasures of travel by car and

bicycle, illustrated by six outstanding rides. Available also are 35 mm color slides (samples enclosed).

If you wish, I can include sidebars with detailed routes, descriptions, small route maps, or information on how to plan other car/bike trips.

Are you interested in this article? I look forward to hearing from you.

While I would not say something like "three weeks after receiving your okay, I can..." it obviously did not hurt this writer. So, while there are query-letter writing rules, this is not rocket science or brain surgery. There are grey areas. Come to think of it, there are probably grey areas in rocket science and brain surgery too. But I digress.

Another query that worked

Another writer sent the query below to *Chatelaine*. Note the informal, almost chatty tone. The author had written for this editor before and felt comfortable using a degree of informality, but look at how focused her idea is. The more work you do for (most) editors, the easier it becomes to pitch them, but you still have to pitch focused ideas suitable for the publication and its readers.

Notice how the query below asks, and promises to answer, a number of questions.

Subject: I Kissed A Girl!

Working Headline: Straight Girls, Curvy Choices

While researching the sex piece I wrote for *Chatelaine*, I came across a couple of women who mentioned they had had (mild) sexual experiences with other women, or had thought about what it might be like. One friend confessed a certain curiosity about being with another woman; a second, happily married, once took a female lover. Like "Jessica Stein" in the provocative new movie that bears her name, these women seem straight.

They have (or have had) boyfriends or even husbands and they feel sexually comfortable—even satisfied—with men.

Still, there's this other kind of drive.

> What does this say about female sexuality? I used to understand homosexuality as an either/or proposition—you were either attracted to the opposite sex or your own; you were either gay or you weren't. (There's bisexuality, but that's different from what I'm getting at.)
>
> The straight guys I know don't seem open to considering the possibilities of gay relationships, or of learning about them second hand. But women are different. I know several who want to hear all about what it's like to be with a girl, even though they would never really try it.
>
> It makes me wonder: instead of a dichotomy, is female sexuality a kind of continuum, with friendship at one end, lesbianism at the other and varying kinds of affection and companionship in between?
>
> I would like to explore this further for *Chatelaine*. I see the article featuring anecdotes from women who have had same-sex experiences but don't consider themselves gay or bi-sexual. I would use comments from an outed lesbian and an expert to give the girls-experimenting-with-girls angle some context and contrast. (However, I would want to keep the tone intimate, friendly, and decidedly non-political.)
>
> I can write to an assigned length but I was thinking 1800 or 2000 words. Looking forward to hearing your thoughts.

Do you see what I mean by *always be curious*? This query oozes curiosity. However, it is also focused. Imagine that sexuality is a continuum, from heterosexuality on one end to homosexuality on the other. (I acknowledge I am greatly simplifying the sexual continuum here.) This pitch is not about heterosexuality. It is not about homosexuality. It is not even about bi-sexuality. It focuses on one niche aspect of the continuum: about people who are somewhat curious about the same sex.

The article was published a few months after the query was submitted. Once the editor said, "Yes!" the writer's work—the interviews, research and writing—began. Writing that query letter, I suspect, was not too difficult; however, the writer had to come up with the idea, be confident about the idea, and find the right market for the idea. That, in a nutshell, is your job.

Another query that worked

Here is another of my query letters that worked. I have written a fair bit about technology and telecommunications and it is my job to always be curious about potential technology and telecommunications article ideas. That means being open to interesting hooks that exemplify issues in those sectors, which I believe this query demonstrates.

Subject: Query: Cell phone 911 issues

The woman in the torn red dress with frazzled red hair appeared dazed and confused as she tried to cross Highway 400 just north of Black Creek Drive on a sunny Saturday morning. Traveling north at 110 km/h, I zoomed right past her. If I had stopped suddenly or veered off the highway to help, I would have caused a major accident. Instead, I reached for my cell phone and called 911.

The emergency operator listened politely, confirmed it was a lady in red crossing the northbound lanes near Black Creek Drive, and told me the police had been dispatched. In other words, I was not the first driver to call 911.

If you think you hear sirens blaring a lot in this city, it's probably because sirens blare frequently in Toronto. Torontonians call 911 anywhere from 2,500 to 3,500 times a day, or over one million times a year. About 45 to 50 per cent of the calls are made from cellular phones. Of those, almost 100 calls a day are made by accident, when the key pad of a cell phone in purse, briefcase, or pocket comes in contact with an object or some part of the human anatomy and speed dials 911.

This is particularly irritating for 911 operators, as they have to stay with such calls until they can confirm the calls have been made accidentally or until they are sure there is no emergency in progress.

Would you be interested in an article that delves into the problems related to 911 and cell phones? For the article, I can relate my 911 call experience, talk to at least one other person who has called 911 on a cell phone and interview <contact name>, emergency 911 coordinator for Toronto Police Services.

> If you are interested in this article, e-mail me or call (416) xxx-xxxx to discuss assignment details. I have written extensively for the *National Post* and a number of other magazines and trade journals. You can view samples of my work at www.paullima.com/articles.

Do query letters always take work?

As you can see, a degree of research goes into most queries. Do they always take work? The short answer is yes. Sometimes, however, a successful pitch has to do with a lack of ideas, as in this pitch below to an editor.

I was following up on an article on SEO (Search Engine Optimization) I had previously submitted to a publication and dashed off this two-line note:

> Hi Peter,
> Can you tell me when the SEO article is due out? Also, are you looking for ideas for upcoming issues?

Peter replied that day:

> The SEO article will appear in our November issue, which means payment will be mid-November. As for our next issue, are you up on the pay-per-click movement? Specifically, I am interested in companies that pay website operators to stick buttons on their sites and then pay the operator when a surfer clicks through.

I was up on the pay-per-click (PPC) movement and let Peter know. We hammered out the details of the assignment and I had another gig. As you can tell, this is not how I normally query editors. I would not have pitched the editor that way if I did not have a solid working relationship with him. As you develop relationships with editors, the pitch can get easier. But it is not always quite as easy as asking one simple question!

With that in mind, let's sum up in the next chapter everything we've learned about query letters in 20 rules for writing stellar query letters.

Chapter 14: 20 Rules for Query Letters

Newspaper and magazine editors receive more query letters than they can use. They quickly toss most of them. Why? The query letters are not stellar. They are poorly written, lack focus, do not develop a big idea, are not appropriate for the publication, or are not received in a timely manner.

To be effective, to be stellar, your query letter should follow these basic rules:

1. Open with a brilliant lead, one that is as brilliant as your article lead will be. Why? The query letter, in part, demonstrates your ability to write.

2. Match the tone, flavour, and style of your query to the tone, flavour, and style of the magazine. That implies you have read the publication.

3. Demonstrate an understanding of what the publication covers. This may seem obvious. However, editors often complain about writers who have not read their publications and whose queries reflect that lack of knowledge.

4. Demonstrate an understanding of the publication's readers. Editors tell me most writers they reject have no sense of what their readers' want or why the reader reads the publication.

5. Demonstrate what the reader will get from the story. Will they be educated, entertained or both? Will they become more productive? More knowledgeable? More informed? Why should they care? Why will they care? Your query should make that apparent.

6. Define the gist (angle or slant) of the article in one sentence. Think of it as writing your own assignment letter. The harder it is for you to describe the story to a friend, the more you need to tighten the idea.

7. Answer "Why this story?" What is it about your story or your take on a particular theme that makes it stand out from all the other queries? And why should you write it? Is it your sources? Is it because of your business, journalistic or a personal experience? Do you have a particular knowledge of the topic?

8. Answer "Why this story now?" What is it that makes your story idea timely? Is it a new study? Is this the beginning of a new trend or the end of an old one? Is it a new way of seeing something? A new twist on an old story? A vital follow-up to a long-forgotten story? Is it because the story has never been told before? Let the editor know "why now."

9. Demonstrate an appreciation of the publication's lead time. What's hot this week may not be hot in three or four months (yes, it can take that long to go from idea to publication). So your story needs a timely hook to pique the editor's interest and the hook needs to be timely down the road.

10. Conduct initial research to support your idea and to demonstrate you have appropriate sources that validate the idea.

11. Keep your query tight and snappy; no more than two pages at most. One page usually suffices unless you are pitching a detailed investigative piece.

12. Include your contact information: name, phone number, address, e-mail address.

13. If you're new to the publication, include some clips (two or three writing samples) or invite the editor to visit your website. (You have a website, with samples of your writing, don't you?)

14. Send the query letter to the right person at the publication. Your query should go to the right newspaper section or magazine department editor. Not sure who to send it to? Look for contacts on the publication's website. E-mail someone at the publication. Pick up the phone and ask. After all, you are a writer and writers know how to find things out!

15. Send your query by e-mail unless the publication's guidelines request queries to be mailed or faxed.

16. If this is your first query, send one idea, although you may send two slants on the idea. If you have written for an editor before, ask if he or she is open to receiving two or three ideas at a time.

17. Spell and grammar check your query. (Not my forte, but don't be like me!)

18. Don't take it personally. If the editor does not respond in a timely manner, follow up (give the editor a couple of weeks). If there is still no response, move on. Pitch your story elsewhere. Perseverance is worthwhile. But don't become a pain!

19. Be prepared to negotiate. You might pitch a query that does not quite connect, but your writing may impress the editor. Be open to negotiating the slant or angle of the assignment. And don't forget to negotiate the assignment details—pay, deadline, word count, and so on.

20. Fulfill the promise of your query. Remember, your brilliant query sold the editor on the idea. Deliver an article that relates to and reflects your query.

Repeat all of the above as often as required to earn a living. And after all that work, don't forget to meet your deadline and word count. (We will discuss the importance of doing so later in the book.)

You will find more query letters in the last chapter of this section. But first I want to discuss more about the business of freelance writing, interviewing, and writing leads.

Chapter 15: Multiple Submissions/Follow Up

Here are two questions I am often asked about the query letter and query process:

Can I submit my query to more than one publication?

How long should I wait after submitting my query to one publication before submitting it to another one?

You can submit a query to more than one publication. That's called a multiple submission. If you send a multiple submission, you are supposed to let the editor know you are doing so.

However, many editors don't like multiple submissions. For some, it's an ego thing. They want to know you have picked their publication and only their publication. But most worry that your article might appear somewhere else before it appears in their publication—a legitimate fear, especially if the publication thinks it is buying first print rights (more on various rights later in the book), so it is just easier to say no to multiple submissions. In short, you are better off sending the query to the publication you think would pay the best and/or be most interested in your story.

That leads us to question two. How long should you wait before following up? Some editors reply immediately to queries. Others take weeks. Magazine editors can take a month or more. Some never reply.

Here's my strategy—and it is an important part of my sales and marketing effort: I give editors up to four weeks to reply. This means, of course, I track when I send out my queries and to whom I send them. It also means I have many queries out there at any given time. When a reasonable amount of time has passed, I follow up—e-mail or phone the editor.

When I call, I have a 30-second blurb ready. Even if I get voice mail, I get my point across, and my point goes something like this:

> Hi, this is Paul Lima calling. I sent you a query two weeks ago on what organizations can do to ensure they profit from office automation through taking a planned approach to training. I'd like to write this article for Human Resources Monthly. I'm wondering if you've had a chance to look at the query? Please let me know. You can reach me at (416) 555-1212.

The last sentence, of course, is for voice mail only. If I get voice mail and don't hear back from the editor within another week or so, I call again:

> Hi, this is Paul Lima calling. I'm following up on my query on what organizations can do to ensure they profit from office automation. I'd like to write this article for Human Resources Monthly. If, for some reason, you want to pass, I'd like to send my proposal elsewhere. Please call (416) 555-1212 in the next day or two if you're interested in the article. If I don't hear from you, I will pitch it elsewhere. Perhaps we can work together in the future. Thanks.

This message is not delivered as an ultimatum. It is stated in a professional and polite tone. Even if I only get voice mail when I follow up, I know within four to six weeks if the editor is interested in the article. If the editor does not reply, I can pitch my query elsewhere.

There are exceptions to this process. If the article has been sent to a daily and is time sensitive, I would call sooner. If it is hot news, I would e-mail my query and follow up by phone within days or hours, depending on how hot the news is. If an editor said he or she was interested and needed more time to think about it or had to review it at an editorial board meeting, I'd give the editor more time (unless the query was time sensitive and I had another hot market to which I could send it).

Hidden benefits of phone follow up

While you can follow up by e-mail, it doesn't hurt to use the phone once in a while. You might even get passed voice mail and get to talk to editors. There can be hidden benefits of following up by phone. If you get the editor on the phone, you get an immediate yes or no response to your query.

Several times, editors have asked me for more information on the article and have bought the article after I gave them more detail over the phone.

The editors who have said "Thanks but no thanks" have always been polite and professional. A few have asked me to submit other ideas; several have suggested other publications that might be interested in the article idea. (And yes, I mention in my query that the editor of *such-and-such* suggested I send the query.)

But what has really paid off for me is that several editors have said, "*I'm not interested in that particular article but do you think you could write an article about...*"

The editor of *Computing Now* (now defunct) rejected a couple of article proposals but then offered me a monthly 2,500-word feature called My Beautiful Digital Office. I wrote 12 features for the magazine. The editor of Fast Forward, the technology section of the *Toronto Star*, rejected a proposal, asked for more, rejected them, and then, during a follow-up call, offered me a bi-weekly communications column. I wrote for Fast Forward for seven years because I followed-up by phone, and I used my work there to open doors to the business section and other sections of the paper.

Remember, one of your goals as a freelance writer is to find steady gigs. Steady gigs mean steady income. It all starts with making a query/phone follow-up strategy part of your business strategy.

If a pitch does not sell, revise it and look for a new publication. Do that two or three times. If you don't sell the idea, cut your losses and move on with other ideas. I usually have three to six ideas in circulation at any one time, except when I am too busy writing to pitch ideas, which happens a great deal with me... because, I have repeat business!

Query timing

If you are pitching an article proposal related to seasons (winter, spring, summer or fall) or an idea pertaining to a holiday celebration (Christmas crafts, Easter celebrations, Halloween safety tips, and so on) keep in mind that many publications plan their seasonal or holiday issues far in advance of the season or holiday—especially monthly magazines.

For instance, *Chatelaine*, a monthly magazine, "puts to bed" its Christmas issue in September. That means you should be pitching

Chatelaine Christmas-related article ideas in April or May, at the latest.

While daily papers have more latitude, they also plan special sections a month or more in advance. Keep this in mind when pitching your seasonal or holiday-related article ideas.

As a rule of thumb, pitch monthly publications three to four months in advance of the time you think your article should run. Pitch weeklies (or weekly sections of daily newspapers) about four weeks in advance. Even pitch daily publications at least two weeks before an event, if timing is important, so the editor can allocate space to your article.

If an idea is hot and timeliness is an issue, you might get away with less lead time, but don't count on it.

Chapter 16: Writing Article Leads

If you take time to produce a detailed query letter, you will often find your lead, the beginning of your article, is in your query. It might not be exactly there, but the query will give the editor (and you) a solid idea of what the article is about and perhaps where the story begins. For instance, if you look at my dog query and compare it to the final article, you will find the two are very similar.

Why is the lead important? If you don't capture your reader's attention in the lead, chances are your article will remain unread. If you don't capture your editor's attention in the query lead, chances are your article idea will not be accepted. In addition, if you produce strong, dynamic leads, you will write in a more structured manner.

Many writers bury their leads. They try to build suspense—as one might with the opening of a novel. What you want to do, in fact, is set the stage for the article in your lead. I am not saying there cannot be suspense, but you have to build suspense sparingly and appropriately. But you would not try to build suspense in a hard-news lead or for a breaking-news story. If your lead is nothing more than cute—if it does not set the stage, establish important themes, and/or introduce significant characters—it will fail.

Only the beginning

Some editors will tell you that you have one or two paragraphs to capture the reader's attention. Some will tell you that you have one sentence. If the first sentence doesn't capture the reader's attention, the reader will not read on. Mind you, if the first sentence works, but the second doesn't, the reader may not continue reading so, as important as the lead is, what comes after it is vital too.

Having said that, the importance of the lead is sometimes—not always, but sometimes—exaggerated. I have read many articles from start to finish that have had dull leads. I have even read poorly written articles. Most of us have because the publication, type of article, subject matter, and/or the purpose of the article resonated with us or fulfilled a need. That doesn't mean you should try to get away with dull, poorly written leads. It just means some articles are read even if the leads are nothing special.

Let's take a closer look at the factors that affect your lead (and, in fact, the entire article):

1. **Publication**: Is it staid, conservative, liberal, sensational, radical, flip, satirical, commercial, non-profit, local, national, or regional? Is it a newspaper, magazine, newsletter, or annual report?
2. **Subject Matter**: The topic you are writing about.
3. **Type of Article**: Investigative, news, profile, column, obituary, filler, how-to...
4. **Purpose of Article**: To inform, entertain, warn, solve problems, create controversy...
5. **Reader**: Readers are not a homogeneous mass. They have a wide variety of needs and a wide variety of opinions. They read primarily because they want to be informed or entertained. Even then, they are not always consistent. Many readers want information presented in an entertaining manner. Others want it presented in a no-nonsense manner. A lot of what the reader expects depends on the overall tone and style of the publication they are reading.

What's entertaining to one reader may be dull to another. What's no-nonsense to one is a complex quagmire to another. Still, readers often share common values or interests. People who want information on computer monitors would probably pick up a copy of a computer publication if, on the cover, were the words: "Special Computer Monitor Issue." And they would likely read an article that started:

> There are many different types of monitors you can buy for your computer. What you buy depends on what you want to do on your computer, and on what type of computer you have.

A pedestrian lead? Yes, but if the subject matter is of interest to me I'll read on, looking for information that is of value. Now, before editors kick me, allow me to say that I am not advocating dull, pedestrian leads that make readers snore. I am saying leads should be written in context and context includes the publication, subject matter, purpose of the article and the target readers.

The monitor article could have started:

> Have you ever wanted to be Alice, absorbed into mystical colors as you fell though the looking glass? Colors so magical they could only be embraced in dreams—if you dream in rainbow-induced Technicolor. Well, this world, or as close as you will come to it without the use of hallucinogenic drugs, is yours to capture—if you have the right computer monitor.

As a reader, I might enjoy that lead, but if I have no interest in buying a computer monitor, I probably would not have read any farther. Conversely, I might find that lead pretentious but continue to read because I want to know more about computer monitors.

The writer may have had more fun creating the Alice lead, but is it appropriate? If I were the editor, I'd embellish the bland lead and tone down the over-written one. Does it seem subjective? In many ways, it is. But there are hard rules for lead writing too. Let's try to demystify leads by looking at what you should and should not do.

Leads in greater detail

How many words should your lead be? As long as necessary to draw your reader in and make a point. In short, there is no ideal number. Ten words may be appropriate under some circumstances, but 100 words may work in other circumstances. Some feature articles have leads that are longer than many news stories. Whatever its length, the lead should leave the reader feeling as if something important awaits, that it will be worth his or her while to read on.

When writing leads, avoid clichés, generalizations, stereotypes, information overload, or any combination of the above, such as:

> It's every parent's worst nightmare. Your child is playing outside and you hear the screech of brakes in front of your house followed by a thump.

Many stories start with "It's every parent's worst nightmare" and many of them focus on a silly or mundane topic. If it is truly a nightmare topic, don't tell me. Show me. Let your writing paint a nightmare picture. And if it not a nightmare situation, don't go there.

> 'Tis the season to be jolly. Ask the man with the white beard, red hat, and that special sparkle in his eye.

While there is technically nothing wrong with the above lead, it is overused during the Christmas season because it is easy to write. I suggest you put more effort into your writing, especially your lead, instead of leaning on something that has been used *ad nauseum*.

> Nine out of ten doctors in Canada feel socialized medicine is on the road to ruin, but nine out of ten Canadians, while expressing some doubts about the effectiveness of the system, prefer it to the free enterprise, American model that leaves many people without adequate medical protection, which is why most Americans, especially those in middle class and lower income brackets, are interested in the Canadian health care system, even though the majority are leery of socialized medicine.

What do the doctors feel? Is it in sync with what Canadians feel? And what are Americans interested in? Furthermore, what do you think this article is really about? You should be enlightened by the lead, not confused by it.

In summary, your lead should focus on the subject matter and convey that focus in a clear and original manner. It should be clear, focused, creative, and original. Do your analytical reading. Read newspaper and magazine article leads on various topics. Try to model the leads you like in your writing. You can find numerous magazines and newspapers online (the list is way too long to compile; Google is your friend).

Lead types

There are three basic types of leads: news lead (W5 or hard lead), the non-news lead (soft lead), and the feature lead (soft lead generally used for, but not restricted to, long magazine articles). Within each category are a number of sub-categories.

The type of publication you are writing for, and the type of article you are writing, will influence your lead. For instance, you could be writing a news story, feature article, column, editorial, how-to article, and so on. We will focus on leads for news stories in this chapter, but will present a bit of information on non-news or soft leads. In the next chapter, we will look at soft and feature leads.

News leads include the W5—who, what, where, when and why (and sometimes how). There are several types of news leads, including the blind lead, summary lead, wrap lead, and shirttail lead, which we will look at.

No matter what kind of news lead you are writing, you need to know your W5. That will help you determine the focus of your article and help you write your lead. The W5 is so important, you should jot it down before writing. Even if you do not use a W5 lead, you will need to cover those elements in your article, so make sure you know who, what, where, when and why (and how) before you start to write anything. With that in mind, let's look at some samples,

Sample W5 leads

Here is a news headline followed by a W5 news lead:

Headline: Wildfire towns declared crime scenes
Police in Whittlesea, Australia declared incinerated towns crime scenes today, and the prime minister spoke of "mass murder" after investigators said arsonists may have set some of Australia's worst wildfires in history. The death toll rose to 166.

Deconstructing the W5, we see the following:

Who: police; the prime minister
What: declared incinerated towns crime scenes … spoke of "mass murder"
Where: Whittlesea, Australia
When: today
Why: investigators said arsonists may have set some of Australia's worst wildfires…

Sample W4 news lead

You don't always have to use every W in your lead. However, you should be conscious of why you use the ones you use and why you leave out any of them.

Headline: Home prices to tumble in '09

Sub-head: Average decline to be 9 per cent

> House prices are expected to fall eight per cent across Canada this year and sales are predicted to slip nearly 17 per cent, according to a new report from The Canadian Real Estate Association.

Deconstructing the W4, we see:

> **Who**: Canadian Real Estate Association
> **What**: house prices expected to fall 8%
> **Where**: across Canada
> **When**: this year
> **Why**: there was no reference to the economic downturn; however, with the spate of articles on the recession, including others on the same page, the why is apparent, so it was left out of the lead.

Summary lead

Summary leads summarize the most important idea in the story. It is often preferred for breaking-news and issue-oriented stories. Here is a sample summary lead:

> The University of Oregon must move more women into higher-level faculty jobs or face federal sanctions.

Here is another sample summary lead:

> International Business Machines chairman and chief executive Louis Gerstner will face a friendlier group of shareholders at the annual meeting in Toronto today, after the computer giant last week posted surprisingly strong earnings for the last quarter.

Blind lead

A blind lead is a summary lead that leaves out potentially confusing detail(s), as in this example:

> The state's land-use planning agency on Friday chose a former city planner from New York to be its new director.

This lead omits the name of the planning agency (the Department of Land Conservation and Development) and the name of the city planner, who was relatively unknown. A catch-all paragraph (or nut 'graph—the story in a nutshell) immediately follows a blind lead and would include specific details omitted from the lead.

Wrap lead

To "wrap" a lead, you combine, refer to, or wrap several items in a lead.

> Thursday's storm caused the deaths of a Hamilton woman who broke her neck in a fall, a Niagara Falls man who had a heart attack while shovelling snow and a Fort Erie teenager struck by a skidding car.

Shirttail lead

Shirttails includes a summary lead focusing on the most newsworthy elements, followed by the remaining items (or shirttails), each with its own lead. Shirttails are often used for meeting stories. The first lead targets the most important item on the agenda; remaining items are introduced with an "in-other-business" transition in the second paragraph.

> A man taking photographs of Portland's skyline about 2:15 a.m. Sunday was struck by a car and knocked into the Willamette River off the Interstate 5 ramp to Interstate 84.
>
> Another accident later that morning, this one involving a hit-and-run driver in Southwest Washington, left a Lynnwood, Wash., man in serious condition.

Complex Shirttail lead

Similar to the Shirttail lead, the Complex Shirttail lead includes a summary lead focusing on the most newsworthy elements. But that lead is followed by a number of related elements.

> The federal government has provided nearly $400 million for desperately needed affordable housing in

> Ontario—but the money may not be spent any time soon.
>
> The province has stashed the money in a contingency fund pending the outcome of a fiscal battle with Ottawa.
>
> Now, housing groups are wondering whether the province will ever spend the money on housing.

Notice the multiple who's and related what's in the above lead. Each source has equal weight. Each who is given its own paragraph and its own what to make it clear there are three sides to the story; the conflict makes this topic newsworthy.

Deconstructing the who and what from the above lead we find:

Who: federal government

What: provided nearly $400 million for desperately needed affordable housing

Who: The province

What: has stashed the money in a contingency fund

Who: housing groups

What: are wondering whether the province will ever spend the money on housing

You should be able to find the multiple where's, when's and why's in the lead as well.

Sample W5 lead

Here is a sample W5 lead from a one-source article:

> Ontario's economy is in for a slowdown, says Canada's central banker, as the U.S. housing and auto sectors cool, spilling across the border.
>
> Although Ontario's economy will continue to grow in the next 12 months, it will probably turn in the worst performance among the provinces, Bank of Canada governor David Dodge said today.

Deconstructing the W5, we see:

Who: Ontario's economy

What: is in for a slowdown; turn in the worst performance among the provinces

Where: Ontario; in Canada
When: the next 12 months
Why: the U.S. housing and auto sectors cool, spilling across the border

Paraphrasing and quoting

Notice how the writer yields to a higher authority by using two paraphrases in the above lead. In other words, the writer does not quote Dodge in the lead; he does, however, refer to Dodge. Why reference Dodge in the lead? Dodge is the governor of the Bank of Canada. If Paul Lima says something about the economy, it's not news and it would not be reported. If the governor of the Bank of Canada says it today, it is news and it must be attributed to him.

Dodge is the only source in this article. He is gave a speech on the economy today. That's news. Reporters can get comments from bankers, economists, and others for follow-up articles that they can write for tomorrow's edition of the newspaper.

But why paraphrase, not quote Dodge? Often, the gist of a comment is all you need to set the stage for the article. To quote Dodge in the lead would require too many words to say the same thing. By paraphrasing, the reporter establishes that comments by Dodge will be the focus of the article. The lead covers the W5 and establishes Dodge as the central figure, and then the writer quotes him several paragraphs in:

> "It is important to think of this as a mild and likely short-lived, cyclical slowdown," Dodge said in a speech televised to the Ontario Economic Leadership Summit in Niagara-on-the-Lake.

Eight paragraphs into a 12-paragraph article, the reporter presents another side of the story, again paraphrasing Dodge:

> Dodge conceded those forecasts could be off, however, if consumers decide to start spending even more. And they might.

Putting this information right after the lead would have undercut the news. Mind you, you might call not putting it in right after the lead "sensationalizing the news," and you might be right.

However, newspapers tend to present the "sexy" side of the story first, and then fill in with additional facts that give a story balance and make it seem objective.

Again, in this article, the reporter does not quote anyone else. This article focused on the speech the day after it was given. The business sections of newspapers can do a more in-depth analysis tomorrow, and quote other sources. In other words, the theme of this story has legs—it will run for several days.

What about *how*?

Read more news stories; focus on the lead to see how the writer has worked the most pertinent W5 details into it. Then see how those details play out through the rest of the story. Look for conflict and consensus—people on opposite sides of issues butting heads in the article or people in agreement.

One thing you might notice as you do your reading is that *how* is seldom used in the lead. As one reporter friend of mine points out, "Sadly, it's most often neglected by journalists who just don't think to ask, 'Just how did this happen?' or 'Just how is this supposed to work'?" Keep your eyes open, though, and see if you can find how in any leads. If you find, ask why it was used. And when you don't find it, ask yourself why it was not use and if it should have been included.

Use active voice

When writing leads, use active voice (who did what to whom), not passive voice (what was done to whom by whom). Active voice uses fewer words and engages the reader more than passive voice does. Let's look at active voice in the first W5 lead presented in this chapter, and then convert it to the passive voice so you can see the difference.

> **Active**: Police in Whittlesea, Australia declared incinerated towns crime scenes today.
>
> **Passive**: Incinerated towns were declared crime scenes today by police in Whittlesea...
>
> **Active**: Fire destroyed a house on Main Street early Monday morning.
>
> **Passive**: A house was destroyed by fire on Main Street early Monday morning.

Why a W5 lead wasn't used

The article below could start with a W5 news lead about the economic downturn. Instead, it starts with a three-paragraph human interest lead, known as a soft lead (rather than a hard news lead). The reason is simple. This was part way through the economic downturn of 2008 and there had been many news articles on the downturn. In other words, the economic downturn was not news. The human interest in this article is known as a poster child lead—one person who represents the toll the downturn had taken on many people. The poster child puts a human face on the issue. But notice how it still gets to the news in the fourth paragraph—the nut 'graph.

In short, if a story plays out over days, weeks, months, or even years ("has legs," in journalism parlance) it often moves from a news story to a human interest story (although it can become a news story again if there are new developments). The human interest story still has to contain elements of the news (again, as you will see by the nut 'graph) but the lead puts a human face on the story.

> **Headline**: "There aren't even jobs to bag groceries" in Calgary
>
> **Lead**: Cassandra Lees has found herself in a situation she would have thought impossible just a year ago—unemployed and unable to find work anywhere in Calgary.
>
> When Lees, 28, moved to the city three years ago from Winnipeg, she couldn't walk down the street without seeing a "Help Wanted" sign in every retail window. Employers were offering trips to new recruits and giving away cars as incentives to employees.
>
> Now, after months of looking for everything from secretarial work to retail positions, Lees said she is painfully aware of a new reality. "There aren't even jobs out there to stock shelves or bag groceries," she said.
>
> **Nut 'graph**: No province is immune to declining fortunes, but Alberta's fall, after such dramatic highs as last summer's oil and gas prices, is steeper than anywhere else. The province's economic activity is projected to fall by 2.3 per cent this year, the sharpest drop among the provinces, according to an RBC report. Capital investments in the province have scaled back significantly, most noticeably in drilling for new wells.

See the feature in a W5 lead?

We will look at additional types of leads in the next chapter. By way of introduction, see if you can find the potential for a feature in the W5 lead below. As mentioned, news stories are often written in inverted pyramid style. In the lead, the writer packs pertinent information or facts, embellished with little or no colour, and covers the story's five W's:

> More American teenagers are having babies, getting arrested, or being killed by bullets each year, according to America's Children at Risk, a grim new portrait of American youth released yesterday. The year-long study said more than 6 per cent of children under age 18—nearly 4 million—are growing up in so-called "distressed neighborhoods." Their future is gloomy.

Who, what, where, when and *why*. And a stunning conclusion: *Their future is gloomy*. All in an amazing 58 words:

> **Who**: More American teenagers
> **What**: are having babies, getting arrested, or being killed by bullets each year
> **Where**: America; distressed neighborhoods
> **When**: each year; new portrait ... released yesterday
> **Why**: growing up in "distressed neighborhoods"

This lead was, in fact, the entire article. No other information followed the lead. It is complete in itself because it answers the five W's. And yet, look at how it ends: "Their future is gloomy." Period. Full stop. As if there is nothing more to say. Or is there?

Maybe there was more to this story and the paper didn't have room to run it. Remember that news editors feel they should be able to cut a news story anywhere after the lead. While this two-sentence story is complete, I suspect you can you imagine the potential here for a 2,000-word human-interest feature based on the two sentences. With that in mind, try the journal exercise, below.

Journal exercise: Finding a feature in the news

Imagine you've been assigned to write a 2,000 word human-interest feature based on the two-sentence news article concerning American teenagers. You are writing this for the Life section of your local newspaper or for a local magazine that explores social issues.

Answer the questions below to help you imagine the process you would go through to research a feature article:

- What is the local angle on this story? Is the future of teens in your city, town, state/province as "gloomy" or at all gloomy? Why? Why not?
- What would you read and who would you talk to for background information on the state of teenagers in your community? Who would you interview?
- Where/how would you start the article? With the study? With a social worker or some other expert? With a teen who has had a baby, been arrested or been shot?
- What points would you cover in your article? How would you structure it to draw the reader in and keep the reader reading?
- Would you look for a conflicting voice—a teen who has overcome difficult circumstances or a social worker who is optimistic, for instance?
- Would your conclusion state that "their future is gloomy" as the study concludes? Might you look for a counter-point, an 'unless' or 'however' statement: 'this is how things are and why they are and how they will remain unless/however....' (As long as you have evidence that there is a counterpoint to this story.)

Chapter 17: Soft and Feature Article Leads

As you have gathered by now, rather than using the W5 to deliver the news, soft leads capture the attention of readers by using a story-related anecdote, painting a picture of a person, place or thing, or posing a question. The paragraph that follows a soft lead—the nut 'graph—often contains the most important W5 elements.

Feature article leads draw the reader into a longer, more leisurely (sometimes contentious) look at a subject, person, event. Feature leads are similar to soft leads but they tend to go into more detail and establish the major theme and conflict of the story. Often setting up opposing points of view, the feature lead might focus on a person, a detailed retelling of an event or a detailed recreation of a scene.

Unlike news articles that often peter out towards the end, feature articles have defined beginnings (lead), middles (body), and ends (conclusion). The longer, more leisurely lead is a staple of feature writing for magazines, but they can be used in longer newspaper articles. The middle builds on the opening, putting flesh on the bones of the themes, characters, or conflict introduced in the lead. And the end often reflects or echoes the beginning of the article.

Let's think about the "American teenagers" news article again for a moment. What if you wanted to write a soft lead or feature lead based on that news lead? Where would you begin the article?

I'd suggest you would lead with a poster child, the one who represents the many. As crass as it sounds, you would want to find an American teenager who has had babies, been arrested, and/or killed by bullets. You would use your poster child to create a human-interest lead that would capture the attention of your readers.

> Sheila Smith was only 14 when her first baby was born. It was December 23, 2008, a week before the resident of Harlem, in New York City, was arrested for shooting a drug dealer during a heroin deal gone bad.

> She survived three years in jail, where she gave birth to her second child after being raped by a prison guard.
>
> Two days after she was released from prison, Smith and her two children were shot dead by the drug dealer's girlfriend, in a revenge killing that has shocked a poverty-stricken neighborhood that thought it was no longer capable of feeling shock.

You could then follow that human-interest lead with a nut 'graph summarizing the gist of the article and telling the readers more explicitly what the article is about and why it is being written. The nut 'graph, the transition from the lead to the body of article, would look a lot like the W5 news lead we saw earlier.

> More American teenagers are having babies, getting arrested, or being killed by bullets each year, according to America's Children at Risk, a grim new portrait of American youth released recently. The year-long study said more than 6 per cent of children under age 18—nearly 4 million—are growing up in so-called "distressed neighborhoods."

But our story would not end there. Following the nut 'graph you might use a quote.

> "As our study indicates, their future is gloomy," says Anthony Times, the author of the report that was presented to a Congressional hearing on distressed neighborhoods in Washington last February.

While news articles sometimes (certainly not always) take one point of view, feature articles invariable present opposing points of view. In other words, you want to set up the reaction that demonstrates a conflict of opinion.

> Social workers and clergymen say it does not have to be this way. Education, training, and jobs—enough to provide a glimmer of hope—is all that is required to turn around the situation.
>
> But that takes cash, and the report's authors concluded that the government's coffers are empty.

> Any funds that could be earmarked for additional services to assist inner city youth have already been committed to fight the debt and support the war against terror, the report indicates.

What comes next? It all depends on your focus. For instance, you might include any of the following:

- Comments from clergymen and spokespersons for social agencies, and the parents of the dead child.
- Background information on the human cost/burden.
- Background information on the financial cost.
- More comments from the author of the report.
- Comments from those representing various government agencies that should be funding programs, ideally juxtaposed against additional comments from the parents of the dead child and perhaps clergymen and spokespersons representing social agencies and so on.

On the other hand, if this article profiled the neighborhood where Sheila lived and died, following your transition you could:

- Talk to more teens in the neighborhood.
- Find an example of someone who bucked the trend and escaped the "gloomy" neighborhood.
- Give some background and history of the neighborhood: Was it always this way? When and why did it become this way?
- Use some reaction comments, farther down, from clergymen or social agencies.

Again, it all depends on the focus (angle or slant) of the article. You make your focus clear in your query letter to the editor; however, remain open to suggestions from the editor pertaining to the angle or slant as well.

Soft lead examples

Don't bury breaking news under a soft lead; however, if the story is not a breaking news story (a follow-up to a news story or a profile, for example), start with a soft lead.

For instance, as I am writing this chapter, there are a number of news stories about the economic downturn. Is it a recession? Will it become a depression? What caused it? How can we get out of it? Whenever you have a newsworthy trend—economic, political, legal, social, cultural, medical, technological, and so on, you will find interesting follow-up articles that explore niche aspects of the trend. They tend to use soft leads, as in the example below.

> **Headline**: In a shrinking workforce, women may surpass men
>
> When Angie Dick heard her husband might be laid off at his factory job, she knew it was time to start working.
>
> "I hadn't worked for 13 years after I was disabled in a car crash," said Angie, 44. In September, she stared working as a sales representative for Kresslor Personnel, an employment agency in Mississauga.
>
> Mark was laid off at his oil-drum refurbishing job two weeks ago.

In the next paragraph in the article, in the nut 'graph, we find the news:

> As the economic downturn gets worse, experts say Dick is part of a trend in which women find it easier to get jobs, and could soon outnumber men in the workforce as jobs in the manufacturing sector decline—an area traditionally dominated by men.
>
> The last time women surpassed men in employment was during World War II…

The soft lead is enticing because this is not a hard news story. It is a follow-up to hard news stories about the economic downturn. It relates directly to the economic downturn but details a by-product of the downturn and speaks to wider social implications of the downturn.

Here is another soft lead example:

> The campaign ad opens with a familiar boyish face, now atop a body that sways uncontrollably. Michael J. Fox, wearing a shirt and suit jacket, talks directly to the camera.

> "They say all politics is local, but it's not always the case," Fox says in the 30-second commercial backing Senate candidate Claire McCaskill in Missouri, a Democrat. "What you do in Missouri matters to millions of Americans—Americans like me."
>
> Fox, who suffers from Parkinson's disease and supports research on embryonic stem cell for a potential cure, also has lent his celebrity to Democrats Benjamin L. Cardin, running for the Senate in Maryland, and Wisconsin Gov. Jim Doyle, who is seeking re-election. Both politicians also back stem cell research.

Again, the news follows the soft lead:

> The ads, released today, have triggered a backlash, with some criticizing them as exploitive. Conservative radio commentator Rush Limbaugh has claimed Fox was "either off his medication or acting."

The soft lead is enticing because this is not a hard-news story, even though the ads were released "today." Had war broken out today, or had a bank been robbed, that would be hard news. This is soft news because it is a spat between celebrities, because Fox is famous and is ill, and because Limbaugh is a jerk. (Sorry, I could not help but editorialize!)

There are a number of other types of soft leads.

Scene-setter lead

Scene-setters open with description. They may contain some action, but the main point is to create a stage on which action can unfold, or to give a sense of place necessary to the focus of the story.

> A woman with tormented eyes talks to herself as she plays a battered piano in Ward D's dayroom. Other psychiatric patients shuffle on the beige linoleum or stare from red-and-green vinyl chairs. A bank of windows opens to a fenced courtyard. Outside....

Significant detail lead

The article this next lead is taken from explored the continuing influence of Communism and central planning on the operation of the shipyard and the economy of Poland.

The statue of Lenin—hidden, but still in the neighborhood—perfectly symbolized the story's central theme and illustrates the use of a significant detail to craft a lead.

> Hidden beneath a heap of inner tubes in a tiny storeroom on an island in the middle of the Vistula River is the statue of Lenin that stood for decades inside the Gdansk Shipyard.

To question or not to question?

Some editors ban question leads, reasoning readers want answers, not questions; however, question leads occasionally work particularly, but not exclusively, for sports stories.

> What's black and orange and the worst nightmare for teams headed to the state football playoffs?

The answer to the question is, of course, the local football team; its uniform is black and orange.

Leads that start with questions often fail because they do not perform the basic function of a lead—stating the central theme that organizes and explains the entire story. Furthermore, readers might resent frivolous questions when they want news. Still, some stories deal with fundamental questions. So, a question lead can be appropriate.

Profile lead

Here is an example of a profile lead, followed by a quote and a transition.

> Paul Lima considers himself successfully retired from reality. He took a one-year sabbatical from Georgian College in Barrie, Ontario, where he worked as a continuing education program manager, and never returned. Instead, he moved to Toronto and launched a freelance writing business.
>
> That was over 18 years ago.
>
> "I could not see myself going back to work, not to a real job, after a year of freedom," said Lima who writes about technology and small business issues for The Globe

and Mail, National Post, CBC.ca and a number of other publications.

While he now considers himself successfully retired from reality, success, as he defines it, did not come overnight. For the first three years, while working as a freelance writer...

Notice in the first line how we give away the ending: Paul Lima considers himself what? "Successfully retired from reality." Then we give a little background information: here is where he was, here's what he did. However, even though we've given the ending away, we build some suspense using the transition line: "For the first three years, while working as a freelance writer..." In other words, the fairytale has a happy ending, but we are going to go through freelance writing Hell to get there.

Based on the lead/transition, readers know that they will experience the lessons that allowed Paul to successfully retire from reality. In that way, the transition holds the attention of readers.

Will we interview any other sources? Perhaps. This depends on the slant or angle of the article. Are you writing a profile on Paul Lima or are you writing an article about freelance writing struggles and success using Paul as your poster child? Are you writing an article on marketing a business, using Paul as your poster child, and then interviewing marketing experts?

If this is a profile about Paul, once you have a lead/transition like our profile lead above, it's all over but the writing. Add three or four hellish experiences. Mix in a few key quotes. Toss in a pinch of background information proving this is a typical (or atypical) situation. Perhaps reference an "authority." Stir in lessons learned. Conclude with a final quote and comment, and you have baked an article.

Sample feature lead

The feature lead goes into more depth and detail than the typical soft lead. It paints a more vivid picture, often introduces large themes, and establishes a conflict similar to fiction: man vs. man, man vs. nature, man vs. self.

The sample lead below does not address a strong conflict. It is more like an extended human-interest lead but it is included here to show you the degree of detail you can use in a lead when you are writing a long feature on a particular topic.

Feature article leads for glossy consumer magazines can be even longer—as long as the lead is used to establish the central themes and conflicts of the article.

> Kevin Huber can differentiate between intense light and dark shadows. Other than that, he sees nothing. Legally blind since birth, Huber can navigate through his word-processing package as fast as any computer user I've seen.
>
> Huber, 38, has his Masters in Science from Guelph University and works as a client support representative for Microcomputer Science Centre in Mississauga, where he tests computer systems and software intended for use by visually challenged persons and shows instructors how to train disabled persons on computers.
>
> While he cannot see the keys, he can touch-type on his standard keyboard. And, while he cannot see his computer screen, he hears what others see, thanks to his IBM Screen Reader and speech synthesizer—two tools that translate visual information into audible information.
>
> Huber's dark, deep-set eyes almost twinkle when I ask him if he can imagine life without computers. "I don't have to imagine it. I lived it," he says and he vividly recalls his university days, when typing a 500-word essay was a chore.
>
> Huber is one of many persons with physically disabilities who successfully use adaptive technology to adjust to their particular challenge.

This is where the lead ends. Notice the shift in tone as the body of the article, another 1,500 words, begins with a nut 'graph that focuses the reader's attention on the topic or issue on which the article is focused. (I find writing a nut 'graph also helps get the writer focused.) So here is where the lead leads the reader:

> As slanted sidewalks, or curb cuts, are used to make streets more accessible to mobility challenged persons, adaptive technology or electronic curb cuts, are used to make computers more accessible to physically challenged persons.
>
> Physical challenges can be divided into three categories—visual, hearing, and mobility. Visual challenges range from reduced visual acuity to blindness. Hearing challenges range from slight loss of hearing to deafness. And mobility challenges range from impaired movement of limbs to limited movement of the head and lips...

Why start with Kevin?

The above lead attempts to draw readers into the article by making them interested in the human aspects of the issues, hence it starts with Kevin, someone who personifies what the article is all about. Notice how the lead tries to paint a portrait of Kevin by focusing on his ability, disability, age, educational background, and even his eyes. Appropriate for an article that opens with a blind person, no?

The body of the article is rather straightforward. It builds on "physical challenges can be divided into three categories—visual, hearing and mobility" by detailing the technology available to help those with the challenges outlined. Kevin appears several times throughout the article, however, and reappears at the end.

> While advances in adaptive technology make computers more accessible for the disabled, access can still be a difficult and frustrating experience. Huber knows that firsthand. But, while he sometimes lags behind non-disabled computer users when learning new programs, he is not afraid to play with the new programs.
>
> "I get into a lot of trouble others don't get into, but I learn more too," said Huber.
>
> Huber's advice to anybody thinking about entering the world of computers? "Embrace it with an open mind," he says, because computers enable the disabled to participate in learning and employment experiences that may otherwise be closed to them.

If the article were a profile focused solely on Kevin and his accomplishments, he would not have disappeared. But the article was meant to provide a service—to inform physically challenged individuals and their employers of the computer "curb cut" options available. Kevin reappears to complete the circle: to connect the end of the story with its beginning. It is the payoff or reward, so to speak, for the reader. It makes the reader say, "Oh yeah, I remember why I started reading this." By closing the circle and bringing the reader back to the beginning, it makes the reader feel good or helps reinforce what the reader has learned.

Does all of this sounds manipulative? It is. Writing is a conscious act. You choose the words, sentences, and paragraphs. You choose what information to put in and what to leave out, when to quote, when to paraphrase, and when to ignore what somebody has told you. You choose where to start and how to end your article.

The more you read and analyze other articles, and the more you write, the more natural it becomes. I was tempted to say "the easier it becomes" but it's never easy. If it became easy, then everybody would do it. It is definitely a craft, something you need to learn and practice.

Lead-writing quick tips

Here are a few quick tips to help you write leads.

1. **Length**: News lead: 25 to 50 words. Soft leads and feature-style leads can range from 25 to several hundred words or longer. Leads of several hundred words are used primarily for feature magazine leads.

2. **Attribution**: You don't need to attribute any information in your lead to anyone you interviewed unless the point of view needs to be clearly established and explained, or unless you are directly quoting or paraphrasing someone who is central to the article.

3. **Quote leads**: Starting an article with a quote rarely works. It has to be a spectacular quote to supersede the news or soft lead.

4. **Cliché leads**: Dare I say it? Avoid them like the plague. "It is every mother's worst nightmare…" Leads like this are overused and are often used for trivial issues, issues that are not any mother's worst nightmare.

5. **Numbers**: Beware of using too many or you will overload the reader. Cite one side of a statistical battle in your lead. Set up the other side in the transition or further down in the article.
6. **Talk to yourself**: Read leads out loud. If they sound awkward or confusing, they are awkward or confusing. If you have to breathe half way through a sentence, the sentence is too long.

Leads tend to become awkward when you engage in overloading. Overloading can easily confuse the reader.

> Dalton McGuinty, the premier of Ontario, today announced he would formally protest what he describes as the decision by the federal finance minister, Jim Flaherty, made on October 16, to not meet the obligations of the $1-billion Ottawa-Ontario Fiscal Accord negotiated between Ontario and Ottawa by Ralph Goodale, former federal finance minister in Paul Martin's short-lived minority government that was swept from office by the Conservatives in part on a platform to resolve the fiscal imbalance. Flaherty denies the allegation that he is....

Who did what? When? Where? Why? At this point, most readers would be saying, "Who cares?"

Journal exercise

Remember the analytical reading I asked you to do in Chapter 3? Continue to read analytically but focus on leads. Ask yourself why the writer starts where he or she starts and figure out how the writer starts. Is it a hard news lead or a soft lead? Analyze how the lead draws you in. Or does it draw you in? What characters, themes, conflicts does it introduce? See if you can find the nut 'graph. How does it focus your attention? Does anyone introduced in the lead come back into the story? Why? Why not?

Look at your idea file for article ideas you have developed. Try to figure out where such articles might begin if you were given an assignment. Who would you have to interview or what would you need to know to start there?

Use this knowledge to help you write your query letters because, in many ways, the opening of your query should be as strong as an article lead. It might not be the same as the lead, but it must capture the attention of the editor and draw the editor into your query.

Finally, if where to start seems subjective, don't sweat it. In many ways it is. But it is your job, as a writer, to determine where to start. And then, of course, you hope the editor agrees! Even if the editor makes changes to your lead, don't sweat it. I've had editors turn my soft leads into hard news and supplant my news leads with soft leads. Once you land an assignment, ask the editor, "What kind of lead would you like me to use?" And follow the instructions your receive.

Don't be surprised if the editor tampers with your lead. As I've come to learn: writers write; editors edit. For the most part, they do a mighty fine job of it, too. At the same time, if you get in sync with your editor, delivering what the editor feels the readers of his or her publication expect, you will find the editor will often—not always!—leave your leads alone.

Chapter 18: Finding Markets

It takes work to run a business, any business. Working as a freelance writer is as much a business as working as an insurance salesperson or a widget manufacturer. I happen to find it more fulfilling than selling insurance or manufacturing widgets, primarily because I like to write. Because I enjoy writing, I avoided the business aspects of my work in the beginning and, by golly, I didn't get paid to do much writing. Now I am running my business like a business. I am doing all the writing I want to do and, some days, I do more than I care to do. And I am paid for it all. So, in this chapter, I'll share some more of what I've learned about the business of marketing my writing services.

Allow me to say (repeat) this: as freelance writers, we sometimes forget we are in sales. The average salesperson may make dozens of calls before closing a sale. Same with freelancing. Don't think of that as rejection; don't let it get you down. It simply is part of the sales process. Of course, sales people tend to have higher "close" rates if they call on companies that can use the products they are selling, if the products are presented in an appealing way, and if the prospects believe they are quality products. Same with freelancing. You have to pitch the right ideas to the right editors at the right publications. Your query has to be well packaged and the editor has to believe the idea is one his or her readers will want to read about.

Submitting my query is like getting my foot in the door. Sometimes the editor opens the door wide and buys. Sometimes I have to be a tad persistent—follow up on my pitch by phone, for instance. When I call an editor, I refer to the query; that gives us something to talk about. Editors have never complained about my follow-up calls, even those who have said 'no thanks' to my proposals. Of course, I often get voice mail. Not every editor calls back, but many do. I have had editors call back and say "no thanks" or call back and say "yes please." I've had editors call back and say "no thanks" but then ask for other proposals or offer me an assignment. In short, you can't control the actions of your prospects. All you can do is sell—and sell well.

Once I realized the initial key to running a successful freelance-writing business was sending out detailed, thoughtful, well-written queries that were tailored to specific publications (computer article proposals to computer magazines, business article proposals to business magazines or business sections, community news article proposals to community papers, author profiles to book sections of newspapers, and so on), my work picked up.

Once I found the courage to follow up on my proposals by phone, my work picked up exponentially.

Of course, as I consistently and professionally delivered the goods (submitted my articles) on time and to word count, editors began calling me to ask me to write for them. They also passed my name on to other editors. In any business, this is called positive word of mouth. It happens in the restaurant business, in the retail business, in the hair salon business. It happens in the writing business, too. Once I acquired several steady gigs, I spent less time developing article ideas and sending out queries and more time writing and earning an income.

Also, as I have come to know my editors and their working styles, I tend to pitch them in a less formal manner. It's not unusual for me to dash off an e-mail to an editor that says, "Hey, how about an article on such-and-such? Whatcha think?" Okay, I use a little more detail than that and I find out if the editor is open to this kind of pitch before I engage in it. But pitching to editors you know is definitely easier than pitching to new (to you) editors. Only you don't get to know editors until you sell them a few ideas and deliver the goods.

Where do you find markets?

As I've alluded to in previous chapters, markets are everywhere. But some days when you are developing pitches, they can seem elusive.

Frankly, there is a great deal of market research you can do online. However, it doesn't hurt to get out of the house occasionally and read newspapers and magazines at the big-box bookstores, at your local bookstore, or at the library. You get a real sense, looking at all those covers, of the sheer variety of publications that are out there.

But there is also a hidden market that does not appear on bookshelves of bookstores or in most libraries. This hidden market is called the trade publication market.

For every sector out there, there is at least one trade publication and often several: doctors, lawyers, accountants, information technology managers, computer resellers, telecom, hydro, automotive manufacturing, automotive sales, shoe sales, manufacturing of every kind, convenience stores, hotels, travel and tourism, small business, financial services, insurance, banking, medical, pharmaceutical, entertainment industry, trucking and so many others.

I cannot list all sectors that have trade publications, but you can find trade magazines (and many other publications) online. Start at any search engine and conduct a search for "trade publications" or "trade magazines." Also, try directories such as the Google Directory (www.google.com/Top/News/Directories) or Yahoo! News Directory (http://dir.yahoo.com/News_and_Media/Newspapers/web_Directories).

There are also directories and writers' guides available from Amazon.com, Chapters.ca, various bookstores, and local libraries and college and university libraries. Again, my advice is that you develop ideas, then go looking for appropriate publications. However, since you now have a number of ideas percolating and several queries ready to go, this might be a good time to look at the writers' directories!

Journal exercise

If you have developed a few article ideas, here is something you might be ready to try:

- Find the appropriate publications for two or three of your ideas
- Read sample articles in the publications you are going to target
- Write and refine several queries to meet the expectation of the publication's readers
- Find (online or by phone) the names and contact information of the editors you would send your queries to

If you feel ready, follow the publication's submission guidelines and submit your query. Of course, if you do that, be prepared to follow up on your query a few weeks later. Also, make sure you are prepared to write the article if you land the gig. If, however, you don't get the sale, stay calm and move on to your next query.

Did I say *next*? You do have more than one article idea, don't you?

You should also have more than one query out there too, once you are ready to start pitching, if you want to generate steady writing gigs. It's how the business works: Pitch, pitch, pitch... Follow up, follow-up, follow-up.... Pitch, pitch, pitch...

As you pitch and land assignments, you then pitch and follow up less and you write more. If you do an excellent job of writing, you generate repeat business by pitching editors who know you and look forward to receiving queries from you or by writing for editors who call you and offer you assignments,

Before we move on to the next chapter, allow me answer a question I am frequently asked: How many queries should I have out there at any one time?

Sorry, but I am going to answer your question with a few questions: How busy do you want to be? How effective and efficient a writer are you? How many assignments can you handle at the same time?

I can handle multiple assignments, now. By multiple, I mean three, four or five, depending on how long the article is and how much research is required. But, when I was getting started, one assignment seemed to absorb all my energy. With that in mind, I would suggest, by way of minimum, you should try to have at least five active queries out there at all times. If you have limited writing experience, that might feel intimidating and there is nothing wrong with starting slowly. But if you want to earn a living as a freelancer, you need to be pitching constantly.

As you get busy writing, you can pull back on the query lever. But don't pull back too far. Remember, when you finish one gig, you will want to move on the next, so you should always be querying or generating repeat business with editors for whom you have done some work.

Chapter 19: Idea Acceptance: Now What?

What you do once an editor says "yes" can be as important as how you pitch your ideas. Upon having your proposal accepted by an editor, you have to discuss a number of details with your editor before you write. After all, once the editor says, "Yes, I'd love to buy that article from you..." you move from the domain of salesperson to that of a supplier of words.

Editors tend to be busy people but they also tend to be professional. They know that clear instructions up front mean they will be more likely to get what they want. But, if your editor should happen to forget this, it is up to you say, "Oh, before I begin writing, there are a few things I think we should go over...."

I suggest you make up a "Yes Checklist" sheet using the headings below. You may not go over every item on the list, but you will find the more you discuss up front, the fewer problems you will encounter once you file (submit) your article, and when you invoice.

Yes Checklist: Overview

The Yes Checklist includes a number of items that we'll go through in a moment. First, you should know there usually is no reason to communicate with your editor once a story has been assigned and the details have been sorted out. However, if the angle of your story changes, if an important source is not available, or if, for any reason, you can't meet your deadline, you need to communicate with your editor as soon as possible and arrange a new, mutually agreeable plan of action.

Also, if this seems like a long list, that's because it is! However, it gets shorter the more you work with a particular editor. You skip the details you know—rights bought, kill fee, invoicing and so on—and move more quickly through the details you have to discuss. In short, use the Yes Checklist information below to help you sort out pertinent assignment details with your editor and to help you create an article assignment sheet that you can refer to once you begin your assignment.

Yes Checklist

Article idea

Short synopsis of your original idea to make sure you and the editor are on the same track or to see if the editor wants to alter the slant of your idea in any way.

Working title

Article title for submission; the editor will usually write the headline but you can create a working title. (Sometimes an editor will assign a slug—an article name or number that identifies what the article is about and, perhaps, when the article is due. If the editor assigns a slug, use it as the working title and file name.)

Slant/angle

The particular approach to the article you are taking or that the editor wants you to take; the aspect of the idea the article will focus on. This may be a reiteration of the query, but it gives you and the editor a chance to discuss any other pertinent details.

Contact information

Contact information should include the publication's name and address (especially if you have to invoice by mail), editor's name, phone number, e-mail address and perhaps fax number (seldom required; ask if you'll need it).

Deadline

Date your article is due to the editor. Meet the deadline if you want to work for the editor again. If you have problems meeting your deadline, let your editor know in advance and re-negotiate. Do not get into the habit of re-negotiating deadlines.

Word count

Minimum, maximum, or exact number of words due. Hit your word count. Do not underwrite or overwrite by more than 5%. If you have more of a story (or less of a story) than discussed, do not write long (or short) without contacting the editor. Explain why you want to go long or short and re-negotiate the word count. But be prepared to stick with the existing count!

Style guide

Many publications have their own style guides or follow *The Canadian Press Stylebook* or *The Chicago Manual of Style*. If the publication has a style guide or follows a particular one, get a copy of it and use it. Also, before writing your article, review the publication you are writing for and model your writing on the publication's overall tone—formal, chatty, and so on.

Contacts

People you will interview; the editor may have a few suggestions.

Background/reports

Reports, white papers, books, and so on you might want to read before writing; websites you may want to visit for background information.

Filing method

How you will submit the article to the editor? Almost every publication wants you to file by e-mail. But make sure. Before filing electronically, discuss whether your manuscript should be embedded in the e-mail message or sent as an attached file—generally as a Word or text file.

Photo/illustration/art work

Editors will sometimes ask you to take a photo. Unless you are a decent photographer, however, they are more likely to request you ask your contact to supply a photo or artwork. Or the editor might want your interviewee's contact information so the publication designer can get an illustration or take a photograph.

Payment and expenses

The amount of money you get for the work done. Most publications pay a set amount per word; some pay a set amount for the assignment (and give you a word count range). Some pay a set amount 'per column inch'. (Work out the number of words per column inch with your editor as the number varies from publication to publication, depending on the type size and the width of the column.) Some publications pay per edited word (the number of words remaining after an editor edits your article for style and fit). More on payment, below.

Ask if the publication covers expenses and discuss what they will and will not cover. Publications used to cover long-distance calls and film expenses but, with long-distance rates plummeting and digital photos not costing anything to process, most publications expect you to pay for long-distance calls and don't expect to reimburse you for film. However, some publications will pay for calls; many will pay you a fee if you supply photos. Discuss it up front. Unless you have to travel, there are few other expenses. But don't travel and presume the publication will cover your costs. Discuss it upfront.

Invoice

Most publications want you to send them an invoice. I always invoice within a week of sending in my work. A few publications I write for have payment systems in place and I do not have to invoice them. But I use my accounting software to track when payments (Accounts Receivable) are due. Find out if you should invoice, when you should invoice, how you should invoice, and to whom you should send your invoice.

Kill fee

What you get if the article is killed (is not published). If a publication can't use your work because (thick skin required here!) the editor didn't like it, their editorial schedule changed, they ran out of room (and it was a time-sensitive article), or for any other reason, they should pay you a kill fee plus any negotiated expenses.

How much is a kill fee? A kill fee can range from 0% to 100% of the fee. I'd suggest you negotiate a kill fee of 50% to 100% (100% in cases where the article did not run for reasons beyond your control). Also, if the editor says the article is not up to snuff, find out why and negotiate some time to rework it. You might just get it published.

Rights sold

Since the development of the Worldwide Web, copyright has become an issue. Simply put, you sell a publication "first X serial rights," where 'serial' refers to print rights (not electronic; you sell first electronic rights to a website that is publishing your original work) and 'X' refers to the specific market the publication serves: local market, Canadian, American, North American, or world rights. Some publications have a standard contract; with others, you have to negotiate the 'X'.

Many publications want to buy serial and electronic rights for one fee because they want to publish the article and put the article on their website or sell it to a commercial database. In fact, they may have a standard contract you have to sign if you want to write for the publication. There was a time I fought for separate serial and electronic rights. I no longer do that because most publications want both rights for one fee. Never sell copyright or moral rights, however. (More on copyright and moral rights coming in the chapter on copyright and other business issues.)

Contract

If the publication doesn't use a contract (and some publications do not), tell the editor you'd like to e-mail him or her the assignment details as you understand them, to make sure you have it right. Submit an article assignment sheet, based on this checklist, with pertinent details. Include a cover note asking the editor to review the details and get back to you by a specific date if anything is missing. You don't want to be working diligently on the article only to discover, after you've put in days of work, that you misunderstood something or the editor forgot to tell you something important.

More on payment

Again, getting the above information up front before you start to write will save you problems down the line. Of course, after writing and filing your article, you want to be paid. If the editor doesn't mention payment, ask about it! You should have a per-word or per-assignment figure in mind. Most publications pay set rates—from as low as 10 cents per word to a $1 or more. However, be prepared to answer the question: "What do you expect?" (That's why you should have a per word or per assignment figure in mind.)

As mentioned earlier, community papers pay anywhere from zero to 10- or 15-cents per word. Most large urban daily newspapers pay anywhere from 35 to 50 cents per word. Industry trade magazines pay 25 to 50 or 60 cents per word; some high-end trades pay a dollar per word. Glossy consumer magazines pay 50 cents to one dollar per word. A few have cracked the dollar barrier and pay $1.50 or $2 per word.

If the editor's offer feels right, say, "Thanks. Let's sort out the details" and go over all the details presented in the Yes Checklist. If the figure feels low, be prepared to say something like, "That's in the ballpark but I was expecting more because..." (go over the amount of research and the number of interviews you have to do). Or say, "That's not close to what I make when I write for XYZ." The editor will either say, "Well, that's what we pay" or "We could bump it up a few cents per word" or "You've got to be kidding."

No matter what is said, you have to make a business decision and decide what you're going to do next.

Don't forget to ask the editor when you will be paid.

Some publications pay on acceptance: payment arrives 15 to 30 days after you file the article, providing the editor likes (accepts) it. If the editor doesn't like it, he should pay a kill fee.

Some publications pay on publication (30 or more days after they publish the article).

Sadly, some publications treat every article, even those based on queries, as if they were submitted on spec: if they don't like it or can't use it, they don't pay you for it; they don't pay a kill fee either.

Make sure you know when and how they pay and when and who you should invoice. You usually invoice the editor, who sends your invoice to the accounting office/department or the publisher for processing, but don't presume. Ask, especially if you want to be paid in a timely manner—or at all!

Chapter 20: Research and Interviews

You may have some expertise on the topic you're writing about but editors expect you to do background research and conduct interviews for most articles (other than opinion columns, which can be a hard sell, unless you are truly an expert). This chapter will examine basic research techniques and help you prepare to conduct interviews.

While you can exercise a great deal of creativity working as a freelance writer, you need to conduct thorough research and interview appropriate people before writing articles. Once you have done that, you need to accurately present the facts you've uncovered and quote interviewees in context. If you fail to do this, you will lose the trust of editors and lose repeat business.

Background research: Web

I am online constantly doing background research, reviewing press releases, finding contacts, and setting up interviews. My Internet Explorer Favourites (bookmark) is full of statistical and information sites and links to market research firms. In addition, I belong to several small business, writing, and technology e-mail lists. I can get answers to almost any question related to business, technology or writing in hours, if not minutes. I also find many article ideas and interview sources in these discussion forums. It's an understatement to say I find the Internet an indispensable research tool.

When I wrote my first health-oriented article on the causes of skin cancer and how to prevent it for the *Toronto Star*, I conducted a great deal of background research on the Canadian Cancer Society's website. The research proved to be invaluable when I interviewed a cancer specialist. If I hadn't done background research, my first question might have been something like, "What causes skin cancer?" To which I'm sure the good doctor would have answered: "What type of skin cancer are you referring to?" Before conducting my research, I didn't even know there were different types of skin cancer.

Instead of using my prime source for background research, I was able to spend more time talking about some of the larger issues related to cancer causes and prevention. The interview took far less time than it would have had I gone in as a total neophyte and I got better information from the doctor than I would have received had I not done the background research.

Background research

As mentioned, a certain amount of background research goes into pitching article ideas. This research may come from your personal or professional experiences or from the material in your idea file, press releases, on the Web, or from preliminary interviews.

Once you are assigned an article, you need to continue the research process. How much research is required? It depends on the nature of the article, its purpose, and its length. It also depends on what you already know about the topic, the type of contacts you have, and what you have negotiated with the editor.

Think of a story as a series of concentric circles. You want to start your research at the outer ring and work your way into the centre—the crux of the story. By defining outer ring issues and researching them, you will be able to define more clearly the inner ring issue(s). This will enable you to formulate appropriate questions for your interviewees.

Good sources of outer-ring research include the Web, information databases, reference books, magazines and newspapers, industry analysts and reports, government white papers, university professors, and even public-relation agencies. Of course, who you go to and what reference material you use depends on the topic about which you're writing and the type of article you are writing.

One of the first articles I wrote for a community newspaper in Toronto was about a government-funded home renovation. Once the renovations were completed, the house was to be converted into a privately run group home. The house was going up in an area that had a number of group homes and there was an uproar in the community—or so it seemed.

At first, it appeared the article would need to address:

- Provincial and municipal non-profit and social housing policies
- Concerns of social housing advocates and opponents
- The issue of government funding for renovations

But because the article was for a community paper, the article had to focus on:

- Neighborhood issues surrounding this particular house
- Interests of local politicians, business owners, and residents
- The thoughts of local home owners

I had all of 500 words (two typed pages, double-spaced) in which to do this. And I knew next to nothing about social housing, other than what I had read in newspapers. The last people I wanted to interview first were the people banging heads on both sides of the issue. I needed to fill in my knowledge gap so I could better understand the issues. How would you handle this situation? Who do you turn to for answers?

I looked through newspaper files and found quotes from groups in favour of, and opposed to, various forms of social housing. I also read a white paper (background paper) on social housing in Toronto. I got the white paper from a local city councillor (whom I would later interview for the article). I read the report, made notes, and called a few of the people who had worked on the report. I told them I was conducting background research for an article on the social housing and that I needed to clarify a few points in the report. As is often the case, they were happy to chat about their work. From these contacts, I was also able to obtain the names and numbers of other people I could call for information and quotes, in particular people who were actively debating this issue in the neighborhood where the home I was writing about was under renovation.

If this sounds like meticulous, time-consuming work, it was. But it was necessary because I was not knowledgeable about social housing.

Once I finished my background research, however, I felt like a social-housing expert. (One of the joys of writing: you learn a lot.) I could have written a 2,000-word essay on the politics surrounding government social-housing policy. However, my editor did not want such an article. He wanted 500 words on the controversy surrounding one particular house.

When my background research was complete, I had to focus on the inner rings. I wrote out questions for those closest to the battle, talked to local politicians and residents about the issues, and reported on all sides of the controversy.

While there was not much about provincial or municipal social housing policy in the article, it would have been difficult to write the article without some understanding of the bigger picture. And, as is often the case, the research I did served me well in other articles.

Is this type of research always required? It depends on the nature and length of the story, what you already know about the topic (I knew very little), and on the contacts you have. It also depends on deadlines. I had two weeks to do research, conduct interviews, and write the story. If I had been given three days, I might have panicked or said no. Today, I would not panic.

I have become better at compressing the research/interview process and am a more confident interviewer. On occasion, I go to the centre with little background information. It's not how I prefer to work, but I can do it because of my experience and confidence in my ability to get the story.

In such cases, I do not try to fake knowledge. Nor do I beg forgiveness for my lack of knowledge. I tell my sources I am writing about an unfamiliar subject and am on a tight deadline. I tell them I will be taking meticulous notes (or recording the interview; more on that below), and ask them if they can fill me in on some of the background issues first. I listen carefully, ask for clarification as required, and formulate questions to get me to the heart of the matter.

It's called "winging it" and it's not how I recommend you work if you are new to this business. However, it is something you will learn to do—and do well—as you progress.

Questions. Questions.

When formulating interview questions, use the 5W's—who, what, where, when, why (and how)—to question yourself: Who am I interviewing? What is his involvement in relation to the story? Where is he located in time and space in relation to this story? Why am I interviewing this person? How can this person help me?

Your subsequent interview questions don't have to start with one of the W's, but make sure you gather that very basic material before you dig deeper. Also, before you conduct your interview, review your query. That's what sold the editor. Make sure you don't forget what the sale was based on.

Listen up

I conduct interviews in person and by phone. No matter how you conduct interviews, you have to be a good listener. Part of being a good listener involves making eye contact now and again and smiling, especially at the beginning of an interview.

On the other hand, make sure you know the cultural norms of the person you are interviewing; if holding eye contact is not appreciated, then don't hold it. And if you are interviewing the family member of someone who has died in an accident or been murdered, you may want to limit eye contact and not smile. In short, let the situation guide you. Once you start taking notes, your head will be looking down at your notebook. If you want to ask for clarification or ask a new question, look up and briefly make eye contact. Listen carefully and don't jump in and finish the interviewee's sentences. Encourage the interviewee to keep talking by nodding or saying 'uh-uh'.

Taping notes

I tape interviews when I require a great deal of detailed information, when I anticipate a long interview, when I am trying to recreate events in a detailed manner, or when I am doing a profile on a person or organization. I don't tape if I need a quick quote on an issue or event, a brief fact or date, verification of a fact, and so on. I always take notes (or type notes in Word) if interviewing using my speakerphone, even when taping interviews. You never know when a tape recorder might malfunction, the battery might die, the tape might jam, or you might press 'play' and not 'record' before starting the interview. (Yes, I have done that.)

Many writers have invested in digital recorders and will never go back to analogue tape again. There are many reasons to use a digital recorder. They are, for the most part, more reliable than tape and you can save digital files on your computer. Back up your digital files regularly, so you don't have to redo an interview if you accidentally erase a file or your hard drive crashes. If you need to have someone transcribe your interview, you can e-mail the file to the transcriber.

I am not a great typist and I find transcribing taped notes a tedious process. I try to work from my written or typed notes to save time. If I am doing a Question and Answer (Q&A) article, taping and transcribing notes is often how I have to go.

Interviewees are often willing to answer e-mailed questions, however, which saves both interview and transcription time. But when I am writing a personal profile, I go beyond just taking and taping notes based on the interview questions. I'll make notes about the person, his/her environment, mannerisms and gestures, tone of voice, and so on, while taping the interview. I do this to capture details that will help me bring the person—hence the story—to life.

My tape recorder sits beside my speakerphone. That way, if I connect with a person who is immediately available for an interview, I can put him or her on the speakerphone, press record, and start taping. If you don't have a speakerphone you should be able to get a device that you plug into your recorder and attach to the phone from an electronics retailer. Always try these devices before you use them for interviews. I found out the hard way that one recording device I had worked on my phone in the home office but not on my phone in the living room.

Taping: Who tells whom?

If you are interviewing face-to-face, it will be obvious that you are taping. However, technically, in Canada, only one person has to know that the interview is being taped. In other words, the interviewee can legally record the interview without your knowledge. Even so, unless you have some reason for subterfuge, say something like, "By the way, I'll be recording the interview to back up my notes." It's the polite thing to do.

In the U.S., both parties must know the interview is being taped. If you are doing a phone interview from Toronto with a subject who lives in New York, technically you don't have to tell the person you are taping the interview; however, as I said, it is the polite thing to do and it will not interfere with the writing of the story.

Note taking

When I first started interviewing people, I left space between my questions and tried to jam entire answers into the space. It seems silly in retrospect, as I often had to write down more information than the allocated space allowed. Now I write and number my questions on one sheet of paper and write answers in my notebook or Word file. I number answers that correspond to the questions.

Sometimes, when a conversation gets rolling I abandon my numbering system (and even my canned questions) and just engage in a conversation, all the while taking notes. When interviewing somebody who talks rapidly, I'm thankful I have a tape recorder.

However, if I have to rely solely on notes, I ask fast talkers to slow down or to repeat things they've said—especially if I've only managed to jot down part of a juicy quote.

I used to take down everything an interviewee said—or tried to. Over time, I've learned how to exercise my judgment—how to listen better and jot down the most pertinent information. Conducting background research also enables me to focus my questions and my note taking on the most important information.

After the interview, I highlight information that seems pertinent so I can skim through my notes more efficiently when writing the article. Also, I bracket any personal thoughts or observations that I've jotted down when conducting interviews so I don't confuse my words with anything the interviewee may have said.

Interview tips

What is the best way to improve your interview skills? Practice. With that in mind, read the following tips, which are meant to help you conduct effective interviews, and then see if you can apply them (see the Ordinary People journal exercise in this chapter).

Get organized

Write out your contact names and phone numbers on a sheet of paper or in a Word file and write out your proposed questions.

Call or e-mail your contact and set a date and time for the interview. You can say something like, "Hi, I'm Paul Lima calling from the *Toronto Star* to set up an interview with you about concerns consumer groups have expressed over the rates people are paying for local phone service from Bell." Presuming you are talking to right person, the interviewee will generally agree to the interview. So all you have to do is schedule the date and time.

You can say something like, "I'm working to deadline, so what time today would be good for you?" If your deadline is not pressing, you might say, "Would later today or tomorrow be better for you?" Even if you have the luxury of a week or so to complete the story, I suggest you catch your fish as soon as you bait the hook.

Mind you, the interviewee might be prepared to do the interview when you reach him, which is why you want to sort out your questions before you call to set up the interview.

Interview call

When you call to interview the person, specify who you are, why you are calling, and what you want to do. "Hi, I'm Paul Lima calling from the *Toronto Star* to interview you about concerns consumer groups have expressed over the rates people are paying for local phone service from Bell."

Establish initial rapport with the interviewee, but don't chat away mindlessly. Remember, you are both busy people.

Ask the interviewee to S-P-E-L-L his or her first and last name. Some people don't spell their names the way you might think they are spelled and it's important to be sure that you have the accurate spelling. If relevant to the article, ask for his/her age, position and the spelling of the company name and where (city/province or city/state) it is located.

Follow your interview outline, but...

Follow your interview outline but be open to investigating new directions that are pertinent to the article as you listen to answers.

Ask follow-up questions: "Can you elaborate on that?" "Can you explain that in greater detail?" "What led you to that conclusion?"

Ask questions that allow your interviewee to react to what others have said: "You're saying that the rates only cover the cost of the service, but others say your company is profiting exorbitantly from the fees. Can you respond to that?"

Don't be afraid of 'dumb' questions or questions to which you think the answers are obvious. The answers may not be as obvious as you think; you may get a quote that lets you state the obvious in a new or interesting way.

Keep opinions to yourself

Resist the temptation to state your opinions on the subject unless, for the sake of the article, you need to provoke a response from the interviewee.

Don't answer your own questions: "How did you feel when the robber pointed a gun at your head? Were you scared?" The person will probably say, "Yes." But the interviewee will be parroting your second question; you won't know how he or she really felt.

Open-ended questions

Ask open-ended questions:

> **Closed**: "Did you rob the First National Bank?" (No.)
>
> **Open-ended**: "To what extent were you involved in the planning the robbery?" (Um, ah...)

Let the interviewee talk but be firm if she moves off topic or simply pushes the party line: "I realize that it's Bell's position that the local phone rates are cost recovery only, but why would three industry analysts say that is not the case?"

Be assertive

Be assertive but not aggressive or obnoxious. If the person you are interviewing replies to the above question with something like "The analysts are wrong" or "They don't have all the facts," then you need to ask for "the facts." But don't browbeat your interviewee with what others have said. When you are writing, you can juxtapose what the analyst has said against what the spokesperson has said. Let the readers draw their own conclusions.

If the interviewee wants to talk about new and wonderful things that have nothing to do with the article, say, "That's most interesting and I hope to be able to write about it one day. What I need from you right now is...."

Upfront and objective

Don't apologize for a lack of knowledge. Be honest. Don't be afraid to ask for help: "I'm not familiar with your new widget. Can you walk me through how a manufacturing company would use it to save time in the manufacturing process?" At the same time, if it is relevant to your article, you might want to ask that question anyway, so the interviewee can describe the process to you.

If an interviewee asks why you want or need a particular bit of information, don't mistake this as hostility. In most cases, the interviewee is trying to put your questions in context and a simple explanation is all that is required.

Don't react to hostility, anger, or abuse with hostility, anger, or abuse. Say something like, "You seem a bit upset with this question. Perhaps we can clarify why I need to know this and go from there..."

Show interest and enthusiasm. If the questions are dull or you are bored, the answers will be dull and the article will be boring. People are likely to be more forthcoming if you show interest in their answers.

Note taking and on the record

Take meticulous notes; record whenever possible. If writing a profile and interviewing in person, record the interview. This will leave you free to take notes about the person's dress, the setting, or anything else that appeals to the senses (sights, sounds, smells, taste, touch, intuition) and is pertinent to the subject matter.

Don't accept off-the-record interviews unless it is the only way the interviewee will speak and, even then, think twice about accepting them or using the information. (You may have to discuss the use of such interviews with your editor.)

Sometimes a person will speak on the record, but ask you not to use his or her name (not attribute the quotes to him or her). If it is the only way you can get the story and there is a legitimate reason for it, you may have to accept the condition. But ask again at the end of the interview if the person still feels the same way. (Respect the person's wishes: a government employee feeling he or she might be fired, or a person hiding from an abusive partner may have good reasons for keeping his/her identity secret.)

If the interviewee says at the end of an interview that the answers were all 'off the record' refer to your opening remarks. "I said I was from the *Toronto Star* and asked if I could interview you about concerns consumers have expressed over the rates people are paying for local phone service. So I will have to consider your answers on the record."

You do not need signed consent forms to use information from the people you interview. However, if you are covering a complex or controversial topic, discuss with your editor if you need a consent form. More often than not, you won't need one. At the same time, make sure you turn on your tape recorder before you start the interview so that you have yourself on tape identifying who you are and the publication for which you are working.

No sneak peaks

Moving beyond the interview, don't show sources your work. If the interviewee wants to see the article before it is published your answer is, "No." Be polite but firm. Any editor would be livid if you let your interviewee 'clear' the article first.

Are there exceptions to the above? Just like there are exceptions to almost every rule of grammar, there are exceptions to the above. I once had a person give me a very detailed explanation about an extremely technical matter. I said, "I'd appreciate it if you could review my interpretation of the technical information to make sure I got it right." I only sent the interviewee the portion of the article on the complex technical matter.

If you are writing an article for an in-house publication (a corporate job), the client (usually the publication's editor) will have an article approval process in place. It might be fine for you to have interviewees review articles; however, ask your editor first. She might want to receive and edit the article before it goes out for approval. If that is the case, you can tell interviewees that you'll be filing the article with the editor who will review it and send it out for comments and approval. Find out what the process is, and what part you will or will not play in it, before you conduct your interviews.

Journal exercise: Getting focused

Focus on something you are writing about or hope to write about. Perhaps you can use one of the query letters you developed (you have written several query letters, haven't you?) as a place to start.

First, describe your assignment in one or two sentences. Something like: "Focusing on the issues of health and nutrition, this article will explore whether there is any truth to the expression 'an apple a day keeps the doctor away'."

Then find and list three sources (websites, white papers or other research documents) you might use for background research. List two or three possible interview contacts. Write out 10 questions you would ask each interviewee.

Journal exercise: *Ordinary People*

Pretend you are writing for *Ordinary People Magazine* (a fictional magazine): "At *Ordinary People Magazine*, we believe ordinary people are extraordinary."

Interview an ordinary person—a relative or friend, or your butcher, baker or candlestick maker—and find something that makes that person extraordinary. Then write a lead and nut 'graph.

You should know the person you interview will probably not consider himself or herself extraordinary. It's your job, through your interview, to find out what is extraordinary about that person.

The extraordinary element might involve the person's entire life; it might involve one element of the person's life or one incident in the person's life. It's up to you to discover the extraordinary in the ordinary person you interview.

You'll do this through:

- The questions you choose to ask
- Listening closely to what the person has to say
- Asking for details and clarification on the things the person says
- Absorbing all that you have heard
- Writing your story from the point of view (angle or slant) that says there is something extraordinary about this particular ordinary person

Before you start your extraordinary people interview, explain you are doing this as part of a learning experience, not for publication. Try your best to get organized but do not fret if you are not sure what questions to ask. Plunge in and have fun. Once you complete the interview, write your article—or at least the lead. Heck, if the person is truly extraordinary, pitch a query to an appropriate publication. (If that happens, you need to get permission from the person you interviewed to pitch a story idea based on the interview, as you told that person that the work you were doing was not for publication.)

Interview checklist

After conducting several interviews, you will feel like a pro. But if you are a novice, review the interview checklist to make sure your are as organized as you can be.

Before the interview

- Introduce yourself, the publication, and article topic
- Explain how and why the interviewee has been chosen to be interviewed
- Set up the interview appointment
- Dress appropriately to interview location and interviewee subject, if you are interviewing in person

- Inform the interviewee that you will be taping the interview
- Check the tape/digital recorder
    - batteries are fully charged or power cord is available
    - tape is blank and you have extra tapes (or adequate file space)
    - forwarded tape past tape leader / created appropriate file
    - check volume control
    - check external microphone switched to 'on'

Beginning of interview
- Introduce yourself, the publication, and the article topic again
- Re-ask permission to record
- Start recording by identifying yourself and the publication for which you are writing the article
- Start interview with a comment such as, "I've prepared some questions but I'm prepared to digress if digressions seem appropriate to the topic…"

During the interview
- Began with general, open-ended questions
- Keep questions short, simple, and clearly stated
- If the interviewee seems to be struggling to answer, ask if you can clarify the question
- Follow-up interesting answers with additional probes to clarify important details

After the interview
- Ask, "Is there anything else you'd like to add? Anything you think I'm missing?"
    - Be open to hearing some interesting information you may want to follow-up on
- Thank the person for their time and let the person know approximately when the article will be published
- Check that the recording was successful
- Make handwritten notes on ideas, interpretations, and other insights; secure recording and notes against lost

Chapter 21: Copyright and Business Issues

Since the development of the Worldwide Web, copyright has become a major issue for freelance writers. Remember that you sell publications first X serial rights. Serial equals print and X equals geographic (Canadian, American, North American or world) rights. You have to negotiate geographic rights with the editor.

In theory, if you and the editor do not discuss copyright, you are selling only first serial rights. Most publications have websites, however, and republish work in electronic databases. They might use your work online and electronically without discussing electronic rights (e-rights) with you. That's more than first serial rights and it breaks the law. To circumvent this, they issue contracts that demand e-rights for no fee to you, the writer. This is perfectly legal and if you sign the contract, the publication can then use your article in electronic databases and on websites. On the other hand, if you do not sign, you might not get the assignment.

If you ask for payment for e-rights, publishers will often plead website poverty. Gee, do they pay to host the site? Do they pay employees or freelance website designers to construct and update the site? Of course they do. Why then are they so reluctant to pay writers? I've not heard a good answer to that question. While there are writers' unions and associations fighting for e-rights, the fact is that many publications will not pay for such rights. That means you have a business decision to make because, as stated above, some publications will simply not hire you if you do not sign their contracts.

Why you want more money for e-rights

As a freelance writer, you own the copyright to your work. You can earn income by selling second serial rights to non-competing publications. If your work is online, it is devalued because anybody with access to the Web can read it. Why would another publication want to buy it if it is online?

Therefore, to protect your income, as well as your rights, at least ask for payments for e-rights. When I sell to a newspaper or magazine, I sell either first Canadian or North American serial rights. When possible, I negotiate 10% to 25% for e-rights. But it is not always possible to negotiate such a deal. Enough said.

By way of aside, when I do corporate work (brochure copy, press releases, articles for in-house newsletters, Web content), I sell all rights for one fee. Corporations want to own what they contract out (it's called work for hire). They also tend to pay more than publications, making the sale of all rights worthwhile.

Some publications that do not pay e-rights pay decent rates and give me steady work. So, begrudgingly, I sell them serial and non-exclusive e-rights combined in one fee. Non-exclusive sale of e-rights allows me to post articles on my website and to try to resell articles to other websites. As I said, it is a business decision.

Beware of the contracts that leave you with copyright but take serial rights, e-rights, and moral rights. If you grant a publication moral rights, you grant them the right to edit your copy any way they want and to run it with or without your permission and with or without your byline in any print or electronic publication they produce. If you sell or give away copyright, you cannot resell your article to any other publication or website. In fact, you cannot even post in on your website. Fight for your e-rights; do not give away copyright or moral rights.

Reselling versus recycling work

Unless you sell copyright, you can resell your article to any other publication within 24 hours, unless you've agreed to time, geographical, or competitive publication restrictions. However, even if there are no negotiated competitive publications restrictions, if you resell an article to a competing publication, the publication you first sold it to would not look kindly upon you. So resell intelligently. If you retain e-rights, you can resell your article to a Web-based publication. (A few pay for material, but not many.)

Rather than reselling my articles, I focus more on recycling ideas to different publications. That way I can reapply most of the background research I have conducted and even reuse some of my interview material. This reduces my per article workload and it means I am paid for first serial rights (first rights tend to be a higher rate) rather than second serial rights by the second publication.

I try not to resell the same idea to a publication that directly competes with the publication to which I have sold first rights. If I do recycle an idea to a competing publication, I find new interviewees and make sure I write a new lead. If I have any doubt, I discuss them with my editors. In fact, many editors hire me because I have previously written on the topic that they want me to write about; they think I actually know what I am writing about! In short, whether you are selling an original idea or recycling one, work with your editors in an upfront and professional manner. It pays off in the long run.

Tracking who owes what

In an earlier chapter, I outlined all you have to discuss with an editor before you submit an article. One of the discussion points was the method of invoicing. If you want to get paid, you need to invoice—in most cases.

I did not have to invoice the *Toronto Star*. The paper directly deposited cheques into my bank account, but I kept track of what they owed me. Occasionally, I had to inform their accounting department it had missed a payment.

Unless the publication pays like the *Toronto Star* does, it is your responsibility to invoice editors (or publishers), to keep track of your receivables (the money owed to you), and to make calls or send e-mails to remind editors or publishers if they fall behind on payment.

You can do this in a computer spreadsheet such as Excel or in an accounting package (Quicken or another package). You can even use pen and paper. Whatever you use, use it consistently so you know who owes you what and when it is due. In addition, if a publication falls behind in its payment, remind them in a professional manner that payment is past due. While it would be nice if all publications paid promptly (most do), it is your job to stay on top of the situation.

Minimize bad debts

Bad debts happen. They are not fun, but they occur. There are a few things you can do to minimize bad debts. If you notice a publication comes out erratically, consider it a sign that the publication may be having financial problems. If the editor of a publication you have never seen or heard of contacts you, ask the editor to send you a copy of the publication so you can see how well it is produced. Also, if you are doing work for a new publication, see if you can chat with other freelancers who are writing for it or who have written for it.

If you are doing work for a small business or a corporation you are not familiar with, check references. Also, ask for an upfront payment of 50% of the negotiated fee (more about this in the next section of the book). If the person you are dealing with refuses, it may be a sign of financial instability. Do not write a second article for a publication if they have not paid you for your first article. (There are exceptions to this rule, especially if you are writing articles on a daily or weekly basis for legitimate publications, or writing a second article for a respectable monthly publication that requires a great deal of lead time.)

If a publication goes under (bankrupt), there is little you can do to obtain payment. It happens. It has happened to me. It's not fun. I hate it. I cut my losses and move on.

Basic bookkeeping

Disclaimer: *This short section is not meant to replace advice a bookkeeper or tax adviser may give you. Unless you have accounting/tax expertise, I recommend that you use a professional to help you with your bookkeeping and taxes.*

One of the nice things about freelance writing is that you do not need a great deal of money to launch your business. On the downside, you can't simply hang out your freelance-writing shingle and expect money to come flowing in. As with running any business (at least any other business I know), it takes time to establish yourself and develop regular clients. That means the cash flow can be erratic the first year or so.

In most countries, you are allowed to deduct legitimate business expenses from your revenues. What are legitimate business expenses? Keeping the disclaimer above in mind, I deduct the cost of the following:

- Computer hardware, software, and peripherals. (Hardware, software and many peripherals are considered a capital investment; a percentage of the investment is deducted each year.)
- Office furnishings. These, too, are often considered capital investments.
- Office supplies: pens, pencils, paper, staples, disks, stamps, etc.
- Magazine and newspaper subscriptions.
- Phone services and long-distance business calls.

- Internet Service Provider and Web space hosting fees; fees paid to website designers.
- The percentage of my rent equal to the percentage of my apartment that is devoted to office space. (If you own a house, you may only be able to deduct a percentage of the interest you pay on your mortgage, rather than a percentage of your mortgage; the rules are not the same for Canada and the U.S. so check with your accountant.)
- Business meals (a percentage may only be applicable).
- Business portion of car expenses, including a percentage of gas, repair bills, and insurance.
- Professional fees (like your accountant and your membership in writers' organizations, such as the Professional Writers Association of Canada or the American Society of Journalists and Authors).
- Professional development expenses.

I keep track of the money I earn (revenue) and the money I spend on my business (expenses) in Microsoft Excel. This makes life easy for my accountant as I can print a full expense and income report (broken down by categories) so she doesn't have to spend hours sorting through a shoebox full of receipts. (I keep a shoebox full of receipts so she can check items if she has any questions.)

As mentioned, I also track money owing to me (receivables). Once I invoice a client, I enter the date of invoice, client's name, article topic and the date payment is due in Excel. (There are accounting programs, as mentioned, that you can use for this as well.) I check my receivables on a monthly basis. If a receivable is overdue, I send a polite e-mail reminder. That usually sorts out the problem: the editor forgot to forward the invoice to accounting, accounting misplaced/lost the invoice, the cheque is in the mail—as it often really is.

On occasion, I have had to re-invoice publications, especially start-ups (new publications) that are underfinanced. Several publications have gone under, declaring official bankruptcy, while owing me money. It's worth repeating: it happens. There are avenues you can follow to attempt to recoup your money, including small-claims court or hiring a collections agency.

No matter how you slice it, collecting overdue accounts is a pain. Everybody who runs a business has had to deal with bad debts at some point. Expect it, but do what you can to minimize it. If it happens to you, fight for every dollar owed—within reason. If the company that owes you money has gone bankrupt, recognize that you won't get much, if anything. Cut your losses and move on. You might want and need the money but do you need the negative energy or aggravation associated with fighting a battle you can't win.

In short, rather than spending your time fighting a lost, negative battle, I believe you should get on with your job and spend your time more profitably—pitching, selling, and writing articles.

Chapter 22: Additional Query Letters

The query letters below were used successfully to garner article assignments. They are reprinted with permission of various members of the Professional Writers Association of Canada (PWAC). The authors hold copyright on these queries, even those who have asked that their names not be used, and the queries may not be reproduced.

If the queries do not resonate with you, don't think they will not resonate with editors. It is your job to send the right query to the right editor of the right publication. If you now nothing about lymphedema, for instance, you would not write the query below.

> Did you know that lymphedema occurs mostly in middle-aged men and women 35-45 years old and happens when there is interference in the movement of lymph fluid?
>
> When movement of lymph becomes impaired, fluid leaks and accumulates in tissues and swelling occurs. This swelling, although not usually painful can be extreme as a limb or body part (mostly in the arms and/or legs) may expand to several times its normal size. In addition, it leaves the skin and underlying tissues more vulnerable to infection and inflammation than normal. And over time, the skin can become hard and thickened.
>
> Conventional treatment for lymphedema yields only temporary results that don't address the underlying cause. The good news is that are there a range of holistic options such as natural herbal remedies, nutritional supplements and manual lymph drainage (MLD) and combined decongestive physiotherapy (CDP) treatments available.

They help keep the swelling associated with lymphedema under control and reduce the possibility of infection and secondary skin change.

As a member of the Professional Writer's Association of Canada, I have written several articles on holistic medicine for Alive, Beyond Fitness, Canada's Healthy Living Guide, Country health, Health 'N Vitality, Vitality, Weight Watchers and other Canadian and U.S. publications. I currently write a feature column on holistic medicine for Health 'N Vitality magazine.

I have a piece coming up in the September issue of *Alive*, "The Healing Power of Pet Therapy" and "Weight No More: Lose Weight Naturally" for the May issue of *Health 'N Vitality*.

Thanks for your consideration. I look forward to hearing from you.

The article based on the query by Barbara K. Adamski (see query below) was published in *Flavours* magazine. Barbara is a freelance writer and editor based in New Westminster, B.C. She has written for several magazines and trade publications, including *enRoute*, *Reader's Digest*, and *The Walrus*. Her work has also been broadcast on CBC Radio. If you want to know more about her, visit her website at www.barbadamski.com.

Japanese food never goes out of style in Greater Vancouver and it constantly changes and evolves, reflecting the diversity and creativity of the community.

Take sushi for example. The word sushi, although it officially refers to vinegared rice, was long thought by Canadians to mean raw fish. But a peek at what local Japanese restaurants are doing with sushi reveals intriguing combinations of fish (both raw and cooked), vegetables, and fruit (yes, fruit).

While the BC Roll (barbecued salmon skin and cucumber) has been a mainstay for several years now, there are some other fresh and tasty rolls appearing on menus.

The above three paragraphs are how I propose to start an 800 word feature on the Lower Mainland's sushi scene.

I plan to cover interesting new combinations, such as Tojo Restaurant's Northern Light Roll (zucchini, prawn tempura, mango, and avocado wrapped in a thin cucumber crepe), and discuss where to buy new and traditional ingredients for your own sushi party at home.

While many of us know about nigiri (fish or other ingredient on rice) and rolled sushi, few know about the traditional Japanese method of preparing sushi for home parties—temaki (literally hand-rolled) or cone sushi. Not only is it easier to prepare, guests can add their own ingredients quickly and easily, using a different combination for each piece.

I plan to visit Matsu Sushi, a Coquitlam-based sushi store, for tips on making sushi, hosting sushi parties, and information on sushi complements such as side-dishes, sake and other wines, and beer.

Recipes that I would use include are vinegared rice, and a few side dishes such as goma-ae (spinach, miso, and sesame) and pickled ginger. I would also interview a sushi chef to find any tips he has, and how he comes up with new sushi combinations. And I'd like to suggest some interesting desserts such as traditional green tea ice cream or, for the more daring, wasabi gelato.

Many queries, like the one below, cover how-to topics and include tips that let readers know how to solve a problem or take advantage of an opportunity. What do you know how to do? Or who do you know who knows how to do something particular well? Think about it, and look for, publications that might be interested in your how-to ideas.

Subject: Working 9 to 5—Valuable Office Etiquette Tips for Moms-to-Be

Nausea, swollen feet, doctor's appointments, and casual clothing are all part of the pregnancy game. Unfortunately, when the game is played in an office setting, what should be an enjoyable time can also become a situation that creates friction with co-workers and superiors.

What is the etiquette of pregnancy in the workplace? Is it okay to talk about cravings and flatulence at the water-cooler? When is the proper time to announce the big news to your boss? Should you work until the last possible day before your due date?

With more and more women in the workplace, there have been many changes in office etiquette as it relates to pregnant women. Office etiquette expert and certified professional member of the Association of Image Consultants International, Donna Chevrier offers this advice: "Once you have decided how long you will continue to work, you need to discuss these plans with your employer before anyone else at the office learns about your pregnancy. This way you will maintain a professional image through your honesty and integrity."

The article I suggest is a list of 10 valuable office etiquette tips for moms-to-be with topics ranging from when to announce the happy news, office baby showers, how to graciously handle morning (and sometimes all day) sickness, proper office attire, doctor related absences and how to politely turn down physical or strenuous work. I would also like to include a sidebar on how to prepare in case baby decides to make an early appearance. Image consultant and office etiquette guru Donna Chevrier has agreed to be interviewed for this article.

I am a Toronto-based freelance writer who has had articles recently published in Canadian Family Magazine, The Globe and Mail, Fazeteen, and What magazines. In 2000, I also had the honour of having my article "The Down Under Wonders" nominated in the National Magazine Awards.

I look forward to discussing this article with you.

The query below was originally sent to *Home Business Report*. The editor didn't reply. The author decided to send the query to *Today's*

Parent. She got the gig, though the angle was changed to a humour piece with the focus on summer challenges because the article was going to appear in the August issue. As mentioned, if you demonstrate flexibility, it can help you land writing gigs.

> "I'm doing an interview on the phone. Come in and wave 'hi' then get a snack and start your homework."
>
> The note is on the kitchen counter where my daughter, Jennifer, will see it when she comes home from school. She peeks in the door, waves and leaves. Half an hour later, I check on her. I have completed my interview with a company CEO who didn't have a clue about what just happened. It was easy to achieve my goal this time. But it wasn't always that way.
>
> When I embarked on my freelance writing career in 1995, my daughter was nine. I made the decision, in part, to be closer to home and my family. My office was situated in a corner of the family room, where I remained for five years. In between I dealt with arguments about not being able to watch TV because I was working, listening to Jennifer and her friends chatting at the dining room table outside my door, and a variety of family emergencies including scraped knees and hurt feelings that couldn't wait until I got off the phone.
>
> But the positives far outweigh the negatives. When there's a special school event, I can usually juggle my calendar to be there. When the school calls to say my daughter is sick I can drop what I'm doing and tend to her needs. When no other parent is available to drive during the day, my kids could always count on me to help out.
>
> In Canada, parents who choose to work at home do so for a variety of reasons. For those of us who stick with it there are numerous challenges and rewards. I would love to write an article for Today's Parent on self-employment and parenting. I could write this in one of four ways:
>
> - A first-hand account of challenges, comical moments and other reminiscences by parents who have chosen to work at home where the line between family and work is often tenuous, or

- A "how to make it work" article, interlaced with first-hand experiences and information from professional sources like Donna Lero from the University of Guelph and Nora Spinks from Work Life Harmony Services, or
- An article focused on parents who might be considering working from home, what the challenges are, what personal attributes are needed and information from experts, or
- An article that combines two or three of these ideas.

I am a veteran freelancer who specializes in writing about parenting and business issues—teen issues in particular. My work has appeared in a number of national and regional magazines and I recently won an IABC Award of Excellence for "Turning your store into cool central"—a thought-provoking article about the lengths retail merchants are going to in order to drive teens into their stores. You can find the article online at www.writeconnection.org along with some additional samples of my work.

Many magazines cover health issues. But seldom can you simply write about an illness or health issue. You need an angle: how to live with the issue, how to avoid it or overcome it, how family members can help someone with a particular issue, and so on. Just as I have written about search engine optimization and pay per click for a variety of publications, you can apply the same slant to various health issues and write similar articles about each issue—for one publication or for a variety of publications.

Subject: Query: Parenting on Low Power

A recent bout of shingles sapped my energy and led to a series of viral infections lasting several weeks. It has meant cancelled engagements, some time off work, imposed rest times on weekends - and, outside in the garden, a gleeful takeover of unchecked weeds. It hasn't meant, however, time away from the demands of being a mom. Sick leave is not included in the perks of parenting. Any mom or dad who's been down with the flu can tell stories of serving dinner with a forehead that burns hotter than the entree, or trying to sing the requisite roster of bedtime lullabies while coping (croaking?) with laryngitis.

Illness, whether short- or long-term, can certainly present additional challenges to the job of parenting. While we deal with fatigue, fever, aches or pains, we must continue to nurture and discipline our children. I would like to write a feature about "Parenting on Low Power" for your publication. I can present coping techniques and strategies for conserving energy, finding alternate care, coming up with creative ideas for keeping kids occupied, and thinking outside the box when it comes to performing daily parenting tasks. I'm sure parents who have managed this situation in the past will be able to offer some proven tips, as will service providers (health and/or social service professionals).

A variety of parents will be able to benefit from this article—including those dealing with chronic illnesses such as chronic fatigue syndrome, those undergoing treatment for acute health problems such as cancer, and other moms and dads experiencing colds, flu or other viruses that may have them temporarily under the weather.

[*About paragraph deleted.*]

Query sent to *The Globe and Mail* arts editor

This query may seem a tad long, but I had never written an author profile. I wanted to convey a sense of my writing style and what the author went through to complete her first novel, as that was the focus of the pitch. I interviewed the author before pitching this and thought there was an intriguing story here, one that deserved to be told.

If interested, you can read the article, "Dreaming of Fat City," online at this page: www.paullima.com/articles. Scroll to the bottom and you will find the link to the article.

Last Summer At Barebones is narrated by Dee Graham, a forty-something journalist who lives and works alone, scribbling stories for a tabloid rag. Graham is a near-anorexic recluse struggling to forget the childhood she spent as a despised and picked on, enormously fat, compulsive overeater.

One night, she inadvertently crosses paths with an obese female comic telling intimate details of Dee's childhood twisted into a comedy routine. The comic is her former chief torturer, her sister, the once lithe and beautiful Theresa. This encounter causes Dee to recall her miserable life, in particular the summer of 1970 she spent at Barebones Lake in Muskoka. Dee begins to plot her revenge.

Diane Baker Mason, a forty-something writer who lives with her twin teenaged sons and her dog, started the novel as a bit of a lark—something to keep her writing skills sharp until she found time to embark on her real novel, a magnum opus about a vampire housewife who drops from the sky like something out of a Blake poem. Over 100,000 words into *Last Summer At Bare Bones*, Mason canned the idea of the vampire novel and began to take her "lark" seriously.

Over the five years it took her to complete *Last Summer at Barebones*, Mason continued to write in spurts because she:

- Had to drive her mother (who had almost died) to various medical appointments
- Started York University as a mature student
- Obtained her English degree
- Endured the break up of her marriage of 20 years
- Took on several jobs to pay child support (her ex kept the twins)
- Entered a new relationship, which came crashing down
- Ran in, and completed, the New York City marathon
- Started law school (she enters third year this fall)...

She despaired ever completing the novel, then one day in June she found time and fortune on her side: she received a letter awarding her a $10,000 Canada Council grant and, on the same day, she received her letter of acceptance from Osgoode Hall Law School. She had three months to finish her novel if she chose to go to law school, and she could afford to work on it full-time.

"I love a deadline," she says.

In early September, McArthur & Co will publish *Last Summer At Barebones*, the first novel written by Toronto resident, Diane Baker Mason. Would you be interested in a profile on her? She is willing to talk openly about the dedication and perseverance it took to complete her first novel as life collapsed around her.

[Concluded with *About Me* paragraph.]

Everything You Wanted to Know About Freelance Writing

Part Three:

How to Find, Price and Manage Corporate Writing Assignments

Chapter 23: Business Vision

In this section of the book, we examine writing for the corporate market—how to find, price, and manage corporate writing assignments. It's not unusual for freelancers to write for periodicals and the corporate market, or for their business to evolve from writing for periodicals to writing for corporate markets (or vice versa). There are similarities to how you approach the periodical and corporate markets, but there are many differences too, as you will see.

The first difference pertains to business vision. If you know you want to write for the periodical market, your business vision should include the topics you want to cover and the types of articles you want to write so you can focus your efforts on finding publications that publish those types of articles on those topics. Although that is over simplifying the job of periodical freelancers, I would suggest that you will have to do even more up front thinking about your business if you want to write for the corporate market.

In short, you need a detailed business vision when writing for the corporate market. It becomes the foundation of your business and marketing plans. You build your business plan and marketing plan upon your business vision so you can focus your energy and time.

Having said that, even if you only want to write for, or primarily want to write for, the periodical market, you still need focus and you have to manage your time. With that in mind, periodical freelancers might want to complete the business vision exercises in this section. A little introspection can't hurt; it can help a lot too.

Why business vision?

Most writers I know do not have a business vision, let alone a business plan. If they have a business plan, it's most likely a long document that is not very practical. For instance, it might define their services and competition and the approximate size of the market they can tackle; however, it might not include a detailed marketing plan—the stuff the writer needs to do to sell services to clients.

Your business vision is your target. It's the business life you want to live—the life of a six-figure freelance writer, perhaps. The business plan includes the goals and objectives and big picture strategies and details that support your vision. The marketing plan, as you shall see, includes the tasks you must do to reach your objectives so you can fulfill your vision. If you do not have a business vision, and business and marketing plans, or if your business plan is collecting dust in a drawer because it's not very useful, it's time for a change. It's time to start doing things differently.

Why do things differently? If you always do what you've always done, you'll always get what you've always got. Because nothing changes unless you make changes in the way you do things. Are you ready to change, to try something different? *If so, let's go!*

Now that you are managing your time better (at least you should be if you read the time management chapter), what are you going to do with all the time you have on your hands?

You are going to establish your business vision and create your business and marketing plans. These tasks are not as onerous as you might imagine, and they are more important than you might think.

As mentioned, your business vision is the foundation of your business plan. Without a business vision, how will you know where you want to go? Without a destination, how will you create a road map to get you there?

Your business vision is not a mission statement. Your business plan can include a mission statement—nothing wrong with that. However, don't confuse your business vision and your mission statement. A mission statement defines the core purpose of the business you are running or why it exists. Your business vision defines your business: who you are, what you do, and why you do it.

To define your vision, think like a journalist. Answer the W5 questions—who, what, where, when, and why (and sometimes how)—from a business perspective.

Who are you now?

Before you figure out who you want to be, focus on who you are now.

You may work full-time, part-time, or be unemployed. You may write for newspapers and magazines on a freelance basis. You may write for periodicals and the corporate market or just for the corporate market. You may do very little, if any, writing.

You may be reading this book because you want to become a corporate writer or because you want to find more or better-paying clients, but put that aside for now.

Take some time to answer the first set of questions. Be honest about who you are now, but don't beat yourself up over anything. You are on a journey, and we are trying to establish where you are now. Then we will look at where you want to go, and how to get you there.

Vision questions: One writer's answers

To make this exercise clearer, I have included a semi-autobiographical set of answers that I created in reply to the "Who are you now?" questions. Notice the informal but honest tone. This is nothing complicated, simply a bit of reflection before we figure out where we want to go, so we can then determine how we are going to get there.

> **Who are you?** Freelance newspaper writer. Occasional dog walker.
>
> **What do you do?** Write articles pertaining to the IT industry as well as small businesses. Write some articles on education and social housing. Walk dogs, as infrequently as possible.
>
> **Who do you do it for?** *Toronto Star* and information-technology trade magazines; community newspaper. Dog walking for a full-time walker who needs help every now and then.
>
> **Where do you do it?** From home by phone; occasionally go out to interview people. Walk dogs in the park.
>
> **When do you do it?** Mostly weekdays, a bit on weekends.
>
> **Why do you do it?** I like to write. I am interested in technology. That led to articles about businesses using technology. I picked up a community paper and called the editor to see if he was looking for a writer. Two years later, I am still writing for him—for very little money.

How did you get here? I have a computer background and worked for a small computer-training company. The technology kept on changing and I didn't want to keep up. An English major, I wrote for my university newspaper and thought I'd try to make some money freelancing while I looked for a job. That was two years ago. I've stopped looking for a job. But I need to make more money. I know I want to write on a freelance basis, but I need to make more money at it.

Vision questions: Who are you now?

Now it's your turn. Answer the vision questions below. Take a few minutes, or more if you need it, and figure out who you are now and how you got here.

Before you start the exercises in this section of the book, I suggest you start a corporate writer's journal or set up a file on your computer where you will do the exercises in this section of the book.

When you are answering the questions below, I want you to write as freely as possible. Use point form if it helps you answer more freely. Keep in mind that this exercise is for your eyes only. So don't censor yourself.

- Who are you?
- What do you do?
- Who do you do it for?
- Where do you do it?
- When do you do it?
- Why do you do it?
- How did you get here?

Please answer these questions before you read on.

Who will you be?

I hope that was not too painful a process. And maybe it was even a little bit fun, or at least insightful. I believe it's important to know who you are if you want to change who you are, so if you skipped this exercise, please go back and spend at least a few minutes on it before you move on.

Next, you are going to answer a similar set of questions, but this time you are going to look ahead. Visualize, through writing, who you want to be and what you want to do. Before you write, read each of the questions and then close your eyes and try to picture the answers. This will help with your writing.

Don't be concerned if you are not quite sure how to answer the questions. As you learn more about how to shape your freelance writing business, you will have an opportunity to revisit this exercise. In other words, you are not carving the Ten Commandments in stone here. What you write can change. But just because it can change, do not short-change yourself here. Give this exercise some thought.

To make this exercise clear, I have modified my own answers to the "Who do you want to be?" questions. After reading the answers, answer the questions for yourself from a business perspective. Write as freely as possible; don't censor yourself.

Read the answers below, and then take some time to answer the second set of questions.

Vision questions: One writer's answers

Who do you want to be? Corporate freelance writer. Occasional periodical writer.

What do you want to do? As a corporate writer, write media releases, promotional copy (brochures, websites), case studies, and related material. As a periodical writer, write business of technology articles and articles of interest to small businesses.

Who do you want to do it for? Corporate sectors I might target: information technology (including security, networking, e-commerce, business software developers); financial services; transportation. Periodicals: *The Globe and Mail* and *Backbone* magazine; search for or be open to solicitation from high-end trade publications.

Where do you want to be when you do it? Write from home. Attend meetings; travel to selected interviews. Open to short-term (couple of weeks) working on-site.

When do you want to do it? Business hours. Not opposed to some evenings and weekends.

Why do you want to do it? I have some writing experience and enjoy writing. I seem to understand what others want to say and can say it, or write it, for them. I like seeing my by-line in print but am more interested in earning a full-time living—making money as a freelancer. I enjoy flexible hours but don't mind working hard to meet tight deadlines. I have had straight jobs and do not like commuting to work and working in offices. I work well without supervision and am an independent person.

How are you going to get there?

Note: Much of this book is devoted to helping you answer the *how* question.

Your turn

Remember, you are looking at who you aspire to be. You may want to develop a freelance writing business or increase your current freelance revenue. You may want to write for periodicals on a freelance basis but pick up some corporate work. You may want to find new or better-paying corporate clients. Like me, you may want to do corporate writing and training, and perhaps write and sell some books (those aspects are part of my full business vision).

This is your vision. Be both as broad and as specific as possible. This information may change as you progress through the book. Nothing wrong, and a lot right, with that. Ultimately, will use this information to help you determine and write your business and marketing plans.

Vision questions: Who do you want to be?

Feel free to answer the *who do you want to be* questions below in your exercise journal or in a computer file.

- Who do you want to be?

- What do you want to do?

- Who do you want to do it for?
- Where do you want to be when you do it?
- When do you want to do it?
- Why do you want to do it?
- How are you going to get there?

Note: You can take a stab at the how question; however, I suggest you skip it for now as much of the rest of this book is devoted to helping you answer how.

Please answer the questions before you read on.

Now what?

Now I suggest you turn your point form statements into sentences. In other words, create a formal business vision.

If you are struggling with what you can write for the corporate market, hang in there. We will look at the writing services you can offer the corporate market later in the book. If you are not sure who you can write for, hang in there. We will also look at the sectors you can target. In short, your vision is an organic statement that you can revise as you progress through this book (and as you progress through your business life).

So what you do now is review the answers to both sets of questions. As you do your review, look for gaps between the answers in Set One (who you are now) and those in Set Two (who you want to be). Those gaps represent the gaps between your current reality and your business vision. As you progress through the book, you work on clarifying your business vision and then on figuring out how to close the gaps.

If you are wondering whether you have to offer as many services as I do to become a successful freelancer, the answer is no. I was a six-figure freelance writer long before I diversified my vision. Changes to my vision, of course, led to changes in my business and marketing plans. As I have said, it all starts with a business vision.

If you have not already done so, finish the first draft of your business vision. Keep in mind that you are writing something that you can change as you read this book and learn more about what it takes to become a successful freelancer and that you can change as your business evolves—as you land new clients, take on new gigs, and develop new skills.

At minimum, you should revisit your vision once a year. Preferably, though, conduct this review once every three or four months over the next year or two if this is the first time you have developed a vision for your business. To remember to do that, book your business-vision visits in your scheduling software. Get into the habit of using your scheduling software so that your computer can tell you what to do, based on what you told your computer you want to do.

So, what is your business vision? Or should I say: what is the who, what, where, when, and why of your business vision?

Chapter 24: Do the Math, Again

Before we move from business vision to the business and marketing plans, we should talk money. And whenever I talk money, I talk time. You know the cliché: time is money. If you work full-time, it may seem as though it doesn't matter what you do with your time: as long as you aren't fired, you are paid. On the other hand, if you are a freelancer, what you do with your time is crucial. If you are not working billable hours, you are not being paid.

Billable hours

You are working non-billable hours if you are in marketing mode, or when you are filing, cleaning your office, doing your books, and so on. A billable hour, on the other hand, is any hour (or part thereof) that you are paid to work.

You may be writing, conducting research or interviews, revising work, or attending meetings. As long as you are being paid, it is a billable hour. On the other hand, freelance writers who write for newspapers or magazines are often paid by the word or are paid a set amount for a word range (an article of 900 to 1,000 words, for instance). These writers often have difficulty thinking in terms of billable hours, but it can be done.

Say you are being paid 50-cents per word for a 750-word article. That's $375. If it takes you two hours to research and to conduct interviews, five hours to write and one hour to revise, that's eight hours. If the editor asks you a few questions and you have to put in another two hours of work on the article, then you've hit 10 hours. In billable terms, you earned $37.50 per hour.

That's better than McWages, but many writers would spend more than 10 hours on such an article. That does not mean you cannot or should not write for newspapers and magazines. However, if you want to be a six-figure freelancer *and* you want to write 50 to 100 articles per year for newspapers and magazines, you may have a tough time reaching your financial goal.

Which came first?

Question: *How many billable hours do you need to work per week to become a six-figure freelancer?*

Answer: *It depends on how much you charge per hour.*

Question: *How much should you charge per hour?*

Answer: *It depends on how many billable hours you can work per week.*

It's a bit like the chicken or the egg question, no? One cannot exist without the other, but which comes first? To answer the question, I like to start with my annual revenue target, which starts with six figures—the Holy Grail of freelancers. Unlike the Holy Grail, earning six figures as a freelancer is not a myth. Writers who earn six-figure incomes are all dedicated and disciplined writers. (But they still manage to take some time off to goof around.)

Six figures may be your revenue target, but don't sweat it if it feels like an unreachable dream right now. To set your annual revenue target, start with your revenue history. How much did you earn last year as a freelancer? It can be difficult to go from a $20,000 or $50,000 income to a six-figure income in a year, so set a realistic target for this year, perhaps a 15 percent increase. If you exceed it, cool! That will help you set a more realistic target for the following year.

On the other hand, even if earning six figures feels like an impossible dream, there is nothing wrong with entering six figures as your target for the sake of this exercise. In other words, there is nothing wrong with, and a lot right with, daring to dream.

What if you are not currently working as a freelancer? What if you have no income history on which to rely? As any small-business owner can tell you, the first year or so is make-it-or-break-it time. You are starting to develop a business from scratch. You are making contacts and marketing your services. It can be difficult to project without history, so simply pick a number—even a six-figure one—and go from there.

With that done, let's figure out how much you need to earn per billable hour to hit your number. In other words, let's...

...Do the math

Annual revenue goal
$ _____ per year.

Now calculate how much you have to earn per week to hit the target. We haven't even started working toward becoming a six-figure freelancer, but I am going to give you two weeks off for good behaviour (or vacation).

Weekly revenue goal
$ _____ per year / 50 weeks = $ _____ per week

Now that you know how much you need to earn per week to hit your target, how much do you need to charge per hour? Most writers will tell you they work, or aim to work, 15 to 25 billable hours per week. Based on that, let's calculate what you have to charge per billable hour. Let's use a six-figure target and an achievable 20 billable hours per week, and continue to do the math:

$100,000 per year / 50 weeks = $2,000 per week

$2,000 per week / 20 billable hours per week = $100 per hr.

So, there is your answer. Or is it?

Will you be able to work four billable hours per day, five days per week, 50 weeks per year at $100 per hour? If you are just getting started, probably not. If you have never charged more than $35 or $50 per hour in your life, the thought of charging $100 per hour might give you pause. At the same time, if you are writing annual-report copy for major corporations, or if you are writing speeches for senior executives, you might be laughing at the thought of charging so little.

There is no set rate for freelance writing. (There will be much more on fees and pricing later in the book.) The amount you charge depends in large part on the services you offer and the sectors you target. But even within similar sectors and for similar services, there is no set rate.

So, here is what you do if you want to be a professional freelancer:

- Figure out what you want to make per year.
- Determine the number of hours (billable) you are willing to work per week.
- Calculate the amount you need to charge per hour.
- Find clients who are willing to pay your rate, and find enough of them so you can work the number of billable hours you want to work.

It's that simple. But it takes a lot of work to get there.

Again, at this point, if you still aren't sure what to charge, don't worry. You'll read much more on rates and how to calculate quotes before we get to the end of the book.

For now, though, do you see why developing a revenue target is so important? If you don't know how much you want to earn, how can you plan to earn it? How do you know how much you need to earn per week or per hour to meet your annual revenue goal? Setting that annual revenue goal is an important part of establishing your rate and creating your business and marketing plans.

If you want to earn more than six figures, you have to work more hours or charge more per hour. If you want to work less than 20 billable hours per week, and still earn six figures, you need to find clients willing to pay more per hour. Or you have to make money in your sleep. (I might have been asleep when you purchased this book. It took a lot of work to write and market it, but now it earns money while I sleep, am on vacation, or do other billable work.)

What about Paul?

When it comes to talking money, I'm not shy. I charge $95 per hour for my corporate writing (and more for my business-writing training). That is more than some small businesses can afford. It means there are a number of companies I do not work for. So, in my non-billable hours, I spend time marketing my services to larger corporate clients, including some not-for-profits that know the value of paying for a job well done. In other words, I market to clients that are willing to pay for "the right words, on time and on budget."

At the same time, I tend to not do really high-end corporate writing—writing annual report copy and speeches for senior executives, writing TV ad campaigns, and the like. Such jobs pay more than $95 per hour but they tend to involve wearing suits to a lot of meetings, something that I am not really into. In other words, you have to know and find your comfort zone. That can influence the hourly rate you charge. (For the record, I own a suit and pull it out of the closet on occasion to help me land high-paying gigs; I just don't actively seek such suit-required gigs when marketing my services.)

You may want a better sense of what the corporate market expects to pay for work but all I can do is repeat: there is no set rate. Sometimes, even different departments of the same company have different rate expectations! We will, however, talk a lot more about money and about issuing quotes. But first, let's revisit a familiar topic.

Three D's revisited

The fact that you are reading this book demonstrates you have desire. And now you know what you have to charge, and how many hours per week you have to work, to earn an acceptable income. So what do you do to get there? Simply put, you have to dedicate a certain amount of time each day to developing your business.

Let's say you want to work 15 to 25 billable hours per week. Let's say you are currently working zero to 10 billable hours. What do you do? In a disciplined manner, you dedicate the difference (at minimum) between the number of billable hours you are working and the number of billable hours you want to work to the task of developing your business.

What do you do with that time? Look for companies and contacts you can work for. Generate repeat business and referrals (if you've had previous corporate clients). Network, network, network. Write, submit, and follow up on pitch letters that market your writing services.

There is no point in dedicating time to this business unless you are going to be disciplined about it. Discipline means you work at your business every week of the year, unless you are on vacation. So, every week, you should either be working your desired number of billable hours or dedicating a minimum number of hours in a disciplined manner to the job of expanding your business.

This book will show you what to do with your time. Only you can do it.

Chapter 25: Corporate Market Services

In writing for the corporate market, the problem is not a dearth of opportunities but a plethora of them in terms of the number of companies out there and the types of written communication they require. That is why we will spend time looking at what you have to do to focus your marketing effort and to find contacts, and on how to best communicate with the contacts you have selected. However, in this chapter, we will look at the types of writing services you can offer corporate clients. Then you will revisit your business vision.

Before you focus your marketing efforts—sell yourself as a writer—you need to know what types of services you can offer the corporate market. You may want to avoid writing some types of documents. For instance, if you don't know what a white paper is, you probably should not bill yourself as a white paper writer. That does not mean you would not write a white paper, if asked. However, you'd want to find out more about it first, before you decided to write it or pass on it. In addition, focusing on particular types of writing helps you focus your marketing. As you gain experience writing a variety of documents, you can broaden the types of writing services that you offer.

Writing services you can offer corporate clients

I have included a brief description of many writing services to help you determine whether they are services you can, or want to, offer. And I've included the department or person (job title) within the corporation who is most likely responsible for assigning the work. The list is comprehensive but not exhaustive. I may have left out something obvious; I may have left out something obscure. If you can think of any other writing services, add it to the list! Also, feel free to e-mail me (info@paullima.com) about any writing services I may have left off the list.

Media releases

This is one of the most common forms of corporate writing. You can see sample media releases online at www.cnw.ca/en. (This is also a good place to find companies that issue media releases and to look for contacts who might hire you to write media releases or other documents.)

The person who writes the release does not always issue it, but there are opportunities to add value to your writing services if you want to issue releases as well. To issue releases, you need to build a database of local, regional, national, and possibly international media contacts. (The Web makes this easier than ever to do, but it still takes work to do it.) You keep this database up-to-date and send releases by e-mail, fax, or mail to appropriate contacts.

You can also issue releases using such companies as CNW, Marketwire, PR Newswire, and so on—but make sure you never issue a release until your client has signed off on it, in person or by e-mail. It takes a particular degree of media understanding to issue and effectively follow up on media releases. That is why most companies employ an internal public relations department or an external PR agency to do so. However, media release writing is often contracted out by the PR department and PR agencies.

Articles for employee newsletters, newspapers, magazines, websites or e-mail

Human resources departments have to communicate policies and procedures to all employees. Sales and marketing managers have to motivate their sales forces. Lowly employees have to be kept in the loop to stay motivated. Whenever new technology is introduced, or new business directions are charted, communication is vital.

Most of this internal communication is done in employee newsletters, newspapers, magazines, brochures and websites, or by e-mail. The writing is often handled by human resources, the corporate communications department, or the manager of the department concerned with whatever issue is being addressed. The writing is also frequently contracted out. Your job is to find out who is responsible (the point person) for assigning the work, and then make contact with that person. (More on how to do so later.)

Articles/documents for stakeholder newsletters, magazines, websites

Companies communicate with stakeholders, such as customers, suppliers, vendors, and investors. The material may go out in a newsletter or magazine, by e-mail, or on a website (often in a password-protected space on the company website where stakeholders can read about the latest developments, new products, special offers, etc.). If you are interested in this type of writing, you need to find the right contact person (often sales or marketing, public relations or the external communications department) and connect with that person.

Articles, case studies, blog posts, and other copy for corporate websites

As with the above, this kind of information is generally intended for stakeholders. However, the public, employees, and media frequently devour it as well. The main contacts can be corporate communications, external communications, or a senior executive managing a major department and working in co-operation with corporate or external communications.

Google ads, banner ads, and landing pages

Coordinated by marketing, companies often contract out the writing of the short ads that appear on Google (and other search engines), banner ads that appear on websites, and the landing pages—the pages that readers are taken to when they click on ads.

Social media (tweets, blog copy, social media profiles)

Coordinated by marketing, companies often contract out the writing of blog copy and Twitter tweets, as well as profiles on Facebook, LinkedIn, MySpace and other social networking sites.

Direct mail promotions; print, radio, or TV advertisements; infomercial scripts

Advertising material is usually meant to generate sales or customer traffic. Advertising may be coordinated by marketing. The writing is often contracted out to an advertising agency. Think like an entrepreneur here. Since some ad agencies contract out writing, who might they contract it to? Why not you? If you have the ability to write ad copy or direct mail brochures, this can be a lucrative market.

Product/services promotional brochures, spec sheets, price lists

Supplementary or collateral material to support the advertising effort; again, frequently coordinated by the marketing department.

Proposals

Agencies, organizations, groups, and companies are constantly seeking funding from government departments or agencies, service clubs, corporations, and other organizations.

For instance, not-for-profit organizations in Ontario often seek funds from the Trillium Foundation, an agency at arm's length from the government that administers the disbursement of lottery funds. Film companies often seek funding from Telefilm Canada and other government agencies that fund feature films in Canada. Most social service organizations apply for funding on an annual basis. Many community groups appeal to corporations for funds to support the arts or local projects. Groups seeking funding require writers to generate proposals. This type of writing is often contracted out.

RFQs, tenders, bids, sales proposals

Companies often contract out the writing of requests for quotes or proposals (RFQs or RFPs), replies to RFQs and RFPs, and the writing of tenders, bids, and sales proposals. The purchasing or accounting department is a good place to start, although individual departments may be responsible for generating their own material, particularly the sales and marketing department.

Recruitment advertisements, job descriptions

Companies have to hire. To do so, they produce job descriptions and recruitment ads. Some freelancers write nothing but recruitment ads and job descriptions. It helps if you know a bit about HR and labour laws to write such material, but that is not always required.

Looking to add value? Offer to place the ads in selected media. However, it requires a particular kind of media buying knowledge to move from being a person offering writing services to a business offering to write, create, and place recruitment ads.

Recruitment letters, e-mail, brochures, websites

Before the dot-com and technology meltdown, high-tech companies were spending tens of thousands of dollars producing recruitment information. Pick a sector that is hot and hiring and you will find companies spending money to recruit new graduates and to cherry-pick employees from other companies.

This kind of communication is not a recruitment ad, although recruitment ad copy may spring from it. It is used to sell the company and all its benefits to potential recruits. The service is often co-ordinated by human resources, but is sometimes farmed out to a recruitment department that works on college and university campuses and at job fairs.

Training manuals, videos, multimedia programs

Once a company hires new employees, it has to orient and train them. The production of training and recruitment material is primarily a human resources function. It may be coordinated by human resources for consistency, but left up to individual departments within some organizations to create. The writing of scripts may be contracted out to freelancers.

Corporate histories, company profiles, and executive bio/profiles

Written for websites, brochures, annual reports, shareholder, or investor videos, these are generally handled by corporate communications and are often contracted out.

Annual and quarterly reports

Writing annual and quarterly reports involves gathering information from a variety of sources for inclusion in the reports. While annual reports include a great deal of dry financial information, they also contain corporate histories, company and department profiles, executive profiles, forward-looking or visionary statements, product information, etc. The writing is often coordinated by corporate communications.

Ghost writing (speeches)

This may be handled by corporate communications or the assistant of the executive giving the speech. Speeches may be given at shareholder meetings, sales and marketing events, conferences and trade shows, employee functions, customer appreciation events, convocations, political forums, and a full range of other occasions. The speeches have to be written. Why not by you?

Ghost writing (articles under byline of executives)

Written for trade publications or newspapers, these articles can be handled by external communications, public relations, or marketing—depending on the nature of the publication and the topic. Think like an entrepreneur. Look at trade publications for articles written by company executives, including guest columns or regular columns. These are most likely ghost written. Find out who placed the article and offer your services.

White papers

Industry-specific papers that address trends, systems, methodologies, and technologies. Tend to be long, research-intensive documents. May be initiated by marketing or senior executives.

Editing

All this writing needs to be edited. Often the writer is expected to do it; in some companies, writing is done in-house but is farmed out to an editor for final review.

Other editing opportunities

Fiction and non-fiction books (for publishers or self-published authors), newspaper and magazine articles, university papers and doctoral theses, research papers, and so on.

Other services you can offer

Communications consulting, strategic planning, business and report writing seminars, and media interview preparation workshops… It all depends on your background, knowledge, and expertise. For instance, to earn passive income, I write books on business writing and freelance writing (www.paullima.com/books).

Do you want to flex other muscles and offer a variety of services? Is that part of your vision? Think about all you can do before you decide what you want to do. Just because you can do something doesn't mean you will want to do it or that you have to do it. In other words, part of developing your business involves thinking about what you want to offer and what you don't want to offer.

What can you write?

There is so much you can write or edit. The problem is often a question of where to begin. To figure out where to begin, ask yourself the following question: What have I done? In other words, based on the evidence (what you have done), what do you know you can do? The evidence is a combination of your education and previous work and writing experience.

Remember, you have to sell yourself as well as your services. That can be a hard sell if you have only done a limited amount of writing. For instance, if you have never written a white paper, or don't even know what a white paper is, you do not want to pitch yourself as a white paper writer. But what if you have never written a media release? Can you pitch yourself as a media release writer? If you have written news articles, you should be able to write media releases. But before you say you can, take time to examine several releases to determine how they are structured and practice writing a few.

If, however, you have never written news articles or media releases, you might want to take a media release writing workshop before you try to sell media release writing services. (If you want to research what a media release is and how it's structured, almost any corporate website contains news releases. The Internet also abounds with information online about writing them.)

If you've done a solid job for people—delivered the right words on time and on budget—they will trust you to do it again. But if you are cold calling a prospect who has never heard of you, you have to convince him you can do the job. That's why you have to sell your writing experiences (and, as we shall see, demonstrate knowledge of your prospect's business sector and business).

Look at the list of writing services you can offer corporate markets. Which ones do you believe you can offer? To help you determine the services that you can offer, see the services evidence list below. Then make a list of the writing services you can offer, based on your evidence. This will form an integral part of your business plan and marketing effort.

Services evidence list

Make a list of the services you can offer based on the evidence—your education and previous work experience. Follow the service evidence list format below.

Services: Write/edit IT white papers and case studies.
Evidence: Covered IT for various newspapers and magazines; worked as copywriter for <Company Name

(high-tech company>; wrote IT white papers and case studies for <list of client names>.

Services: Write/edit magazine ads, brochures.

Evidence: Wrote promotional brochures for <Company Names> in 2005 and wrote product catalogue copy and magazine ad copy for <Company Name> for last two years.

Service: Media training workshops.

Evidence: Conducted over 500 newspaper/magazine interviews. Have adult education training background and have taken media training workshops. Have trained several dozen executives, business owners, and authors. Received excellent feedback.

Service: Edit and translate legal documents, client letters, and promotional material

Evidence: Trained as a legal secretary; have previously edited and translated documents for three law firms and the Ministry of the Solicitor General

Service: Write user manuals and technical documentation

Evidence: Degree in software programming; taken technical writing workshops with Technical Writers Association; wrote training manual for <Company Name>|

What services can you offer? Think about your previous experience—your full-time, part-time, and freelance work experience. Explore your education, hobbies, passions, and interests. Based on the evidence, list three to five services and related evidence. If your list contains any services you do not want to offer, eliminate them. If your list includes services you would like to continue to do, keep them. If you think you can offer any services that did not make your list, add them. However, change "evidence" to "PD Required"—Professional Development Required. In other words, don't offer the service until you find a workshop, course, or other form of training that will enable you to offer it with confidence.

Service:

Evidence:

Service:

Evidence:

Service:

Evidence:

Please create your service evidence list before you read on.

Revisit your business vision

Now that you have a list of services, backed up by evidence, that you can offer corporate clients, revisit your W5 business vision questions. Add the appropriate services to your "What do you want to do?" list and revise your business vision. Include any services that require professional development. The professional development required will become part of your business plan.

If you reviewed the list of services you can offer corporate clients and became curious about services you are not familiar with, investigate them. Find and review samples of the kind of writing you are curious about. If, upon review, you think you would like to try your hand at such writing, look for a workshop or course that will help you become more familiar with it.

Where do you find samples? Do you know people who work for different companies? Ask them to bring home samples of material from human resources or other internal departments. Ask people to bring home samples of marketing material that the company they work for produces or that they get in the mail from other companies. This is a great way to see what is being written. It's also a great way to start networking, which we will discuss in detail later.

Also, go to the websites of different companies (later in the book you'll find out how to select companies you want to target) and look at the wealth of written material on display. At a minimum, you will find media releases and marketing material. You may also find articles from annual reports, bios of executives, corporate histories, white papers, and other samples. Review this material and ask yourself whether you can, or want to, write it.

Your goal is to focus on the type of writing—the writing services—you can do and would like to offer corporate clients. This will help you target your marketing effort. With that in mind, revise your business vision if it is appropriate to do so. Once that is done, we will work on determining the corporate sectors you can target.

Please revise your vision before you read on.

Chapter 26: All About You

When looking for corporate work, you have to focus your marketing. And you focus your marketing based on services, as we have seen in the last chapter, and on sectors. But how do you determine which sectors? The sectors you target are based on your education, previous work experience, hobbies, and interests. Without focus, you will be all over the map, and often looking for work in areas where you have little or no expertise or knowledge, which makes it difficult to sell yourself.

What do I mean by sectors? The next chapter has a longer list, but allow me to show you three examples of sectors (and related sub-sectors) here:

- Construction—residential, industrial, commercial, highways
- Education—primary, secondary, post-secondary, continuing education; public and private; corporate training
- Finance—banking, insurance, mutual funds, brokerage, advisors...

Construction is a sector. Residential construction is one of several construction sub-sectors. If you know nothing about construction, why would you pitch your writing services to construction companies or companies that supply and service construction companies?

You do not have to be a sector expert to do most corporate writing. You do not need to know a sector or company within a sector intimately to market your services there. You improve your chances, however, of being selected for a project if you have knowledge of—and can convey knowledge about—a sector and company. Your prospect will figure that if you can talk the talk, you should be able to walk the walk or, in this case, write the words.

I am not a geek, but I can talk technology at a consumer and business level. (Just don't ask me to solve your computer problems.) I can ask the questions required to get the information I need to write about telecommunications, electronic commerce, online security, and many other technology-related subjects. That knowledge, combined with my writing skills and experience, gives me an edge when marketing my writing services to technology companies.

I also have a continuing education background. When I approach educational institutions or training companies about writing, I stress that part of my life. And I have written about printing services. When I pitch companies in the printing sector, I stress that part of my writing experience. In other words, as I approach different companies in different sectors, I adjust my pitch based on my experience in relation to the company and sector I am targeting.

How many sectors do we focus on? I always suggest three to five. If that sounds too restrictive, think again. Focusing on three to five sectors is not too narrow a field to target. Once you pick three to five sectors (and their related sub-sectors), you will find countless opportunities to pitch your writing services. In addition, focusing on three to five sectors does not mean you have slammed the door shut on other work that might come your way.

Even if you are sceptical, stay with me for the next couple of chapters. Remember, you can always include more sectors later, but I am suggesting three to five is more than enough to begin with.

So let's get focused. What about you? What connections do you have to various corporate sectors? Before you answer that, and before I present you with a list of some of the corporate sectors out there, I want you to do some clustering or brainstorming.

Clustering/Brainstorming

Allow me to reintroduce you to clustering. Clustering helps you jot down all you know about a topic before you write. This helps you write in a more focused and efficient manner. If you need a clustering refresher, read Chapter 7 (Clustering Introduction) again. If you have not done much clustering since reading that chapter, try a few clustering exercises as well to loosen up.

Before you cluster, read over the instructions in Chapter 7. Once you are ready, cluster one of the keywords below.

Keywords to cluster:

Help or ***Spider*** or ***Needles***

> **When you have completed your cluster, continue reading.**

Journal Exercise: Clustering

If you are working your way through this book as it was written, you may have already done this clustering exercise; however, it can't hurt, and it might help, to try it again.

Make sure you have a fresh piece of paper for this exercise. Once again, the keyword you are going to cluster is:

ME

Cluster *ME* as comprehensively as possible. Ready, set, go.

> **Please do your clustering before you read on.**

What next?

By now, you should have a messy page full of circles, lines, and scribbled words that are, more or less, about you.

So what do you do next? Now you look at yourself in relation to the corporate sectors out there. It's possible your *Me* cluster contains little or nothing in relation to corporate sectors. It's also possible you are not seeing what it contains. And it's entirely possible you can extract a list of sectors from your cluster strings. It's also possible that, through clustering, you will discover some other writing services (or perhaps even other services) you can sell to corporate markets.

So, go mining for gold in your cluster strings. List any sectors you can relate to and any other services you can find. If your list feels sparse, don't worry. We are not done yet. Before we move on, I want you to try several more clusters. As you prepare for that, I will let you in on my hidden agenda: You are not just looking for sectors. You are getting to know yourself in an abstract manner. Doing this makes it easier to sell yourself (write about and talk about yourself) in a concrete and focused manner.

I cannot stress enough how important focus is.

Marketing, in many ways, is a numbers game. If you want to improve your odds of winning, you have to sell services (that you can validate) to as many companies as possible in sectors to which you can relate. Again, that does not mean you close the door to other opportunities that may come your way. It does mean you focus your marketing based on your strengths.

I have written many documents for companies in sectors I knew little or nothing about. There has to be a first time for everything, like my first white paper. Once I had written one, I added it to the list of services that I offered. However, I focused my initial marketing efforts on services I could sell and sectors I could relate to. All this, I promise, will become clear once you see the sample pitch letters later in the book.

What you need to know

Before you start marketing, you need to know what services you have to offer, based on your work experience, education, or other aspects of your life. You need to know what sectors you can serve as well, so you can find and approach companies within those sectors. You need to know all this so you can sell yourself to the right company as the right person for the right job.

This is a targeted approach to marketing, rather than a scattergun approach. This is an effective approach to marketing, rather than an ineffective approach. This works. It takes work to make it work. But it works.

More clustering

With all that in mind, I want you to spend time clustering each of the following words:

- *Education*
- *Work Experience*
- *Hobbies/Interests*
- *Passions*

If you are ready, pick your first keyword, write it down, and begin to cluster. Cluster each of the keywords in the list above.

If you are stymied by clustering, give it another shot. But if you have tried and tried again, read the section on the linear approach to brainstorming, below. However, revisit clustering first to see if you can get it working for you. It's a powerful brainstorming tool.

> **Please do all four clustering exercises before you read on.**

Linear approach

If you have difficulty with clustering, a right-brained approach to conducting internal research, look at yourself using a linear approach. Use a point-form list to examine your education, work experience, hobbies, interests, and passions.

Open a page in your word processor, or use a clean sheet of paper. Write down the word you want to brainstorm—education, for instance. Using bullet points, jot down all the words and phrases you associate with education. You are not just looking for sectors here. You are getting to know yourself in an abstract manner. This will make it easier to sell yourself (write about and talk about yourself) in a concrete manner. However, it will also help you identify sectors you can write for. Follow the linear approach for the other cluster words listed above: work experience, hobbies/interests, passions.

> **Please do all four clustering exercises or all four linear exercises before you read on.**

Looking at your freelance work

Before you list the sectors you think you have some affinity for, and your reason for listing those sectors (which I will show you how to do), I want you to do one more thing. This may have come out in your clustering or your linear exercises, but if not, tackle it here.

If you have done some freelance writing for the corporate market, make a list of current and previous clients you have had. List the sectors they represent. If you have done some periodical writing, make a list of the publications you have written for, the people you have interviewed, and the companies or organizations those people have worked for. List the sectors represented by those publications, people, companies, and organizations.

Add the list of sectors to the list of sectors you discovered through your clustering and/or your linear brainstorming.

> **Please do the above exercise before you read on.**

Focus versus scattered

In case you have not bought into the need for marketing focus, please read on.

Even if you want to scatter your marketing, you still have to start somewhere. Why wouldn't you start with sectors you are familiar with or are somewhat familiar with? And why wouldn't you start with the type of writing you have some knowledge of or experience with?

Do you have previous work or writing experience in travel and tourism? Why wouldn't you focus on that sector and related sub-sectors? Are you an engineer, lawyer, sales person? Sectors immediately open up. Have you studied political science, nursing, history, biology? Again, sectors open up. Are you a geek? Are you involved with particular charities in particular not-for-profit sectors? There is that word again: sector!

Are you into automobiles? Can you discuss them intelligently (unlike me)? Ask me what kind of car I drive and I'll say, "A big black one." So don't expect me to write for the automotive sector. It doesn't mean I can't write for the automotive sector. It does mean I'm better off marketing to companies within sectors I understand and to which I can relate. You want automotive? It's yours.

However, guess who has written about software that allows the automotive-parts- manufacturing sector to monitor plant production more effectively and keep machine downtime to a minimum? Me. Why? I write about technology, and that cuts across many sectors. But I did not market my writing services to the automotive sector. The company found me through my website. So, while I am suggesting you become focused, I am not suggesting that you shut the door on sectors that, at first blush, seem to have nothing to do with you. But, as I have said, you have to start somewhere—and close to home is as good a place as any.

What if you have a great deal of experience in the legal sector, for instance, and hated every minute of it? Ask yourself whether you can write, or want to write, documents related to that sector. Maybe you didn't like practicing law but wouldn't mind writing marketing material for law firms or for legal departments within companies or organizations in other sectors that you are familiar with. On the other hand, if you want nothing to do with sectors relating to the law, drop law from your list. After all, you're building your business and marketing plan based on your business vision.

But I'm a generalist

Maybe you are an English major. Maybe you can write well, but have no particular experience in any particular sector that you can think of. Ever work in retail? The food and beverage or hotel industry? Even if you did this part-time, you have knowledge and experience, enough to get you started, to get your foot in the door.

Maybe you have hobbies and interests that can help you figure out which sectors to target. Perhaps you have second-hand knowledge of particular sectors through parents or friends. You don't have to blow anyone away with your knowledge of a sector (I sure don't). Your goal is to target sectors based on your writing skills and abilities, augmented by some aspect of your experience. You want to say, "I have this connection to what you are all about. I understand to some extent the nature of your business. You won't have to spend hours bringing me up to speed just so I can string two sentences together for you."

That's what you say. Only you say that in a much more professional manner when pitching your writing services. Once you get your foot in the door, you no longer have to sell yourself. All you have to do is a damn fine job. Do that and you will generate repeat business. Repeat business means less marketing, and less marketing means you are working more billable hours. So, it gets easier. But you still have to start somewhere!

Cross sectors

It's entirely possible your skills and knowledge cross different sectors. For instance, you can apply basic sales and marketing knowledge to many sectors, so you could focus on writing for the sales and marketing departments of companies in various sectors. If you look closely at your background, however, it probably makes sense to tackle the sales and marketing departments within companies in several sectors rather than in every sector out there.

The ability to write general articles or profiles is a skill that can be applied to communication opportunities in many sectors. I still encourage you to focus because you can find only so many contacts and you can send out only so many pitches in a day.

In short, this is what I want you to do: be open to any opportunity that comes along, but start your marketing where the opportunity for future success is greatest based on your previous experience: work, education, interests, and so on. In other words, based on *you*!

To kick-start your corporate writing business, go with your strengths. If that sounds too narrowly focused, wait until you do your research and start pitching. You will be glad to have a focus. When opportunity knocks, answer the door. Use what you learn to expand your marketing efforts. But you still have to *start* somewhere. So, focus first. Expand later.

Determining sectors

The exercises you did above should help you get to know yourself so you can figure out where to begin your marketing. Just as we created a services/evidence list, we are now going to create a sectors/evidence list. I'll create a list here for you to review. You can then create your own list.

Sample Sector list

Sectors: Information technology, e-commerce, Internet, network security, telecommunications.

Evidence: Covered IT and telecom issues for various newspapers and magazines; wrote articles relating to e-commerce and security. Wrote an e-commerce trends white paper for Jupiter Research.

Sectors: Printing (business/industrial).

Evidence: Familiar with printing industry through work on <Company Name> product catalogue; took design and print course at community college.

Sectors: Publishing.

Evidence: Worked on publicity for launch of first novel; conducted media interview training for three authors; edited two self-help books; self-published three books.

So, what sectors will you target? By now, you should have a number of sectors you can target. Using the service evidence list format above, make a list of the sectors you can write for, based on the evidence—your education, previous work experience, hobbies, interests, and passions.

List three to five sectors

Sector:
Evidence:

Sector:
Evidence:

Sector:
Evidence:

Sector:
Evidence:

Sector:
Evidence:

Please create your sector evidence list before you read on.

Revisit your vision

Now that you have determined the sectors you can target, revisit your W5 business vision questions. Add the appropriate sectors to your "Who do you want to do it for?" list and revise your vision.

Please revise your business vision before you read on.

Chapter 27: Target Corporate Sectors

By now, you should have a good idea of the sectors you want to target. A list of sectors (and related subsectors) is nevertheless provided below.

Exactly how many corporate sectors are out there? More than I can come close to listing. If you want to overwhelm yourself with sector possibilities, search for "Standard Industrial Classification" on Google. The index lists every sector from A (abdominal) to Z (zoological gardens).

I will list just a few sectors and some of the sub-sectors. If I missed any appropriate sectors—sectors you can justify based on your experience—add them to your sector list and your business vision. But keep your target list to five sectors (and their appropriate sub-sectors) maximum, based on your experiences and on the extent to which you want to work in those sectors.

Once you find sectors you want to conquer, you need to find companies within the sectors and then find contacts within the companies (which will be discussed in detail later in the book). Then you begin your marketing campaign. But if you are shivering at the prospect of cold calling or cold mailing, rest assured that I am going to show you more than one marketing technique.

Sectors and sub-sectors

Some of the many sectors (and sub-sectors) that freelance writers target include:

Arts & Entertainment: ballet, opera, classical music, visual arts, film, television, radio...

Construction: residential, industrial, commercial, highways...

Education: primary, secondary, post-secondary, continuing education; public and private; corporate training...

Finance: banking, insurance, mutual funds, brokerage houses, financial advisors...

Food and beverage: grocery chains, stores, hotels and restaurants, bars, breweries, and various beverage companies

Government: federal, provincial, regional, municipal; government ministries, agencies, departments; politicians; non-governmental organizations (NGOs); lobbyists...

Health (public and private sector): hospitals, clinics, physiotherapy, nursing homes; pharmacies, pharmaceutical...

Information Technology: computer hardware and software, Internet, electronic commerce, security, Web design, computer dealers, system integrators, robotics, biotech....

Marketing: advertising, public relations, sales, consultants...

Manufacturing: automotive (cars, trucks, parts, etc.), furniture, industrial machinery, hardware, appliances, sporting goods, shoes and clothing...

Non-profit: social services, charities, cooperatives, NGOs...

Printing: commercial (large, medium, and small format; customized; creative; art) and consumer (retail)…

Publishing: fiction, non-fiction, specialty presses, self-publishing, print-on-demand…

Professional Services: legal, accounting, financial planning, engineering, medical, dental…

Resources: oil and gas, mining…

Retail: clothing, furniture, hardware, appliances, sporting goods, liquor, big box....

Telecommunications: landline, wireless, satellite, long distance, Voice over Internet Protocol; consumer, business...

Trades: plumbing, electrical, cabinetry, woodworking, renovation, contractors…

Transportation: trucking (local and long haul, residential and commercial moving, distribution), planes, trains, automobiles, buses...

Travel and Tourism: airlines and charters, trains, marine, bus; travel and tourism agents; travel websites; resorts, theme parks, eco-tourism, zoos, hotels, municipal, provincial and national attractions...

The list, as I said, is by no means an exhaustive one. It's meant only as an overview; you should start with sectors related to your education, work experience, hobbies, interests, and passions. With that in mind, feel free to add your sectors and sub-sectors to the list, but keep the list of sectors you will target at three to five. You don't need to have extensive experience within a sector to add it to your list; however, it will help your marketing effort if you have some sector-related education, work experience, or knowledge.

What I would like you to do now is combine your services with your sectors and sub-sectors—where possible. If you have some freelance or business writing experience for particular companies, mention those clients or companies by name. You will understand why later. Put it all down on paper, or on your computer screen, so it's there in black and white before your eyes.

Allow me to demonstrate below.

Sample sectors/services list

Sectors: Information Technology, e-commerce, Internet/network security; telecommunications.

Services: Write/edit IT white papers and case studies.

Evidence: Covered IT for various newspapers and magazines; worked as copywriter for <IT Company>; wrote IT white papers and case studies for <clients>.

Sectors: Printing (business/industrial).

Services: Direct marketing brochures, sales letters, and ads. Replies to RFQs. Website copy about sales, services, and equipment.

Evidence: Familiar with printing industry through work on product catalogue for <Company Name>; took design and print course at college. Wrote promotional brochures and sales letters for <Company Names> in 2005 and wrote promotional copy (sales, services, and equipment) for website of <Company Name> for last two years. (We are presuming the companies listed here are printing companies.)

Sectors: Legal—law firms, courts, Ministry of the Solicitor General; legal departments in large financial institutions.

Services: Proofread and translate legal documents into French, client letters and promotional material. Write/edit magazine ads and brochures.

Evidence: Trained as a legal secretary; have previously edited and translated documents into French for three law firms and the Ministry of the Solicitor General.

Before you do the exercise, read on.

Lateral thinking

What are financial institutions doing under the legal sector above? For the sake of argument, let's presume you have experience in legal and finance. It would then make sense to target legal departments in financial institutions. But say you had legal experience and experience in manufacturing or in politics. Then you might include legal departments in manufacturing sectors, or you might include non-governmental organizations or political lobbyists who are trying to influence laws. I call this lateral thinking.

At this point, you might have accidentally stumbled upon lateral thinking through your brainstorming. If not, see whether you can apply lateral thinking to the sectors you could target. For instance, I have a tech-writing background. I have written for a number of technology and telecom firms. Recently, a lawyer read some of my work. He was introducing an application that would help lawyers monitor the status of their cases and bills. He asked me to write some promotional copy and support documents. I had never thought of selling my tech-writing services to law firms. Now that I know some law firms hire tech writers and I can justify adding the legal sectors to my target market. I would not, however, offer to write legal documents for them because I have no experience in that area.

That's how lateral thinking works, and why focus is not limiting. You expand your sectors, and the type of writing you can do, as your experience expands. Just to be clear: I don't have to add legal to my sector list, but if I want to write technology-related documents for law firms, or for tech companies that target law firms, I can add the sector.

Sometimes lateral thinking is as simple as taking your background and expanding the sectors logically. Say you have a background as a nurse or nursing assistant. Sectors you might logically target include nursing homes, nursing schools, and hospitals. But you might also target pharmaceutical firms and medical supply companies. In other words, if you have a nursing background, a pharmaceutical firm is far more likely to hire you than it is to hire someone like me.

To put that into practice, make sure you add to your list any sectors you think you could write for based on your education, previous work experience, hobbies, interests, and so on. If you have previous writing experience in one sector, you can probably apply that experience to a sector, or sectors, you have not written for. For instance:

> **Sectors**: Accounting; accounting and finance departments in automotive manufacturing.
> **Evidence**: Certified General Accountant; five years accounting experience with auto-parts manufacturer.
> **Services**: Document I have written for other sectors: media releases, case studies, and replies to RFQs.

What are we doing and why?

The need for all of this work is difficult for some people to grasp. You want to start marketing and I have you examining your past. There is a reason. You will most likely find your immediate future is built on your past, even if you have recently graduated from university and have limited work experience. When pitching corporate clients, you have to make some connection between who you are and what they are. What you are doing here is preparing to start your marketing effort where the opportunity for future success is greatest, based on past experiences. You are aligning the types of services you can offer the corporate market with the sectors you can target.

You may also choose to leave out some sectors and services, based on any negative experiences. For instance, based on experience,

I know I never want to write for the fibres and threads manufacturing industry again! If you want to do so, go ahead. It's all yours.

Journal exercise

Combine your services with your sectors and sub-sectors. This is an important exercise; do not skip it. The exercise is the beginning of your business plan and your marketing plan.

Sectors:
Evidence
Services:

Sectors:
Evidence:
Services:

Sectors:
Evidence:
Services:

Please do the above exercise before you read on.

Chapter 28: Business Plan

Before you start to read about the business plan, allow me to recap what we know so far:

- How to better manage your time and your e-mail
- That the corporate sector needs freelance writers
- How to develop your business vision and revenue forecast
- How many billable hours per week you need to work, and how much you need to charge per hour to reach that forecast
- The types of writing services you want to offer corporate markets and your rationale for offering those services
- The sectors you want to target and your rationale for targeting each sector

What is a business plan?

Now it's time to put what you know, and some additional information, into a business plan. The business plan is the foundation of your marketing plan. I like to think of a business plan as a road map that helps you reach your business vision, which is why it includes your business vision (or destination).

In addition to including your business vision, your business plan includes the services you plan to offer, the sectors you plan to target, and your revenue forecasts or projections. So the work you've done to date will pay off as you put your business plan together.

You forecast your revenue annually and quarterly, based on the services you plan to offer, to keep yourself on track. For instance, if you forecast you will earn $20,000 in the first quarter and you earn only $5,000, then you know you have to pick up the pace—do more marketing!—or you will miss your annual revenue target. If you forecast that you will earn $10,000 in the first quarter writing IT and telecom white papers and you earn only $5,000, then you know you have to pick up the pace—do more marketing!—or you will miss your annual revenue target. Unless...

Let's say you forecast that you will earn $10,000 in the first quarter writing IT and telecom white papers and $10,000 writing copy for IT and telecom sector annual reports. However, let's say you actually earn $5,000 writing white papers and $18,000 writing annual report copy. You have exceeded your overall revenue targets for the quarter and you can keep on doing what you are doing. Unless...

Unless you really like to write white papers more than annual report copy. If that's the case, you have to pick up the pace—do more white paper marketing. But at least you will be marketing from a position of financial strength.

Once you have your business plan in place, you create your marketing plan—a schedule of tasks you will complete during non-billable hours to generate billable freelance work.

Some people make their marketing plan part of their business plan; others consider their marketing plan a separate document. I make it sound as though the business plan and marketing plan are two separate documents, but I don't care if you keep them in one file called Business Plan or in two separate files. Here's what I care about: your marketing plan should be based on, and support, your business vision and your business plan, including your revenue forecasts, the services you want to sell, and the sectors you want to target.

In short, the business plan includes your vision and the financial goals that support your vision. The marketing plan, as we shall see, includes the tasks you do to support those goal so you can fulfill your vision.

Finally, your business plan may include a list of professional development training required to shore up any business weaknesses you have. For instance, you might want to take a specific writing course, a website design course, or a course to teach you how to better use Word, Outlook, or other appropriate software applications.

Can you afford to miss revenue targets?

Determining how much you need to earn each month—to pay for food, rent, or mortgage, utilities, transportation, basic business expenses, and so on—goes beyond the scope of this book. However, you should have a good sense of what you need to earn to survive (or thrive) before setting your freelance business revenue projections.

If you earn less from your business than you spend on life and have no other sources of income, then you will experience cash-flow problems. On the other hand, if you earn less from your business than you spend on life but have investment income or a partner who has a decent job, then you might be fine—other than suffering from a slightly bruised ego.

But if you fall off your bike (using a metaphor here for *miss your revenue target*), and it is your goal to ride it no matter what, you may have to step back and revamp your plan or double your marketing effort. Before you do that, look in the mirror and ask yourself if you have done all you could. Have you done the following:

- Outlined your business vision?
- Created realistic business and marketing plans based on your vision?
- Followed your plans?
- Followed them in a dedicated and disciplined manner?

If the answers are *yes*, get back on that bike and commit to riding it better than ever. If the answer is *more or less* or *not really*, get back on the bike and commit to riding it. Either way, expect to fall several times, especially in the first year or two. Any business owner does. In this business, as with most businesses, persistence pays off—as long as your plan makes sense (if you've done the work I've asked you to do, it should) and you are implementing the plan in a dedicated and disciplined manner.

Remember, as we read in Chapter One, the difference between business winners and business failures is that business winners do the work that business failures don't know they should do or are, for whatever reason, unwilling to do. If you need more inspiration to help you roll up your sleeves and do the work you need to do to succeed, I recommend the following book: *8 to be Great* by Richard St. John (available online at www.richardstjohn.com).

Business expenses versus life expenses

Why don't I base my revenue projections on my business expenses? That is how most businesses are set up. They forecast expenses and revenues, and as long as revenues exceed expenses, they are in the black, or profitable.

As a freelance writer, you will find that once you get your office set up, you do not have to spend a lot of money on running your business, as long as you are working from home and have no employees. If your revenues do nothing more than exceed your business expenses, you will probably not be able to live off the money you make. With that in mind, I base my revenue needs on my life *and* my business expenses, rather than just on my business expenses. The money I make should cover any business expenses (phone and Internet, computer, office supplies, some travel, and so on) and life expenses (mortgage, car, food, dog food (for the dog, not me), entertainment, and so on).

Business plan: What it is not

I have seen many long, convoluted business plans, the kind of documents you would produce if you wanted to go to the bank to secure a loan. These plans are appropriate for small and medium businesses with offices, capital expenses, employees, and so on. Or, they are appropriate for companies seeking bank loans or angel investors. None of that applies to the business of freelance writing, unless you are planning to start a full-service public relations agency or an advertising agency. If that is your vision, then by all means go for it. You can apply many of the principles in this book. But understand that you are setting up a whole other kind of business.

If you want to be a freelance writer, your business plan does not need to demonstrate, in detail, your market research, competition, and rationale for establishing your business.

Companies hire writers. There is your market research. *Other freelance writers are out there.* There is your competition. Oh, and guess what? For the most part, they do not have business or marketing plans. *Can you write well and meet deadlines?* If so, there is your rationale.

Knowing the above is no guarantee of success. But my point here is this: you can spend several months conducting research into all of the above and come to the same conclusion, or you can get on with running your freelance writing business.

To sum up: Your business plan should not be a long, convoluted, complex, full-color document that includes pie charts and bar charts, graphics and appendixes, all published as a PDF or PowerPoint file.

Your business plan should not take three months to research and six months to write. You have better things to do with your time, such as marketing your services and making money.

So, how long should your business plan be? Five to ten pages, more or less. How long should it take to write? A week, more or less. The second time around (as in a year later) it should take even less time to write, unless you dramatically revise it, which is a possibility and perfectly acceptable. As your business vision evolves, so to do your plans.

After the first or second time through, revisit it on an annual basis to make sure your business vision hasn't changed, or to alter your vision based on your experiences. You update your revenue targets and the services and sectors you want to target, and revise your marketing initiatives based on your revised business vision and business plan. That can be done in a couple of days.

Take some time and write your business plan. (Not your marketing plan; just your business plan.) Feel free to model the format of the plan below or set up your own template.

Business plan

Business vision

Here is where you would insert the who, what, where, when, and why business vision you developed earlier in this section. Make sure it is up to date with the sectors you want to target and the services you want to offer.

Services/sectors/prospects

Here is where you would go into greater detail about the services you want to offer, the sectors you will be targeting, clients you may have had and prospects you have already thought of. Don't worry if you haven't thought of many, or any, prospects. We will go digging for prospects when we talk about marketing. But if you have worked for clients in some of your target sectors, list them here. You will be working with this list later in the book. You can also list your rationale for targeting sectors or particular prospects here.

In other words, this section is literally what you want to do and who you want to do it for. It builds on your business vision. What you are doing here is aligning your business vision with your business plan, which you will then align with your marketing plan, so you can achieve your business vision.

List your services, sectors, and evidence. Remain focused, but where applicable, apply lateral thinking as you follow the Services/Sectors format you used above. Include "previous clients" and "prospects" as well, like so:

Services/Sectors/Prospects

Sectors: Information technology, e-commerce, Internet/network security, telecommunications.

Services: Write/edit IT white papers, case studies, media releases, and Web content.

Evidence: Covered IT for various newspapers and magazines; worked as copywriter for <Company Name (IT firm)>; wrote IT white papers and case studies for <list of client names>.

Previous Clients: <list of companies you have done work for in these sectors>

Prospects: Companies in the IT and telecom sectors; also look for prospects that are heavily engaged in e-commerce.

Moving on to revenue projections

The next section of the business plan includes your revenue projections, annual and quarterly, based on services you want to sell.

If you have been working as a freelancer, you have some history to go by. You know how and when you have generated revenue. You could simply try to build on that, but that would not be very challenging, would it? After all, you now have a vision and know what services you want to sell and the sectors you want to target. Also, you may wish to jettison some clients. Consider all of that when making your projections.

If you have not been working as a freelancer, your goal here is to project your revenue targets as best you can. Aim high and see what you can do. Next year, you will have a better sense of what you can achieve.

Does that mean you cannot hit an acceptable revenue target in one year? Not at all. However, the more experience you have as a writer and the more experience you have conquering corporate markets, the better equipped you will be to set clear targets and boost your revenue. Bottom line: whether or not you have been working as a freelancer, it takes desire, dedication, and discipline to generate work. Base your projections on what you aspire to achieve, and do the work required to achieve it.

Make room in your projections for last year's figures, this year's forecast, and this year's actual revenue. (See Revenue Projections below.) When you revisit your business plan next year, you will have your new actuals in place and you will be able to base your forecasts on your those revenues.

If you have been working as a freelance writer, I hope you know where to find last year's revenue figures, and that you can break down your revenue by month, quarter (a fiscal quarter is three months: usually January to March, April to June, July to September and October to December), and client. But if you have not been tracking your revenue closely, or you are new to this, use an Excel spreadsheet to set up your revenue projections as best you can.

When it comes to quarterly projections, don't divide by four. Your quarterly revenue projections should be based on your business vision, which might call for you to take time off in the summer or at some other time of year. That means your quarterly revenue might fluctuate. You might work the summer, but work less than in the fourth quarter, and so on. On the other hand, you might currently have clients who give you work on a seasonal basis, so your revenue projections might fluctuate until you find other clients you can work for at different times of the year.

Start projecting using the charts below. However, plug in your own figures and your own services. If you have never done this before, it might feel like tossing darts in the dark. But you have to start somewhere. If you have some revenue history, apply it as best you can. Next year, this will be much easier.

Revenue projections

Set up charts similar to the ones below, but put your actual and projected revenue in the first one. Also, create your own list of services in the second one and fill in the projected revenue blanks.

Revenue	2010 Actual	2011 Projected	2011 Actual
Annual	85,000	100,000	
First quarter	18.000	20,000	
Second quarter	23,000	25,000	
Third quarter	19,000	25,000	
Fourth quarter	25,000	30,000	

Revenue: Services	2010 Actual	2011 Projected	2011 Actual
Business Writing: White Papers / Media Releases / Annual Reports / Direct Mail / Brochures / Sales Letters / Google Ads / Website Copy			
Business Editing: White Papers / Annual Report copy			
Periodicals: *Globe and Mail* / New Publication 1 / New Publication 2			

Professional development

We have almost completed our business plan. I suggest you also add a heading called Professional Development and list any courses you plan to take and books you are going to read. You determine what courses to take and books to read based on your business vision.

Review the sectors you want to tackle and the writing services you want to offer. What do you need to do to brush up your skills and make your vision a reality?

Think also about the fact that you are now running a business. If you have never run one before, you might want to take basic bookkeeping and marketing courses, or perhaps attend seminars on personal selling or networking. You might want to learn how to use particular software applications or how to create a website. As you read this book, other ideas might come to mind. Be open to them and add them to your professional development chart, which might look something like this.

Item / Location	Date / Cost	Rationale
Business writing (night school)	Tues. evenings, April to June; $675	To improve business writing
Microsoft Word—workshop through <company>	2 days in August, $375	Apply advanced Word concepts such as mail merge to sales letters and media releases
Basic bookkeeping (night school)	Winter 2008, $265	To better track revenue/expenses; & organize my books for tax time.

Now what?

Now spend some time on developing and writing your business plan. If you have been doing the exercises presented in the book as you've been reading it, you are all but there. If you haven't, take some time now and work on the exercises so you can develop you business plan. The fact is, you want to have your business plan in place before you put your marketing plan together.

As a step toward developing your marketing plan, we are going to look at the various arrows you have in your marketing quiver. Once you understand the weapons in your marketing arsenal, you will be able to build a marketing plan that helps you fulfill your vision and business plan.

Remember, the business plan includes the goals that support your business vision. The marketing plan, as we shall see, includes the tasks you complete to reach those goals so you can fulfill your business vision.

Chapter 29: Five Marketing Arrows

When it comes to marketing, corporate writers are like most other businesses. We do not have the marketing budget or muscle of a Nike, McDonald's, or Wal-Mart, or even of many medium-sized businesses that you've never heard of. However, we have many of the same marketing options that companies large and small have.

We have at least five arrows in the marketing quiver, including:

1. Generate repeat business, testimonials, and referrals.
2. Network with friends, relatives, associates; through organizations.
3. Advertise and promote.
4. Cold calling and direct mail.
5. Online strategies (website, blog, and social media)

Most businesses—large, medium, or small—have the same five arrows. What the marketing plan allows you to do is shoot them all in a planned and systematic manner to generate new and repeat business. That's the key to any successful marketing campaign: implementing the marketing tasks that support your business objectives in a planned and systematic manner.

A planned and systematic manner doesn't mean you can't wake up one day feeling inspired and try something spontaneous. Occasionally, I shoot off one or two marketing arrows when ideas strike me. I wake up most days, however, knowing what I am going to do and why.

What I am going to do here is help you understand the purpose of each of the marketing arrow and show you how to apply each one in a planned and systematic manner, all based on your business plan.

Why so many marketing elements?

Seldom does a writer who wants to conquer corporate markets send out one pitch or make one call and strike it rich. You cannot control the needs of prospects, but you can let them know you will be there when the need arises. You use multiple marketing strategies because it can take weeks or months for any one company to get back to you. It all depends on when, and whether, the need for your service materializes. So unless you have one client keeping you busy on a full-time basis (I think that is called "a job"), you have to shoot multiple marketing arrows.

Marketing, don't forget, is a numbers game. We want to improve your chances of winning the game. We do this by producing effective marketing material, targeting prospects based on our business plan, and getting our marketing information out there using a variety of means.

Not every arrow in the marketing quiver will hit the target every time you shoot it, but if you are not taking shots—if you let your fears, or procrastination, hold you back—you will never hit the target.

So, remind yourself that you are in business, and start marketing as though it matters. Because if you are in business, marketing does matter. Which is why you need a marketing plan. And building the marketing plan, one step at a time, is what we will do over the next few chapters.

Chapter 30: Generating Repeat Business

Before you put your marketing plan together, you need to select the marketing arrows, or tactics, that you will incorporate into your plan. Then you need to determine how best to use them and when to schedule the tasks required to sell your services to potential clients.

In this chapter, we look at generating repeat business, testimonials, and referrals. If you are thinking you need to generate business before you can generate repeat business, you are right. However, I want to start here for readers who have, or have had, some corporate clients. In addition, I want those of you who have had no clients to start here too. That way, when you land new clients, you'll be thinking about how to keep them coming back.

You can be lazy, but….
You can pray for manna to fall from heaven. Or you learn how to bake bread…. As a lazy person, I love it when the phone rings and someone wants to hire me, or when e-mail lands in my in-box with a request for a quote. I've been a full-time freelance writer since 1993, and I worked part-time as a freelancer for a few years before that. On occasion, old contacts call me or pass on my name to some of their colleagues. In addition, some people search online for writers and find me through my website because it is optimized (more on this later in the book) to show up in search engines when people use search terms such as "freelance writer Toronto," "copywriter Toronto," and several other search terms.

My website is a passive form of client generation (people find my website and contact me). Having one is part of my marketing plan, but it took marketing action—the construction and optimization of my website—to make it work. So it takes work to generate work. In other words, I would starve if I only waited for the phone to ring or for e-mail messages to land in my in-box. Instead, I actively market myself. And one of the best ways of engaging in active marketing is to generate repeat business, referrals, and testimonials.

Retail concept: Repeat business

I like to think this entire book is important; this section is particularly important if you are currently working as a freelance writer or if you are going to invest time generating new leads and clients.

If you are cold calling on a prospect who has never heard of you, you have to convince her that you can do the job. In other words, you have to build trust. (That is one of the reasons why you have to demonstrate knowledge of the sector and validate your writing experiences.) On the other hand, if you have done, or if you do, a solid job for clients—deliver the right words on time and on budget—they will trust you to do it again.

Look at it this way: When you are generating repeat business you are selling to established clients, ones with whom you have a relationship. When you are generating new business, you are selling to strangers (companies or organizations) with whom you hope to build a relationship. The latter take more time and effort. Or as any retailer will tell you, it costs six to eight times more to sell to a new customer than it does to resell a previous customer. Therefore, it's easier, and more profitable, to sell to previous customers than it is to chase new ones. Although I suggest you do both, many freelancers do not have a plan in place to generate repeat business.

Putting such a plan in place does not mean you sell only to previous customers. It means you sell to them while working to find new ones. As you find new ones, and complete jobs for them, they become previous customers. You then apply the principles of generating repeat business and resell your services to them.

Previous clients hear from me at least three times a year. I touch base to see whether a previous client requires my writing services (generating repeat business). Sometimes, I contact selected clients to ask for referrals. Or, if I am updating my website or putting together a direct mail brochure, I ask selected clients for testimonials.

When I am looking to generate repeat business, I call or e-mail previous clients and remind them that I am out here, still available to work for them. Often, they thank me for contacting them, and then... Nothing. If there is no work, there is no work. But sometimes they thank me, and give me a new assignment. Or sometimes they remember someone else in their company or at another company who was looking for a writer. All of a sudden, I have a referral.

Why didn't they call me if they needed my writing services or knew someone who needed a writer? There are as many reasons as there are clients. They were too busy putting out fires and left a writing project on the backburner. They forgot my name, sad as it might seem, or lost my contact information. Another freelancer called them just as they were developing a new project, and they went with that person. And so it goes.

Are there clients you have worked for over the last year or so that you have not heard from? Call or e-mail them. If they don't need your services, they don't need your services. No big deal. But if they need a writer and have been too busy to call anyone, then you are doing them a favour by putting yourself top-of-mind.

How do you generate repeat business?

Some writers say they feel funny asking for work. I do too. After all, I am a writer, not a sales and marketing expert. I am an English major from York University; I am not a businessperson. However, I also have a family, a home, a car, a big dog, and other expenses. I have made a conscious decision to earn my living as a freelance writer. I have had to get over a number of "funny" feelings to become good at what I do. I hope you can get over such feelings too.

So, how do you generate repeat business? There is no magic to generating repeat business, referrals, and testimonials. But it helps if you break the process down into steps and schedule the steps in a planned and systematic manner. Here are the steps:

1. Identify clients and/or editors for whom you have worked. Go back as far as you can; several years is not too far.
2. Develop your sales pitch (what you are going to write or say).
3. Schedule your calls or e-mail messages.
4. Call or e-mail contacts; ask if they require your services (or any new services you now offer, according to your business plan).
5. If you call, have a 30-second sales pitch ready. If your contact answers, deliver it and go silent; let the client reply. If you get voice mail, leave your sales pitch as a message.
6. If you send an e-mail, follow up by phone in a week or so.
7. Perform each of these steps several times a year.

As you land new clients, complete the work, and get paid for it, you add them to step one. If an old client has moved to a new company, find a new contact at the old company and add that person to your "repeat business" list. Then, track down your old client and contact him at the new company to see if you can generate new business with the company (but repeat business with the contact).

Your job here, simply put, is to let previous clients know that you are still out there, available for work. You are contacting people you have had a positive business experience with, people you would like to work with again. You are doing what almost any business does: marketing to your previous customers. You are doing this because your next customer is most likely to be a previous customer. You are doing this because you cannot count on clients to contact you, even if they need a writer for a new project. Sad but true. The onus is on you to keep in touch with your clients, not the other way around.

Scheduling repeat business steps

We will look at what you can say when generating repeat business in a moment. First, I want to show you how to schedule the steps. How long will it take you to identify clients—find their names and contact information—you have worked for? Less than a day? A day or two?

Schedule that task (*identify previous clients*) on a specific day in Outlook Tasks, your scheduling software, day planner, or calendar. Now look ahead four months and schedule the task again. Then look ahead four more months and schedule *identify previous clients* again.

Also, schedule the day or days on which you will develop your pitch (what you are going to write or say) to each client. Can you do it on the same day that you make your list of previous clients you will contact? You can, or you can pick another day. The key is to schedule the task so you will do it.

Schedule the days you will make your calls or send your e-mail. If you have 20 previous clients, you might want to space out the days you contact clients. If you have a few previous clients, you might want to contact them all on the same day or during the same week. Again, the important thing here is that you schedule the action.

Let's look at these tasks scheduled in a calendar:

Repeat Business	January	April	August
Identify previous clients	Jan. 10	April 10	Aug. 10
Develop pitches for previous clients	Jan. 15	April 15	Aug. 15
Contact previous clients	Jan. 17	April 17	Aug. 17

Congratulations. Your marketing plan now has nine scheduled tasks!

What to say when generating repeat business

What do you say to these previous clients? A lot depends on what you did for the client and what your relationship with the client is like. Whatever you say or write, keep it short. For instance, you can remind clients of the work you did and let them know you are available to take on similar assignments.

You can send an e-mail like the one below. Only be more specific and articulate. After all, you are the writer. And you know your client.

> Hi Chris,
>
> Three months ago, I wrote a direct mail brochure for you. Thanks for sending me a completed version for my portfolio.
>
> I am following up to see if you require my writing services again. In addition to writing brochures, I also write copy for websites and articles for employee and customer newsletters.
>
> If I can be of assistance, e-mail me or call me at 416-555-1234.

It's that simple.

However, you can say or write other things. Say you have added a new service to your portfolio of services, or have launched or redesigned your website. That can be the catalyst for your e-mail or call.

Hi, Chris,

Three months ago, I wrote the copy for a direct mail brochure for you. Thanks for sending me a completed version for my portfolio.

I am following up to let you know that I now write media releases for clients. You can see several samples online at www.mysite.com/media.

If you need a copywriter or require someone to write media releases, e-mail me or call me at 416-555-1234.

Hi, Chris,

Three months ago, I wrote the copy for a direct mail brochure for you. Thanks for sending me a completed version for my portfolio.

I am following up to let you know I have recently launched a website with samples of my copywriting, media releases, and articles I have written for employee newsletters.

Feel free to drop by www.mysite.com and look at some of my work. I would like to add the copy for your brochure to my online portfolio. Let me know if this is acceptable.

Also, if you need a copywriter again, feel free to e-mail me or call me at 416-555-1234.

Notice that in that last e-mail, you are asking for permission to add the brochure copy you wrote to your website. You don't have to ask for work to contact an old client. You come up with the reason for the contact. What is important is that you connect with previous clients on a regular basis.

What if you have not launched a website or are not offering any new services and you feel funny about (fear) touching base to ask for work? Do yourself a favour; harness that fear and get on with your marketing.

What if you have touched base twice, have not heard back and don't want to bug the client? You are not bugging the client. You are marketing your services, which is what any business owner does! At the same time, do recognize the limits. If you get no reply at all, not even a "thank you for contacting me," the next two or three times you pitch, remove that client from your list. Or alter your pitch—ask for a referral or testimonial—if that makes sense based on the work you did for the client.

Using the seasons

My client follow-ups are often seasonal messages. I find that mid-spring and early November are good times to contact previous clients.

In mid-spring, I send a vacation alert to clients that I am working for and have worked for. The alert includes the date that I will be on vacation and a message that says I have time (if I do) to take on new projects before I start my holidays.

In early November, I send clients an e-mail letting them know when I will be shutting down for the holidays and I let them know that I have time to take on new projects (if I do) before I start my holidays. I also remind clients that they can contact me early in the New Year if they want to discuss new projects.

Of course, if I am particularly busy and do not have time to take on new work, I would not solicit work this way; however, I still let clients know that I will be on vacation.

Current clients become previous clients

When does a current client become a previous client? Good question and one that I am often asked. As soon as the work is approved and paid for, a current client becomes a previous client. You might not want ask for more work right away, but you can do it subtly when you receive payment for the job.

When I invoice my clients, I thank them for the work and let them know my invoice is attached. (I invoice all clients by e-mail unless they request an invoice by mail.) When the cheque arrives, I e-mail the client and express thanks for the payment. In addition, I say I am available to help with any other writing projects that might be in the works. I don't count this as one of my three planned touches. It's just something that makes sense to do. The cheque arrives and I send the client a simple thank you e-mail message:

> The cheque for the direct mail brochure copy I wrote for you arrived today, thanks. If I can be of assistance again, let me know. In addition to writing brochure copy, I can write case studies, media releases, articles

for employee and customer newsletters, and copy for your website.

Notice how I tell the client what else I can do. That's called planting the seed. How is the client supposed to know if I don't tell her? The client might know, but why take that chance? Why not plant the seed? I also add the client to my list of clients to contact when generating repeat business.

It's your job to keep your name in front of your clients. You don't have to hit them over the head, but you do have to let them know you are in business. Speaking of letting your clients know you are in business, have you ever asked previous clients to let their suppliers, vendors, customers, and other business associates know what you do? If not, read on!

Referrals and testimonials

Once you have worked successfully for a client three times, you can solicit referrals and testimonials. Why three times? Truth is, I just made that up. But I want to feel as if I have an established relationship with a client before I ask for favours. However, when you ask for a referral and/or testimonial depends on the rapport you establish with the client. If you develop an excellent rapport on the first project—you did a bang-up job under tight deadline pressure and the client was extremely pleased—and ask for a referral and/or testimonial when the cheque arrives or when you are working on your next "develop pitches for previous clients" task.

If a client uses you on a regular basis, you may not need to ask for repeat business. Instead, ask for a referral and/or testimonial. If you've worked with a client a couple of times and want to do more work in that sector, ask for referrals. This is your marketing plan. You determine what you want to do and why. However, make sure you schedule it in, or there is a good chance—an exceptionally good chance—that you will do nothing at all.

If a client is happy with your service, why wouldn't that client pass on your name to others who could use your services? Why wouldn't that client send you a letter or e-mail of recommendation—a testimonial—that you can post on your website or use in a sales letter or brochure?

The answer to "why wouldn't" is simple. Clients do not think of sending you referrals or testimonials. Occasionally one might thank you, but don't get into this line of business if all you want is gratitude. While the occasional client might refer your name to someone who needs a writer, or offer to write a testimonial, the onus is on you to ask for referrals and testimonials. That's part of your marketing plan.

With a referral comes a degree of trust. When your phone rings, you would like to hear this from a potential client, I would wager: "Mr. James says you've done an excellent job researching and writing white papers for him. I'm looking for someone to write case studies for my website, and..."

So, how do you ask for referrals and testimonials? It's very similar to the way you ask for repeat business. Here are the steps:

- Identify clients and/or editors for whom you have worked. Go back about a year.
- Develop your pitch (what you are going to write or say).
- Schedule your calls or e-mail messages.

Call or e-mail your contacts and ask if they would pass on your name and contact information to suppliers, vendors, customers, and/or associates. You can also ask your contacts to give you information on who they're passing your name so you can follow up, but some clients are reluctant to do so. Respect that.

When you call, have a 30-second elevator pitch ready. If your contact answers, deliver it and go silent; let the client reply. If you get voice mail, leave your pitch as a message. If the client gives you contact information for a referral, follow up by phone or by e-mail. If you follow up by phone, have a 30-second elevator pitch ready to leave on voice mail or to deliver in person if the new contact answers. Start with: "So-and-so suggested I call you..."

Mostly, I ask for referrals. But when I update my website or brochure (speaking of which, I have to schedule that in my to-do list!), I call a few clients and ask for testimonials. In short, what you ask for depends on what you need at the time. But schedule the *ask*, or there is a very good chance that you will not do it.

You are not bugging clients

What I have done here is spell out a number of ways you can connect with previous clients to generate repeat business, referrals, and testimonials. I am suggesting you do this three times a year. However, ultimately it's your job to figure out when to do it, and how many times to do it—when to connect with clients, and what to say when you do.

You are not bugging clients when you do this. So ask for testimonials when it makes sense—if you are updating your website or producing a brochure to promote your services. And schedule asking for referrals from previous clients. You can mix the generate referrals or testimonials task in with your generate repeat business task, so you can do one or the other or both—whichever makes sense based on your relationship and contact history with the client.

I conduct a workshop called The Six-Figure Freelancer, and 90 percent of the people who take the workshop look all sheepish when I ask them if they actively work to generate repeat business, referrals, and testimonials. Don't be one of those sheepish people.

Focus initially on asking for repeat business. After you have worked with a client on several jobs, ask for referrals and testimonials. Once you have had several positive experiences with a client, the client is more likely to put his or her name on a testimonial that you can use on your website and is more likely to pass on referrals.

If you have had positive experiences with clients in the sectors you are targeting, you want to be particularly assertive. Your vision and business plan are telling you to do more work for companies in those sectors and asking for referrals is a legitimate way of drumming up business. Be polite and professional. Thank your clients for their time, even when they cannot help you. They may not be able to help you immediately, but you have planted the seed. You never know when it may sprout.

So, you have many ways you can approach your requests for repeat business, referrals, and testimonials. Decide what you want to ask of each client, schedule the task, and then take action. If you are not doing this, you are not thinking like an entrepreneur. And if you want to earn a professional level income from freelancing, you have to start thinking, and acting, like a professional freelancer.

Chapter 31: Networking Success

Allow me to re-introduce you to a concept with which you are probably familiar. If you are like most freelance writers, it's one you probably ignore or use informally. The concept is called networking, which is a fancy word for talking to people about what you do.

Asking for referrals is a form of networking. You are networking with previous customers. However, what about all the people you know who are not customers? Why wouldn't you network with family members, friends, other writers, associates, and other people you know? Why wouldn't you join associations that represent your target sectors and go to events where you can network?

True story

As mentioned, I conduct a workshop called The Six-Figure Freelancer. At the beginning of the workshop, I ask people what they hope to accomplish during the day. One time, in response to the question, a woman said she felt she had not begun to tap into the full potential of the corporate market.

I asked her how many billable hours per week she was working. She said 15 to 25. I asked her if she felt she was earning a fair hourly rate. She said yes. I asked her whether she enjoyed the work she was doing. She said she had a good mix of writing—reports, media releases, and articles for newsletters.

"Hmmm," I said. "It sounds as though you have what everybody here aspires to. Enlighten me. What exactly is the problem?"

She explained she had mentioned to her brother that she was going to set up shop as a freelance writer. He said his employer was looking for a writer and suggested she call his boss. She made the call and landed a fairly steady gig, working from home for the company. One day, her client asked if she could take on additional work. He had a customer who needed some writing. She said she could. Between the two steady clients, she was earning a decent living.

She paused.

"And?" I said. "And?"

"It's been too easy!" she sputtered.

She had achieved what every freelancer aspires to, but was beating herself up because it was too easy—because she had not starved and suffered!

Why do writers do this to themselves? Don't answer. The question is rhetorical. I've been guilty of it in my way too.

The point?

Becoming a successful freelancer may not be that easy for you, but if you eschew proven marketing methods—networking, in this instance—that can lead to work, success will be that much more difficult to achieve.

I know freelancers who will not tell friends and relatives what they do. They feel it's cheating or asking for favours. Poppycock! Networking is a legitimate business practice.

When you network, you are not necessarily asking friends, family members, associates, colleagues, and other contacts for work. Heck, unless they are executives or run their own businesses, most are probably not in a position to hire you. So, what are you doing? You are asking whether they can give your business card (you have a business card, don't you?) or your contact information to someone who might need a writer.

Mind you, if the people you are networking with can hire you, why not ask them if they are interested in your services?

Three types of networking

There are three basic types of networking:

- Networking with previous clients to ask for referrals, which we covered in the previous chapter
- Networking with people you know: friends, relatives, associates, and so on
- Networking with people you meet at events for writers, industry events ("industry" being the sectors you are targeting), or formal networking events

To become a successful freelance writer, you need to engage actively in all three types of networking. I have dramatically scaled down my networking at industry events. Why? I generate a great deal of repeat business and referrals. However, before you can generate repeat business, you have to generate new business. Networking is an important means of doing that.

As with generating repeat business, referrals, and testimonials, you should schedule your networking opportunities.

People you know

Before you can network with people you know, you have to make a list of all the people that you know: friends, relatives, associates, other writers, and people in or around your social and professional circles. Then you have to write out what you are going to say or e-mail to your various contacts. You can produce a standard message, but you will want to customize it based on your relationship with each of your contacts.

Once you have your list of contacts and your message written out, you have to start networking. And once you have completed your networking, you do it all over again, according to your marketing schedule. I would suggest networking with people you know at least once or twice a year.

Whether you call or e-mail everyone on your networking list is up to you. It depends, in part, on how long your networking list is and how well you know people.

For instance, if you came up with a list of 99 people (you will be amazed at how many people you know once you start thinking about it), you might want to network three times a year, contacting 33 people each time. (At the same time, remember to review and add new contacts to your list on an ongoing basis.)

If you are really looking to kick-start your business, contact everyone on your list in your first round of networking. Contact selected and new networking-list members in subsequent rounds.

Let's schedule people-you-know networking activities in a calendar (see the next page).

Networking	**January**	**April**	**August**
Make a list of people I know, with contact information	Jan. 10	April 10	Aug. 10
Select people to network with and develop networking scripts	Jan. 15	April 15	Aug. 15
Network with selected contacts	Jan. 17	April 17	Aug. 17

Congratulations. Your marketing plan has nine more scheduled tasks!

Schedule these activities using dates that makes sense to you and your business. Pay particular attention to your business vision's when. For instance, if you want to take July and August off, you should not do any networking in June. Why try to drum up business when you don't want it?

Alternative scheduling method

While I have used the calendar method to divide networking into three tasks that you conduct three times a year, I want you to know that you can chunk these tasks in any way that makes sense to you.

Let us say you spend the next day or two coming up with a comprehensive list of people you know and you end up with 50 contacts. If you networked with five people per week for 10 weeks, that would equal 50 contacts in just over two months. Not a bad start.

You can do your first wave of networking in January, February, and March, and then do a second wave of five people per week over 10 weeks in the fall. In the second wave, you contact people who were on your networking list as well as new contacts you have added to your networking list.

Scheduling networking activity does not preclude networking at any other time of year. If you think of someone you know in May, contact that person. The important thing here is that you establish a formal networking schedule, the times of the year when you network. Be open to networking at other times that make sense based on how your business unfolds.

Again, if you do not schedule networking, you might talk to a few people on occasion. However, you will not connect with all your contacts on a regular basis. And you will miss opportunities for generating work.

How to network with people you know

When you network with people you know, you simply tell them what you do or what you plan to do and—here is the hard part—ask for their help.

"But these people already know I'm a freelancer!" you protest.

Cool. Your work is half done. You don't have to tell them; you have to remind them. Why remind them? Why do advertisers run the same ads repeatedly? Consumers have short attention spans and advertisers run ads repeatedly to keep products or services top-of-mind.

Tell your network of contacts what you do, or remind them. Tell them that you are looking to expand your roster of clients. Ask your contacts if they know someone who might be able to use your services. If so, ask your contact to pass your business card or name and contact information to their contacts or to provide you with names and contact information.

When networking, keep your business vision and business plan in mind. In other words, tell your contacts what you do (writing services you offer) and for whom you do it (sectors). Let people know you are open to other opportunities in other sectors, but lead with your business vision!

Here is a sample networking e-mail script:

> Hi, Terry,
>
> It has been a while since we last connected. In part, that's because I've been working hard to expand my freelance writing business. In fact, I'm wondering if you might be able to help me with that?
>
> I write media releases, website content, and promotional material for companies in the automotive and automotive-parts manufacturing, furniture manufacturing, and information technology sectors. I am looking to connect with executives and business owners in these sectors, to tell them more about my writing services.

If you have contacts in these areas, or can think of others who might need to hire a freelance writer/editor, feel free to forward names and contact information to me or to pass on my name and contact information to those you know:

> Paul Lima
> info@paullima.com
> www.paullima.com
> 416- 628-6005

If you have any questions about what I do and for whom, e-mail or call me. I'm always happy to demystify the exotic world of freelance writing.
Cheers,
Paul

Note: I used a rather informal tone to end this e-mail. The tone you use—and the actual words you use—depend on your relationship with the person you are contacting. For instance, if you were contacting a sibling or good friend, the entire e-mail message above might be too formal. At the same time, remember that e-mail can be easily forwarded. Ask yourself how you would feel if the person you are networking with simply forwarded your message to several other people. With that in mind, you want to use a degree of formality when networking by e-mail.

If you were networking by phone or in person, you would want to convey the same information: a request for help, what you do and for whom and your contact information.

To summarize the "people you know" networking process:

1. Identify personal contacts—friends, relatives, associates—you can talk to about your business. Your contacts do not have to be business people, but make sure you include any business people you do know. They do not have to be clients or prospective clients to make your list. You just have to know them.

2. E-mail or phone them (or meet in person) and ask for their help in contacting people who might be interested in your services.

3. Be specific about what you do and for whom you do it, and about what you want—the type of contact information (company name, name, title, e-mail address, phone number, or mailing address).

4. Follow up if people provide you with contact information or have them forward your contact information to their contacts.

Outside your personal network

Networking can involve talking to people outside your personal network as well—to others in your profession or others in the sectors you are targeting. In other words, you should talk with people you meet at events for writers, at industry events ("industry" being sectors you are targeting), or at formal business networking events.

Depending on where you live, consider joining the Chamber of Commerce, Board of Trade, professional trade associations (in your sector), or writing, editing, small business, and consulting associations. Many associations send out job notices or have job hotlines. In addition, the groups tend to hold regular professional development seminars and socials, and even formal networking events.

Don't just look for other writers to network with. Look for industry contacts. Almost every sector (and you have a list of three to five sectors) has an association. Pick a sector, add the word "association", and Google the phrase. See what you can find.

Sometimes you have to be working in the sector to join the association. Other times, you only need some background connection with the sector to join. Most associations hold formal networking events or informal networking opportunities: breakfasts, dinners, professional development events, and so on. Such events tend to be great opportunities to learn more about your targeted sector and to meet people in the sector. The events might even be opportunities for you to speak on how to develop effective writing, editing, or communications skills. I've spoken at a number of professional development events held by associations and often came away with new contacts and new clients.

When you are looking for networking opportunities outside your list of personal contacts, make sure you look at formal networking organizations too. They tend to hold monthly breakfast meetings or evening meetings. You can conduct Google searches to find networking directories and events in specific areas.

What to do at networking events

When you are networking at events, bring your business card. If you do not have a business card, have a designer create one for you and have it properly printed so you look business-like and professional. In other words, no inkjet cards printed on perforated stock. (More on this later in the book.)

When you attend networking events, you should have two goals: to help people and to let people help you. You help people by listening and summing up what you think they need. ("So, you are looking for contacts with two left feet and who require custom-built orthotic devices. Is that correct?") You also provide people with contacts if you know someone who can help them. To let people help you, you have to clearly state what you do, who you do it for, and the type of contacts you require.

Let's say you have a financial background. If so, you would be looking for executives in the finance sector or for finance and accounting executives in other sectors with which you are familiar. If you have a manufacturing background, you look for executives in manufacturing and perhaps distribution. If you have a legal background, you look for partners in law firms and executives responsible for areas such as legal affairs and government affairs in other companies.

Do you see how your business vision comes into play when you are networking?

Schedule networking activities outside your personal contact list as part of your marketing plan. Instead of presenting you with a task calendar (you get the picture by now), let me to break down networking into tasks or activities that you can schedule in your marketing plan:

- Source organizations that provide networking opportunities. Include writers' and editors' organizations or associations, professional and trade associations (that represent the sectors you are targeting), local chambers of commerce, boards of trade, and formal networking groups.
- Through assessment and investigation (talking to existing members, attending events that are open to non-members), determine which organizations you will join (if membership is a requirement for attending events and meetings).
- Join selected organizations.

- Attend events and functions presented by organizations.
- Look for opportunities to attend other events and functions sponsored by organizations that you do not have to join formally.

In addition to networking face-to-face when and where possible, you should investigate social media such as Facebook, LinkedIn, and Twitter. We will discuss social media in more detail in the next chapter.

Congratulations. Your marketing plan now has even more scheduled tasks!

Collaboration

Although this chapter is on networking, I want to take a moment to discuss collaboration. I am a writer, not a graphic designer or website designer. Occasionally, potential clients will ask me if I can write and design a brochure or website. The honest answer is no, I can't do both. However, I have connected with several designers who can take on the design portions of such projects. I am upfront with the client: I tell them that I can do the writing and partner with a designer to complete the job. The client is often happy to let me bring in my partner. Sometimes the client will want to visit the designer's website or check references. That is up to the client.

Collaboration raises a minor degree of complexity when it comes to quoting on projects, managing them, and billing. Both parties have to define the scope of their end of the project (see chapter on quoting on jobs) and you have to decide if you are going to issue separate or a combined quote. Most clients want to receive one quote only. If you land the job, work schedules have to be co-ordinated, which can involve some give and take. If you've issued one quote, you have to issue one invoice at the end of the job, which means one of the parties gets the cheque and has to pay the other party.

Again, collaboration is more complex than working on your own, but I'd rather deal with the minor complexities than not bid on a potentially lucrative gig.

I also sometimes take on complex writing or editing jobs. I'd like to think that I am a decent writer and editor, but I know I am not a good proofreader. Sometimes I subcontract the final proofreading of a job to a dedicated proofreader. The client does not need to know that I am contracting out the final proofreading, but I have to budget time and money for doing so, and work that information into my quote and my schedule.

So collaboration can help you land gigs you might otherwise have to pass on, and it can help you do a better job on other gigs. With that in mind, you can using networking to find other freelancers, such as designers, editors, or proofreaders, with whom you can collaborate. At minimum, consider joining a formal writers' organization. If you need to collaborate with someone, you can ask other writers in the organization if they can recommend anyone. But before you start to work with another freelancer, check the person's website and ask to talk to references.

Finally, with collaboration in mind, you might want to try to network with graphic artists, website developers, and other independent practitioners who might need to collaborate with freelancer writers now and again. Keep your sectors in mind and try to find people who do work in the sectors that you are targeting. That will give you a more natural initial connection with the people you are contacting.

Chapter 32: Advertising and Promotion

You're reading the newspaper, and on almost every page you see... ads. You're reading your favourite magazine or a trade journal, and on every other page you see... ads. You're watching TV, and every 15 minutes you see... ads. Even if you watch an ad-free cable station, you still see promotions (ads) for other shows on the station. You're listening to the radio, and you hear... ads. You're walking down the street and you see billboards and transit posters, or ads. You are surfing the Web and you see... text ads, banner ads, video ads, all sorts of ads.

You are taking a continuing education class at your local community college, and you go to the washroom, and above the urinals or on the stall doors, you see... ads!

Advertising is ubiquitous, but ask freelance writers if they advertise their services and they look at you as though you are daft. "Spend money promoting my business? Why would I? I am a freelance writer!" Beyond spending money on business cards and maybe a website, most writers do not spend money promoting their businesses. The number of writers I meet who do not yet have websites constantly surprises me. Yes, it costs money to register a website address. It costs money to host your domain. It costs money (or time, if you can do it yourself) to build the site. But the pay-off can be phenomenal.

Why don't writers spend money? Besides feeling broke and being thrifty, not that I am stereotyping, most writers don't realize they are in business. All I can say is this: if you are not investing in your business, who is? Advertising, done properly, is an investment that pays dividends. And yes, at the same time, it may be a risk that does not pay off. With that in mind, I suggest that freelance writers think about where and how they want to advertise and start slowly to test the waters.

Once you have a business plan, based on your business vision, you use your plan to drive your advertising and promotional marketing decisions.

First two promotional tasks

Here are your first two paid promotional tasks:
1. Set up a website following the steps that I outline below.
2. Create a business card. Make sure it reflects what you do and is professionally designed and printed.

Why set up a website before you create a business card? Your business card should have your website address on it, so set up your website first. There will be much more on websites later in the book, so let me address the business card here.

Business card

My first business card was homemade and printed on poor-quality perforated stock. I was not earning much money at the time, and I rationalized my decision to spend no money on my cards. In retrospect, the rationalization made no sense. I was not thinking of my card as an investment in my business. I remember giving cards out reluctantly because they were so poorly designed and did not look professional. What's the point of having a business card if you aren't going to hand it out?

Here is my new card. I am not saying it's perfect, but I've had positive feedback on it and I give it out with pride.

If you are in business, business cards are important, so spend a little time and money on your card and do it right. However, before you print a business card, get your website up.

Company name?

When I conduct workshops based on this book, and start talking about business cards and websites, people often ask me if they need a company name to be in business. It depends on several factors.

I have been operating my freelance writing and training business under my name since 1993. However, if I ran a public relations agency or advertising agency, or wanted to tackle high-end jobs—such as strategizing, designing, and writing annual reports for large corporations—I would register a business name.

Look at your vision. Think of the writing services you want to offer and the types of companies you want to work with. Then decide if you need a company name.

Before you pick and register a company name, make sure you can register a website name that is the same as your company name. If you go to www.paullima.com/domain, you can search (at no cost for the search) for available domain names.

Advertising and promotion

Websites and business cards involve the expenditure of money. Creating and using both (such as handing out business cards at networking events) are significant parts of your promotional effort. However, advertising and promotion should not end there. Below is a summary of advertising and promotional opportunities that you should also investigate.

Advertising: online and print

There will be more on online advertising and promotion strategies in the online strategy chapter in the book. Here is a summary:

- Create a website.
- List your site with search engines (Google, Yahoo!, Bing).
- Run Google, Yahoo!, or Bing ads (requires that you have a website).

But don't stop there. Remember the work you did researching trade associations you might join so you can network? Most of these associations have websites, and many run ads on their websites. The associations also publish electronic newsletters that often run affordable ads. Run an ad for three months on a website an/or in an e-newsletter and monitor the results. If your investment pays off, continue to run the ad. If not, look for other advertising venues.

You can also produce your own e-newsletter and solicit subscribers from your website and/or blog. And, as mentioned earlier, you should create social media profiles using sites such as LinkedIn, Facebook, and Twitter.

You can run ads in selected magazines, trade magazines, newspapers, community newspapers, and in newsletters and publications of trade associations, community and business organizations, unions, churches, and other organizations.

To get started, experiment with one or two publications that reach your target market. Let an ad run at least three times so you can evaluate its effectiveness before you decide to pull it or run it again. In other words, you wouldn't run full-page ads in the *Toronto Star*, *The Globe and Mail*, or the *New York Times*. You would run business-card size ads or classified ads in print (or online) publications that reach companies and organizations in your target sectors.

To make sure your ads speak to the needs of your target market, focus on the primary services you offer, and include your name (or business name), contact information (phone and e-mail address), and your website address.

At the risk of sounding like a broken record, set up your website first. The ads you run can be considered the tip of the iceberg; your website can be considered the base. Your goal is to drive traffic from your ads to your website, where potential customers can read about you and your services and view your writing samples and testimonials.

Advertising tasks

I am not going to create a promotional calendar for you, but here are some broad strokes that will help you chunk your advertising and promotion efforts into manageable tasks that you can schedule:

- Source print and/or electronic media that reach your target market.
- Contact advertising department to get the price of ads.
- Decide on the publications that you will use, based on cost.

- Write and design your ads. (Some publications will design ads for you; however, you might have to hire a designer to get ads into some publications.)

As mentioned, I suggest you run an ad at least three times before you make a decision on whether to stick with a particular publication. Sometimes, a person has to see your ad a couple of times before they act. Other times, someone might notice your ad but not need your service right away. The second or third time they see it, they might need a writer. So give your ad a chance to work for you.

Remember, you are doing this so you can generate new business. If you land new clients and do a bang-up job, you will turn your new clients into repeat customers and customers who are sending you referrals. The more that occurs, the less advertising and promotion you have to do. But if you are trying to get your business off the ground, boost your revenue, or change the direction of your business, you need to schedule advertising tasks so you will get them done.

Public relations

Not all advertising and promotional activities take money, but they all take time. Public relations, for instance, is a form of promotion that costs little or nothing beyond the time it takes to promote yourself.

If you write for newspapers and magazines, you might be on the receiving end of public relations campaigns—media releases sent to you by public relation agencies that hope you will write about their clients. (By the way, many of these agencies contract out the writing of media releases, which is something to keep in mind when looking for companies to pitch your writing services.)

Why not learn from the PR agencies? Are there publications that might be interested in the fact that you have launched a new business? If so, write a media release about your business and services and submit it. Or why not write a release or a pitch that touts you as a communications expert, someone the media can call on when writing articles about the importance of communicating? Write it, and then submit it to publications in your sector or to appropriate TV or radio shows (on which you might appear as a guest speaker).

Let me show you what I mean by promoting yourself as an expert. Here is a media pitch that touts a manners expert. Notice that there is no "news" here. The pitch is simply promoting a person who can speak to the issues of manners. The pitch also raises a business problem and offers the expert as someone with a solution.

Subject: Is Your Etiquette Blowing Business Deals?

Many job interviews and sales meetings are held over breakfast, lunch, or dinner. And many jobs and sales are lost because of it. Why? The guest may have arrived late, may have held his or her eating utensils incorrectly, may have ordered the wrong kind of food, may have discussed a company's internal politics, or may have unknowingly made another major faux pas.

Learning business manners has not been part of a business professional's upbringing, and this can limit success. Learning and using proper business manners would appeal to any professional who is constantly looking for ways to improve business performance.

Adeodata Czink is a manners expert who specializes in helping professionals avoid common etiquette mistakes. Czink, called Canada's Empress of Etiquette, consults on manners and, with grace and humour, teaches people how to avoid common etiquette mistakes and how to properly

- Seat business guests,
- Order a meal that matches your guest's,
- Hold your wine glass,
- Propose a toast with grace and ease,
- Decide who should pay the bill, and
- Many other small but important actions that make a big impact on others.

If you are interested in interviewing Adeodata Czink for an article, please contact <Name, e-mail address, phone number>.

The above pitch was sent out by a PR firm; however, you can write your own pitches (or media releases) and send them to appropriate publications, ideally those in the sectors you are targeting. Of course, your pitch would promote you as... as what? Go back to your business vision to see who you are. Depending on your vision, your release could promote you as a communications consultant, media release expert, white paper writer, editor or grammar expert, communications trainer, and so on. Ideally, it should promote you as someone who can do things that will help others communicate more effectively.

You can also write articles for newspapers, magazines (and even blogs and websites). These articles would be "how to" or "why to" articles that focus on writing and communication topics related to your sector and would position you as someone who is knowledgeable about whatever topic you have proposed. You would not just write and submit the article. Instead, you would schedule and complete the following tasks:

1. Identify publications, blogs, and websites that reach companies in your sectors.
2. Identify the name and e-mail address of editors at each publication.
3. Pitch a short synopsis of your article (similar to the query letter covered in section two of this book) to the contact. Ensure the synopsis contains valuable information rather than an advertorial blurb about your services; suggest an article length of 600 to 800 words. Offer to write the article at no cost but request a short bio with your website address be included at the end of the article.
4. Follow up in about two weeks if you don't hear back.
5. Write and submit the article; meet the word count and deadline.

By way of aside, if you are comfortable with public speaking, you might even arrange to speak at events that attract your target market. You would do this by networking through associations that include members of your target market. Many associations hold professional development events—workshops, seminars, lunches, conferences—and are often looking for people who can speak on a variety of topics. Speakers do not always get paid but some associations offer speakers honorariums.

These association events are often covered by trade reporters, so if you could find yourself quoted in a publication that reaches your target audience, which builds your credibility. Even if the events are not covered by the media, you still get to talk directly to members of your target audience about a topic related to your business.

Finding time to market your business

So, as you see, advertising and promotional possibilities abound. To get started, consider the services you want to offer and the sectors you want to target. Based on those criteria, explore your advertising and promotional options. Pick the appropriate advertising and promotional activities and determine how you might use them to reach your target market. Chunk these activities into manageable tasks and schedule the tasks in your marketing plan.

In short, your job, during your non-billable hours, is to investigate advertising and promotional possibilities and pick those that seem most appropriate for your business, all based on your business vision and business plan.

If you're wondering where you'll find the time to do all this, remember that you are spending less time fooling around with e-mail and surfing the Web so you have more time to invest in your business. Also, how many billable hours per week do you want to work? How many are you working? As discussed earlier, devote the difference between the number of billable hours you want to work and the number of billable hours you are working to these important, non-billable tasks—the tasks that will generate billable hours for you.

Some writers pack all their marketing into one day a week. On Marketing Monday (or whatever day they choose), they literally devote that day to marketing. I prefer to chunk my marketing tasks into smaller bits and spread them over the week. (Actually, I prefer it when the phone rings and people say, "We need you to write for us..." But I find that happens more often when I am marketing my services.) Do whatever feels right for you and fits the way you work.

What if you are working a lot of billable work but are not making a whole lot of money because you have low-paying clients? Spend at least five hours per week and focus on the marketing tasks that you believe will help you find better-paying clients.

Congratulations. You now have a whole whack of marketing tasks to schedule in your marketing plan!

Chapter 33: Cold Calling and Direct Mail

We are now entering the domain of cold calling. I use the term cold call to cover unsolicited phone calls, sales letters, and e-mail messages that deliver your sales pitch to potential customers you have neither met nor been referred to. Cold calling is one of the most difficult and, frankly, tedious aspects of conquering corporate markets. But if you are currently working minimal billable hours, it is one of the most important marketing tasks you can schedule, beyond generating repeat business and referrals, networking, advertising and building (and optimizing) your website.

With that in mind, by know you should know what you want to write. You know the sectors you want to target (and why). Now all you have to do is:

1. Identify companies within your sectors.
2. Find the appropriate person at each company.
3. Write your sales or pitch letters.
4. Fire off your pitch letters/e-mail (or make your calls).
5. Follow up and deliver the goods.

If your initial wave of direct marketing produces clients who generate steady, repeat business, you may not have to use direct marketing to sell your services for quite some time. Most writers, however, market their services, get busy for a while, and then go into marketing mode again. Having to do this drives me crazy, but that is the nature of freelance writing, and I would never exchange this business for a straight job!

Fact is, when it comes to direct mail, a two to five percent rate of return is considered excellent. That means, if you send out 100 pitches and land two to five prospects you are doing well. (You then have to convert those prospects into clients by quoting on the gig, which we will look at.)

You may be thinking, "One hundred pitches? Is Paul nuts? I quit!" Take a deep breath. It took nine months or so for your mother to get you ready to be presented to the world, didn't it? And you are giving birth to a new business, so expect to take some time, and expect to feel a few labour pains on the way to success. In other words, you do not have to send out 100 pitches (or make 100 calls) in a day. But if this is your first year of freelancing and you have no clients, try to send out at least two pitches each business day. If you touch base (by mail, phone, or e-mail) with 10 prospects a week (two per business day), you will have sent out 200 pitches in 20 business weeks.

Does that sound like something you can do? Once you get rolling, there is no reason you cannot do it. Or double it. Seriously. Four pitches a day is entirely possible. That's 20 a week or 100 pitches in just over a month.

We will look at what to write or say when cold calling in the next chapter. For now, let's look at getting your cold call lists organized.

Making contact: Companies

You determine who your potential customers are by reviewing your business plan and then sourcing companies within sectors you are targeting. (Now aren't you glad you decided to focus on a limited number of sectors?) How do you find the companies? Who should get your promotional message? How do your format your message? All will be explained.

Fact is, I cannot give you a list of companies in your sector. However, there are resources that you can tap into. To start with, the Web has made conducting this kind of research a lot easier. For instance, I went to Google and typed in "furniture manufacturing." (I wanted to pick a sector with which I was unfamiliar.) Good old Google returned over 25 pages of links. Your goal, if you want to write for the furniture-manufacturing sector, is to sort through the links to find the names of companies to which you can pitch your services. That's a lot of sorting, and you minimize your work by narrowing your search. You can do that by looking for particular types of furniture manufacturers or for furniture manufacturers in your city, province, or state.

Most companies belong to associations. If we can continue with the furniture manufacturer's example, you can search for "furniture manufacturer association." When I did it on Google.ca, the first hit was the Ontario Furniture Manufacturers Association. The second was the Canadian Furniture Manufacturers Association. I have not checked out the websites of the associations, but associations often list members on their websites, which will help you find companies in furniture manufacturing.

Conduct searches using "American association" or "Canadian association," or "<your city or state or province> association" and you will find scores of associations, many of which list their members. Sort through the links to find the names of companies to which you can pitch your services, and then look for contact information on the association site or by searching the Web.

Many associations publish newsletters or electronic newsletters that contain industry news and member profiles. The richer the association, the more likely it is to hire writers to write articles for its newsletter. If you are thinking like an entrepreneur, you should be thinking this: Why not hire me? And, as discussed in the last chapter, you might want to advertise your services in these newsletters or pitch yourself to the editors as a communications expert available for interviews. *But I digress*.

You want to get your hands on these publications because they run articles and ads that feature companies in your sectors or that target your sector. All the companies named in articles and that advertise in the publications are companies that you should be targeting. Within three to five sectors (and their related sub-sectors), you will find literally hundreds of potential clients to whom you can pitch your services.

Let your fingers do the walking

In addition to the Web, there are other ways to prospect for clients. The *Yellow Pages* directory, for instance, is an invaluable resource for finding company names, especially if you want to target the small and medium enterprise market.

Isn't it delightful how the *Yellow Pages* folks have done so much work for you, listing all the companies by sector or category? Of course, you can let your fingers do the walking online by using the various *Yellow Pages* and yellow-page-like directories. Google "Yellow Pages" or "business directories" and find directories you can search.

In Canada, magazines such as *Profit, Report On Business Magazine, Canadian Business*, and *Maclean's* publish lists of the best companies in Canada to work for, the most profitable companies, and the fastest-growing companies. In the United States, *Forbes, Entrepreneur*, and other business publications publish similar lists. Use these lists to spark your sector and company research. Find contacts at companies that are appropriate for you to approach.

Do you subscribe to the *Wall Street Journal, New York Times, National Post, The Globe and Mail, Toronto Star*, or other business publications or publications with strong business sections? Ever thumb through the career want ads? If not, you should.

Career want ads are an incredible source of corporate information. If companies are hiring at the executive level, then they are growing companies. And growing companies are the kind you want to work for. If they are growing fast, they may not have time to hire all the staff required to support their growth, or they may be hiring only employees who are essential to the core business. Such companies frequently contract out services such as writing.

The want ads generally give you the company name, some background information, and an address or website. The ads often include contacts, which is a great way to add to your cold call list. Also, check out online job sites such as Monster, Hot Jobs, Workopolis, JobShark, and others. Look for companies in your sector that are recruiting. Follow the links back to the corporate websites and find appropriate contacts. In addition, specialized online job boards target various sectors. Use Google, Bing, or Yahoo! searches to help you find specialized job boards so you can find more contacts.

Make it part of your marketing plan to find five companies and five contacts within those companies per day or per week so you can cold call the contacts. But who exactly do you contact when cold calling?

Making contact: People

For the most part, you are looking for management contacts:
- CxO (chief executive, financial, operations, information officer)
- President, executive president
- Vice president, senior vice president, executive vice president
- Manager, director, executive director
- Partner, senior partner, managing partner
- Owner (in the case of smaller businesses)

These are the people who hire contract employees and freelancers. Even if they delegate the hiring, it's easier to find the names of senior people to pitch. Let the vice president of marketing pass your name on to whomever with a note that says, "This writer looks promising...."

These managers and executives are located in many departments within large and medium enterprises and organizations. Depending on the type of writing you want to do, the departments you can contact include:

- Human resources, recruitment and training
- Sales and marketing
- Public relations and/or advertising
- Corporate communications (sometimes a company has internal and external communication departments)
- Finance, operations, manufacturing, information technology or other departments related to your areas of expertise

Pick the department(s); find the contact(s). If you are targeting small or medium businesses, often you need to contact the owner, office manager, or sales manager. You can use the Web to help you find appropriate contacts. Depending on the nature of the services you are pitching, you might be able to find the appropriate contact (name and e-mail or mailing address or phone number) on the company website. Then you craft your pitch and fire away.

If you do not see the contact listed on the contact page or an online company directory, look for a media release, which are often posted online. Releases tend to quote senior executives and often include a name, title, and contact information. Even if they do not include a mailing address, phone number or e-mail address, at least you will know who you are trying to track down. Find the company mailing address on the website, craft your pitch, and fire away.

If you cannot find appropriate contacts on company websites, you should be able to find company phone numbers and e-mail addresses. Call or e-mail and ask for the name and contact information of the human resources manager, corporate communications director, marketing manager, or whomever you are targeting.

Don't be afraid to pick up the phone and make a call. Much of the work you want to do involves calling and interviewing people, so the practice can't hurt. Besides, receptionists tend to be helpful people. They generally have the information you want at their fingertips. However, if you hit a stressed-out person who bites, don't take it personally. Move on.

If you reach a voice menu system, listen carefully to your options. Chances are the department you want is listed. You press the appropriate number, reach an underling (treat him with respect), and ask for the information you need.

When asking for information, you need a short pitch:

> Hi, I'd like to [mail/e-mail] some information to your vice president of marketing, Mr. So-And-So. Can you please give me the [e-mail/fax/mailing] address? Thanks.

Often, the person you are talking to will simply oblige. Sometimes he might ask what this is pertaining to. Be prepared:

> I'm a freelance writer and want to submit some information about my writing services.

You will then be given the information, or not. Again, if not, move on. You might also be told something like: "All contract work goes through the HR department or communications department." Cool. Ask for the contact.

Action leads to action

Do you think you can use these techniques to identify five to ten contacts a week? If so, you can identify 50 to 100 contacts within 10 weeks. How about identifying five or ten contacts per day? That is possible to do if you spend a full day at it. Within one week, you can have 50 to 100 contacts.

You do not have to gather all your contacts before you begin to pitch. Gather contacts one day; pitch the next. It's up to you how you schedule the work, but schedule it or you might not do it. If you want to write, you have to pitch, especially if you are just getting started or if you want to develop your business or shift your business focus.

Does the system work? Around the time the dot-com boom went bust, I lost most of my corporate clients and several major periodical gigs. I took it easy for a while, thinking the bust would bottom out and work would come back to me. Neither happened. So, I reviewed my business vision, revised my business plan, and started pitching prospects in other sectors. I sent out over 100 pitches to companies for which I had not previously worked and I was soon a busy freelance writer again. Some days, I cringed when I opened my e-mail and found that another company wanted to discuss possible work. A nice problem to have, no?

As is the case with most freelancers, my work still ebbs and flows—although it mostly flows—and I still put together an annual marketing plan. I kind of like being in marketing mode. It re-energizes me when I land work with a new company. I have chosen to pursue this line of work, and sales and marketing are an integral part of my business.

It all takes work to make your business work. The companies and the contacts are out there. It's your job to track them down so you can sell your writing services. If anyone knows a better way to make these companies come to you (beyond advertising and snagging hits with a well-designed website), I'm all ears.

Cold call summary

Here is a cold call summary that should help you break your cold call efforts into manageable tasks that you can schedule:

1. Determine sectors you will target.
2. Source 50 companies (or fill in your own number) within each sector within one month (or create your own timeframe).
3. Source contact names and contact information within companies.
4. Write your pitch letters or phone scripts.
5. Mail your pitch letters; make your phone calls.
6. Follow up as required.

Start to map out and schedule your marketing plan of attack. If you do not have a scheduled plan of attack, you will spin your wheels, work in a hit-and-miss fashion, or waste time surfing the Web, responding to non-business e-mail, posting on Facebook, playing solitaire or watching TV. In short, this is not rocket science. To make it happen, it takes desire, discipline, and dedication. It takes research. It takes persistence. It takes work.

Note: See the last chapter of this book for a number of practical cold call telephone tips and hints.

Chapter 34: Cold Calling

Do you have your contacts all lined up? Do you have some clips (samples of your writing), handy, or have you put some samples on your website? If so, you're ready to rumble. But before we rumble, here are a few words for writers who have no, or limited, experience.

Getting experience; generating clips?

Prospects generally want to see clips before they hire you. Instead of sending clips to prospect, I direct them to a page on my website (www.paullima.com/writing) where they can read samples of my work. However, if asked to e-mail clips to a prospect, I would happily oblige.

You don't need corporate clips to get corporate work. Initially, I used newspapers and magazines clips (www.paullima.com/articles) to sell to my corporate clients. If you have no clips, however, or only a few unrelated clips, you may have to do some writing for free to build your portfolio. If you have no clips, I suggest you write for a friend, relative, or associate who can use your writing services. Or consider writing for a charity, not-for-profit organization, or your church, synagogue or mosque.

Let your contact know you are building your portfolio and that you are willing to write two or three documents—perhaps a couple of Web pages, a sales letter, or a case study—at no cost. Better still, you might barter. For instance, try to exchange your writing services for Web design services or advertising space in a newsletter.

Be professional, both in terms of the quality of your work and how you work with your contact. In other words, make sure you understand what your contact needs and the purpose of the document. Establish a word count or page length and a deadline. Deliver the right words on time. Accept feedback from your contact and revise as may be required.

If you are happy with how the final document reads and looks, add it to your portfolio. If you believe your contact is happy with the work, ask for a testimonial. If it makes sense, you might even want to ask for a referral.

The long and short of it is that everybody has to start somewhere. So, if you have no experience or limited experience, do what you can, within reason, to gain experience before you start to market your services.

Pitching: Mail, phone, or e-mail?

Before you make your first cold call pitch, write a generic pitch letter or pitch script. You can follow the pitch letter outlined below and look at the other samples in this book. However, make sure your pitch reflects your writing style, personality, attitude, and experience.

I used to pitch my services by e-mail. I like e-mail. The contact can easily delete it, reply to it, forward it, or file it. But spam has put a crimp in pitching that way; however, I still generate repeat business and follow up on referrals by e-mail. When establishing new contacts, I tend to use mail or the phone. Sometimes I phone first to find out if the prospect is open to receiving an e-mail pitch. If so, I follow up by e-mail. (Having said that, I still pitch editors by e-mail because that is how they expect writers to communicate with them.)

When pitching by mail, you have to put together an impressive package (see "Pitch package" below). When pitching by e-mail, however, do not send a bio or clips as attached files. Some people do not open unsolicited attached files. Instead, offer to e-mail (upon request) sample clips to the contact. If the contact gives you permission to e-mail clips, don't inundate the person. Send three files maximum, or one file with three samples. Of course, you can always point the recipient of your pitch to your website to review samples of your work, which is another reason why you should have a website.

Even when I pitched primarily by e-mail, I knew freelancers who pitched exclusively by mail. They believed that corporate clients, especially executives, like to hold paper in their hands and like to take paper home to read.

A professionally produced mail pitch package can be quite impressive, especially if you are targeting high-end work (annual reports, national advertising campaigns, executive speeches), or if you are offering additional services beyond writing, such as graphic design, communication consulting, project management or strategic planning.

At the same time, some writers conduct custom-made postcard campaigns. The postcards are fairly simple graphically and include a neat slogan or question. ("Looking for the right writer? Look no further..." and makes a point or two about the writer.) The postcard also includes the writer's company name (if the writer has a company name; it's not something that's required), contact information, and website address.

In addition, there are writers who pitch by phone. They call contacts and try to set up meetings or call and ask whether the prospect is interested in receiving a brochure with more information on their services. I'm not a fan of cold calling, but I don't mind following up pitches with phone calls. That way I have something to refer to. "I'm following up on the letter I sent you regarding my writing services and..." If you like to work the phones, however, by all means do so. Call contacts and deliver a short—30-second—sales pitch directly to your contact (or to voice mail).

Feel free to try some pitches by mail, some by e-mail, and some by phone. Monitor what works best for you and do more of it,

Pitch package

A pitch letter should be no more than one page. However, you might include several pages in your package—a one-page bio or résumé, sample clips, and perhaps a brochure, which would be like a paper version of your website, and/or a rate sheet (see below).

If you have a company name, you might want to invest some money to have a designer create a logo and then design letterhead and envelopes for your company. Use this design on your website, business cards and on any other marketing material so you present a unified look—a brand—no matter how you connect with clients and prospects.

Having said that, I do not have a logo or matching stationery. The main thing you want to do is be professional. If you are tackling high-end corporate markets, then you want to have that corporate look and feel. If you are tackling small and medium enterprises, or not-for-profits, you want to be professional, but you don't want to reek of overhead!

Elements of a pitch letter

Whether pitching by mail or e-mail, the pitch letter is similar. Obviously, the e-mail pitch would include a subject line. But a business letter can also use a subject line, as letters often include Re: Pithy, attention-grabbing, professional line.

There are pitch letters in the next chapter, but here are the elements of a pitch message:

> **Subject**: Pithy, attention-grabbing, professional subject line
>
> Dear Contact Name:
>
> **Paragraph 1**: Make a statement about the need for clear, concise communications in the business world, particularly in the contact's sector, and identify yourself as someone who can help the contact/company communicate.
>
> **Paragraph 2**: Demonstrate knowledge about the company and/or sector. (You might include some information about the company you picked up on the website or in an advertisement or want ad.)
>
> **Paragraph 3**: Describe yourself and the writing services you offer. Emphasize your experience in relation to the sector and your writing and the benefits you can bring to the job.
>
> **Paragraph 4**: Invite the prospect to visit your website to read samples of your work (if pitching by mail, include three clips), and to contact you if any other information is required. Or let the contact know you will follow up by phone within a week.
>
> Regards,
>
> Your Name
> Company Name (if you have one)
> Phone Number
> E-mail Address
> Web address

Follow up

When do you follow-up on a pitch? I'd say about ten days to two weeks after you send a pitch by mail. Any longer, and your pitch is stale; any sooner, and the pitch might not have arrived. Even if e-mail is instant, give it at least five days before following up on it.

When you follow up, be prepared, be professional, and be brief. Often you will get voice mail, so be prepared to leave a 30-second "I'm following up on..." pitch, complete with your phone number. You might hit your contact, so have a 30-second "I'm following up on..." pitch ready. Deliver it and then go silent. Let the person reply. Write out your pitch before you start to call. That way you will not ramble, stutter, or sputter.

When cold calling, the worst thing that can happen is that you find out your services are not required. Move on. Most people you pitch will not hire you. But if you don't pitch, nobody will hire you. So be prepared mentally for a high rate of so-called rejection. But remember that every prospect you land equals work and potentially equals repeat business, referrals, and testimonials.

As for the best thing that can happen? The person you e-mail, mail, or call says, "Am I glad to hear from you. Let's talk business." If that happens, you are no longer in marketing mode. Now you have to price the gig. And if you land it, you have to produce the work and manage your client. However, these are topics for other chapters.

Staying organized

If you send a pitch a day, and then follow up each one a couple of weeks later, things can get a tad disorganized—unless you keep track of who you pitched, when you pitched, and when you said you'd follow up. In addition to tracking your pitches for follow-up purposes, keep track of the results of your follow-up (you may be asked to call back a month or so later or send samples of your work) and of any calls you receive from prospects.

Set up a tracking chart in Word or Excel to help you keep track of it all. Include the following:

- Company and contact
- Date you sent your pitch
- Date of follow-up and any required action based on the follow up
- Date of the next follow-up and any required action, and so on.

Rate sheet or not?

I knew you were going to ask me about rate sheets. Should you send one when pitching prospects or use one on your website?

I'm torn. I've removed my rate information from my website. I felt that my rate sheet might screen out some jobs that I would take even though they paid less per hour or per word than I would normally charge. I went on retainer (more on retainers later in the book) with one company for less per hour than I normally charge, but it was a steady, lucrative gig. It was well worth giving the company a rate discount for steady hours. It was a job I might have missed if I'd had a firm, fixed rate posted on my website.

Rather than give someone an hourly rate, I would rather discuss the scope of the project and quote on a job. Often, I don't even discuss my per-hour or per-word rate with the client. Having said that, I know some writers who will not touch work for under a set amount per hour or word. They are upfront about it and if it scares away the occasional prospect, they don't mind.

In short, you have a business decision to make. If you are contacted by a lot of bottom-feeders looking for great deals on your writing services, you can always put a rate sheet on your website after you set up your site. If, however, you want to use a rate sheet or rate card, make it short and to the point, and show some flexibility, as with the one below.

Sample Rate Card

ITEM	RATE:
Media releases, case studies, brochure copy, Web content, and copy editing	$95/hour
Feature articles (includes research, phone interviews, first draft and a revision)	$2/word
Note: A per project rate or per diem rate is negotiable.	

Can you be more specific? For instance, can you give a specific price for writing a media release, case study Web page, and so on?

I know some freelancers who give specific prices for specific jobs; most do not. There is much more about pricing in the chapter where we explore quoting on jobs. Allow me to say, by way of introduction: two similar jobs can be very different, so I suggest that you do not include specific prices for specific jobs on your website.

Let me give you a quick example. Say you quote a price of $500 per media release. Company A calls you and wants you to write one. Your contact says all the information you need on a specific website page and wants to chat on the phone for a few minutes about target market and goals. The approval process will be simple—the director of marketing is the only person who has to read and approve the release. Your fee of $500 might be fair.

Now Company B calls. The contact wants you to come in to meet the director of marketing and the president to talk about a new product, the target market, and goals of the promotion. She also wants you to interview in person several clients who are using the product to get quotes for the release. After you write the first draft, you will be asked to come in to discuss revisions with the director or marketing and president before submitting a second draft.

Compare the amount of work you have to do for Company A to the amount of work you have to do for Company B. Do you really want to charge both companies $500? Again, we will explore this issue in detail later in the book. I just want you to start thinking about it now.

Chapter 35: Sample Pitch Letters

After all that work—determining sectors you want to target, finding companies within sectors, sourcing contacts within companies, and scheduling when to send out pitches—you want your pitches to be excellent. What do you say in your pitch letters? Following the format in the previous chapter should help you organize your thoughts, but don't feel you have to slavishly follow my format. Develop your own style. Whatever your style, make sure your opening grabs your readers' attention and the rest of the letter holds their interest. In fact, think AIAA when writing your pitch letters.

> **A: Attention.** Your opening paragraph should capture the attention of the reader. You can do this by demonstrating knowledge of the sector and presenting yourself as someone who has a business solution required by the company to which you are writing.
>
> **I: Interest.** Your letter must hold the interest of the reader. None of this "Please sir, may I have some writing assignments?" that I often see when reading pitch letters. You hold interest by making a connection between you, your services, and the company's communication requirements, and between you, your experience, and the company/sector.
>
> **A: Attitude.** You cannot sell anything unless you influence attitude. Your letter should convince the reader that you are the right person with the right skills to do the right job for the right company. In other words, demonstrate the business fit and benefit.
>
> **A: Action.** Call for it. Ask the reader to contact you; give him your e-mail address and phone number. Or tell the reader you are going to follow up, and then do so.

With that in mind, let me share a couple of pitch letters with you.

Pitch letter #1

As the junior mining market accelerates into an up-cycle, so does the workload. [Company Name] is entering an exciting new phase of development from grassroots explorer to gold producer. Shareholders are eager for accurate, up-to-date information on the company's evolving African projects.

The list of important writing tasks is extensive: media releases, website updates, annual and quarterly reports, promotional materials for upcoming conferences, technical materials. They all need careful attention, but who among your staff has the time?

I can help. As a former geologist, one with international exploration experience, I understand the technical side of the business. As a writer for and about the mining industry, I know how to translate these technical concepts into clear prose that the shareholder, the broker, or the regulator can appreciate. And as a self-employed practitioner, I can offer you fast turnaround times. Just give me the raw data and facts from your various projects, and I will produce a cohesive narrative.

If you are interested in exploring my writing services further, visit my website at [website address]. Please contact me if you require any other information.

Notice how the work I've asked you to do can pay off with a letter that makes a connection between you, the writer, and the sector and company you are targeting. The writer emphasizes her strengths, spells out what she can do (the types of services offered), raises a problem (who has time?), and offers her writing services as the solution.

The second letter below could be sent to sales and marketing departments of almost any company in any sector as is. But notice how the writer subtly includes the names of several sectors for which he has done work. It would make sense, wouldn't it, to target additional companies in these sectors? In addition, notice how the question posed in the opening line focuses on the business benefits of effective communications. Finally, notice how the letter is structured with bold headings for emphasis and easy reading.

Pitch letter #2

Could you benefit from the services of a professional writer who knows how to get your message across? I'm a Toronto-based freelance writer who has the solid skills and experience you can depend on when it comes to writing media releases, newsletters, and brochure copy.

Here is how you will benefit when you hire [*your name or company name*]:

Grab the attention of your target markets with media releases that shout your praises. Whether you want to tell the world about your new business, a new product or service, or an executive's promotion, you need a well-written media release to extol your virtues.

Communicate effectively with your employees through newsletter copy that informs, educates, and entertains. A company newsletter is a simple, yet effective, method to keep employees onside with the latest corporate news. It can help educate staff about industry trends and can be an efficient way to maintain employee team spirit.

Boost brand recognition with copywriting that sizzles. Locally or globally, the marketplace is extremely competitive. How do you differentiate your services and products from the rest? With solid copywriting.

I've helped a variety of businesses—including retail, high-tech, and professional services—get noticed by the media; have edited two staff newsletters and contributed to several others; and have written advertorials, brochures, website copy, radio advertising copy, video scripts, and case studies.

I will contact you in a week so we can discuss your writing needs. If you have any questions, call or e-mail me—(416) 555-5555 or email@domainname.com—or visit my website (www.domainname.com) to see writing projects samples.

Journal exercise: Write a pitch letter

Now it's your turn. Demonstrate that you can write an effective pitch letter. After all, writing effectively is what you want to do for the companies you are pitching. So, go forth and write a stellar pitch letter. Follow the AIAA format, but put your own spin on the content to make sure the letter reflects your services, sector(s), experience, and even your personality.

Before you send your letters out to prospects, try to get some feedback. If you belong to a writers' organization, such as the Professional Writers of Canada (www.pwac.ca), the National Writers Association (www.nationalwriters.com), or any other formal or informal group of writers or editors, see if you can get feedback on your letter from other members. If not, see if you can hook up with some local writers and exchange feedback services, or hire an editor to take a close look at your pitch letter.

If you think you are ready for prime time, you can start to send your letters to prospects. When you start to get nibbles, issue accurate quotes. When you start to land gigs, manage the process, produce excellent copy, and generate repeat business. But if you want to know more about issuing quotes and managing the process, read on.

Chapter 36: Online Strategies

My website—paullima.com—is extremely important to me. It brings me several new prospects per month. Not all of the companies that contact me through my website become clients, but then not all companies that I send promotional material to become clients either.

Many of my repeat clients found me first through my website; if not for the Web, I can't imagine how I would have met them otherwise. It's just too difficult to reach every potential client, no matter how much time you spend marketing your services.

Websites do not have to be as complex as my site is. At the same time, they can be even more extensive. My business has evolved over time and my website has evolved with it. In fact, I am always looking for ways to streamline and simplify my site, and I try to keep my home page uncluttered and easy to navigate.

Your website can be simple and effective. The point is to get a website up with information about you and your services and a few writing samples before you start any major marketing endeavours.

Do you need a website to work as a freelance writer? No, you don't. Having a website can, however, boost your credibility and extend your marketing effort. Unless you have all the business you can handle and are making the kind of money you want to make, I can think of no reason for passing on getting your website online.

As you create your website, you should optimize it for search engines so that it ranks as high as possible when potential customers search for writers using various search engines. However, you can also pay for ads on Google, Bing, or Yahoo! that show up when potential customers conduct a searches for freelance writers. The ads contain three or four lines of promotional copy (that you write) and are linked to your home page or a specific promotional page, known as a landing page, on your website.

Online strategy summary

Here is a summary of the online strategies you can use to promote your freelance writing business:

- Write, design, and build your website, or contract out the construction of your site
- Optimize your website for search engines (Google, Yahoo!, Bing, and so on)
- Submit your website to search engines
- Investigate ads on Google (www.google.com/adsense); set up a Google AdSense campaign; set your Google ad budget; write your Google ad copy
- Based on sectors you want to target, look for websites on which you can advertise and look for e-newsletters in which you can run ads
- Create an e-newsletter of interest to companies in your target sector; promote it on your website and blog and through social media
- Investigate social media such as Facebook (primarily used for personal interaction, but can be used for business), LinkedIn (set

up a profile and connect with others), and Twitter (find me at https://twitter.com/PaulWriterLima); also, if you have Facebook and LinkedIn profiles, investigate ads on those sites

- Set up a blog; you can use WordPress blog software to set up a static website and blog; talk to others who have websites and blogs and pick the application that will work best for you, or contract out the construction of your blog
- Create and upload YouTube promotional video trailers; insert links to the video trailers in your website and blog and promote on LinkedIn, Facebook, and Twitter

Caveat: You can spend a great deal of time trying to raise your business profile using social media. Don't spend all your marketing time on social media. Create a social media presence but use the conventional marketing tools outlined in this book too. They are important—especially if you are just getting started in this business. I am not saying new media does not work; I am saying shoot multiple marketing arrows, including new media, and monitor results so you can spend time and money on the arrows that work best for you.

Chunk website construction

While you want to monitor the time you spend on social media, you really want to get your website online.

As with Rome, most websites take more than a day to build. So, you can't simply pick a day and put "write and build website" in your marketing plan. I suggest you break the process down into chunks, or manageable tasks, and slot the various tasks into your calendar. To help you schedule the creation of your website in your marketing plan, allow me to do some website chunking for you.

Register website domain and find host

You can register your website and find a host online through www.paullima.com/domain or you can allow the person who will build your site (if you are contracting out the task; see "hire a website designer") do it for you. If you register it yourself, the person who builds your site can either work with the domain and host you have selected or move your domain registration to the company that will be hosting your website.

Determine your website sections

Most websites are composed of several sections or pages. At minimum, I suggest you include the following pages: Home, About, Contact, Writing Services, Writing Samples. You can also add Testimonials or include testimonials on your services or samples page.

Write each of the above sections

You're a writer. You should be able to write your website copy. Keep your copy concise and focused. Ensure it reflects what you can do and for whom you can do it.

Hire a website designer

If you can't design your website, hire a designers. Here are the steps you should take when hiring a website designer:

1. Source several designers; get at least three quotes
2. Check references.
3. Ensure your designer is familiar with basic search engine optimization (SEO) techniques.
4. Negotiate price. You should be able to get a simple site online for anywhere from $500 to $1,500 (unless you want high-end graphics, flash, and animation), plus the cost of hosting ($100 to $200 per year).
5. Negotiate deadlines. Deadlines should include the dates on which you will review design ideas, select final design, test your site online, and go live.

Now that the construction of your website is chunked into manageable tasks, schedule the creation of your website in your marketing plan. And, presto, you have five more marketing tasks scheduled for completion. Again, if you do not schedule these tasks, you might not complete them.

Search engine optimization

Search engine optimization (SEO) is the process of improving the rank of website in search results when people search for the type of information, goods, and/or services you offer.

How to fully optimize your site beyond the scope of this chapter. However, anyone with a website should be aware of basic SEO. (If you want more information on SEO, consider *Do You Know Where Your Website Ranks? How to Optimize Your Website for the Best Possible Search Engine Results* www.paullima.com/books.)

Why SEO?

Search engines are the starting point for most Web surfers. Almost 80 percent of the Canadian Internet population conducts at least one search each month. More than 75 percent of the online U.S. population use search engines. To show up in search engine results, a website must be submitted to the search engine or found and indexed by search engine robots (bots). It can take anywhere from several days to several months to index a website.

To rank high in search results, your site must be optimized for relevant search terms. And when it comes to search engine results, rank matters. Traffic drops significantly by rank. According to the Atlas Institute, the research and education arm of Atlas DMT, an advertising-technology provider, the first site listed in search engine results receives three times the hits of the fifth site; the first 10 sites (generally the first page of results) are visited 78 percent more often than sites listed eleventh to thirtieth.

Keywords are key

Before you optimize a website, you need to define your keywords and phrases—words and phrases prospective customers might enter into search engines when looking for the services (or products) that you sell. Once you have defined those keywords, you should use them in well-written copy on your website because search engines send out bots to read site content. The search engines use the content, and other factors, when determining site relevancy to search terms. The more relevant your site, the higher it ranks.

To optimize your site for the best possible search engine results, do the following:

1. Use a consistent, text-based navigation menu that incorporates your keywords.
2. Include keyword tags (*alt tags*) with all graphics. Every image on a website has a name, such as imagename.gif. These image names mean nothing to the bots. When you add an alt tag to your image, you are adding readable content that the bots can use.

3. Combine keywords with Flash or other non-text objects. The bots cannot read Flash animation pages, so include keyword text on Flash-based website pages, or avoid Flash all together.
4. Build a text site map, one page that includes links to every other page on your site. Link to your site map from your home page so the bots can find the site map.
5. Write your meta tags using keywords. Meta tags are embedded in HTML code on websites. Three basic tags are particularly meaningful: title, description, and content. Only the title tag is seen by visitors. Title displays the name of your website pages in Web browsers. You can change the page title to reflect the products, services, or information on each page. You can also change the description and content meta tags. However, unless each page of your site changes dramatically, you will most likely use one set of description and content meta tags.
6. Use keywords in all your site content. Every descriptive paragraph on your site should include keywords or phrases. Make sure hotlinks include keywords too. Instead of using "Click here for information on our services" use wording that includes your keywords, such as "Information on copywriting writing services" or a simple link, such as, "Web content writing services."
7. Beg, borrow, and barter reciprocal links. When determining page rank, most search engines look at link popularity, or the number of links that point to your site from other sites. For instance, Google's PageRank system determines the value of pages and sites using links from Site A to Site B as a vote for Site B by Site A. Google and other search engines see links to a site as a validation of the site. The greater the validation, the higher a site shows up in search engine results (as long as it is also well-optimized for keywords). So, if you can get non-competitive sites, especially if they are industry-related, linking to your site, you can improve your search engine results.
8. Submit your site to search engines. The bots may find your site if you have links to it, but you should not sit back and wait. Instead, visit the major search engines and find out how to submit your website.
    a. Google: Go to www.google.com/addurl.html
    b. Yahoo!: Go to: www.search.yahoo.com/info/submit.html

c. **Bing:** Go to www.bing.com/docs/submit.aspx

d. Submit your site to the Open Directory Project; once your site is listed, it can be picked up by bots from other search engines. To submit your site, visit http://dmoz.org, click on suggest URL and follow the guidelines. You will have to pick a category for your site and provide a title and description.

Blogging

Blogging can also boost your SEO quotient.

If your blog content is focused on delivering information pertaining to the kind of business writing you do and the sectors that you are targeting, then it will contain many of your keywords. Also, if others like what they read on your blog, they will link to your blog posts, creating links to your website. Both your blog content and links to your blog will help SEO. Make sure your blog looks professional and links back to the primary pages on your website, such as to Home, About, Services, and Contact.

As mentioned previously, blog software like WordPress can be used to create both a static website and a blog. The blog can be set up with links to your permanent pages, such as About, Services, Contact. The page with your blog posts can be your home page, but more likely you will have a permanent home page that links to your blog. If it sounds complex, don't sweat the details. Find someone who can set up your website and/or blog. Although you don't have as much website design flexibility if you choose to go this route, you can have a professional-looking website/blog in a short time and at a fairly affordable price.

Google Ads

If you use the search term "Google Ads" in the Google search engine, the results will include over 20 million links. It costs nothing to have a Web page indexed in the Google search engine.

If I had information on my website about Google Ads and my site was ranked one million links down in the search results, or even 50 links down, visitors would never find me. If I were selling the secrets of how to effectively use Google AdWords to make money, I would not make any money.

There is something you can do to combat a low search engine rank for your website. You can display an ad on Google (or other search engines). On Google, ads appear to the right of the free links and look like this:

Google Ads Secrets
Be up and running in Just 29 Minutes
Fast Results Guaranteed, Risk-Free
AdWordsVideo.com

This particular ad is listed number one (search results may vary) when someone uses the search term "Google Ads".

The Google AdWords pay per click (PPC) advertising program is popular, in part, because you don't pay until someone clicks on your ad. You create the ad (within line count and character count limitations), choose keywords so Google can match your ads to search terms, and pay only when someone clicks on the ad. You also set the per-click fee you are willing to pay and control your budget—how much you will spend per day and month.

The AdWords character (letters, symbols, spaces) limitations are strict. You cannot go over character count when you create your headline and two lines of ad text and your display URL. Here are the maximum character counts:

- Headline: 25 characters.
- Line 1: 35 characters
- Line 2: 35 characters
- Display URL: 35 characters

Your destination URL (the code behind the display URL hotlink that takes user to your Web landing page) can be up to 1,024 characters and Google has an online system to help you create your ad within the allotted character count.

Because your ad's rank (how high it appears on the search results page) compared to other ads is a combination of the price per click you are willing to pay and how popular your ad is (how often it is clicked on), your copy must be written to motivate clicks!

If each click or view brought you more business than the cost of the click, you would not care how much you had to pay per click.

However, clicks often bring tire kickers—visitors who are browsing, but not buying—so you want to be able to set a ceiling on what you pay, monitor results (Google has budgeting and reporting tools), and make marketing decisions based on results.

Chapter 37: Marketing Plan: Big Picture

Let's do a mini review of some of what we've covered so far. To support your professional freelance vision, your business plan should include the following elements:
1. Your W5 business vision
2. A list of sectors you will target and your rationale for doing so
3. A list of services you will offer and your rationale for doing so
4. Your annual and quarterly revenue goals
5. Your revenue goals based on the various services you offer
6. Any writing professional development you need to help you reach your goals

Your marketing plan should detail and schedule the specific tasks you will undertake to reach those goals and make your vision a reality. You have five arrows in your marketing quiver:
1. Generate repeat business, testimonials, and referrals
2. Network with friends, relatives, associates; through organizations
3. Advertise and promote
4. Cold calling and direct mail
5. Online strategy (website, blog and social media)

The marketing plan pulls it all together. It tells you how to spend your non-billable time so you can generate billable work that enables you to meet your objectives and achieve your vision. That is why it is so important to create your vision and business plan before you develop your marketing plan.

Key marketing plan words are *details* and *schedules*. What you need to do is to break down into manageable chunks (details) the five basic marketing components outlined here. Then you schedule each task, deciding on the various dates by which you will complete them.

With e-mail and the Internet, you can, in theory, work for anyone, anywhere. I live in Toronto, but I have American and European clients. Still, I focus my marketing effort in Canada, where I am most likely to find clients. Don't be limited by geography, however. Where you focus your efforts depends upon your vision and the sectors you want to target.

For instance, a friend of mine, a writer and communications consultant with a strong environmental background who lives in Toronto, targets the United Nations and non-governmental organizations involved in environmental issues. He makes excellent money and travels the world.

What does a marketing plan look like?

In the days before computers, tasks that made up your marketing plan would have been listed on a paper-based calendar so you could see you when you had to complete marketing tasks. Today, you can set up a similar calendar of events on paper or in an Excel spreadsheet or a Word document. You may have a favourite scheduling program, smart phone, or even an online calendar that sends reminders to your e-mail program or smart phone.

As mentioned, I use Microsoft Outlook. I use Tasks and Calendar in the full version of Outlook to schedule my marketing activities. The activities pop up on dates of my choosing, reminding me what I was going to do. I also schedule my billable work activities in Outlook. If a non-billable task conflicts with a billable task, I focus on the billable task. But I reschedule the non-billable task so that it does not drop out of sight. While billable hours are always my first priority, my non-billable tasks are always popping up to remind me what I have to do to generate billable work.

You might pick one day a week—Mondays, for instance—to work on marketing. Or you might spread your marketing tasks out over several days. You might review all planned marketing tasks each Monday and schedule specific tasks for specific days based on your billable workload. It's up to you to find the method that works best for the way you work.

To give you some sense of what a marketing calendar looks like, however, I will share a modified version of part of my marketing plan with you. This is the plan I put together before I shift tasks into Outlook.

The chart here is meant to be a big-picture chart. I have not broken the tasks down into their most granular levels and I have left the dates blank. Notice, however, how I have used the five main marketing arrows.

Marketing Plan Task Calendar	Date

1. Generate repeat business with previous clients
   a. Identify previous clients
   b. Write pitch e-mail
   c. Send pitch e-mail
   d. Track replies and follow up	

2. Ask selected clients for referrals and testimonials
   a. Write pitch e-mail
   b. Send pitch e-mail
   c. Track replies and follow up	

3. Create list of networking contacts
   a. Write pitch e-mail and phone scripts
   b. Make calls; send e-mail
   c. Track replies and follow up	

4. Create media interview training website (landing page) a. Create Google ad and link to landing page	

5. Write article on importance of AIAA when writing
   a. Source publications and contacts
   b. Communicate with editors
   c. Write and file article
   d. Select next topic
   e. Repeat above	

6. Pitch myself as a communications expert to <publications>
   a. Source publications and contacts
   b. Write and issue media release	

7. Run business-card ads in three publications
   a. Source publications and contacts
   b. Price ads; select publications
   c. Write ads; find a designer if required
   d. Run ads
   e. Monitor responses; plan next ad series	

8. Cold calling
   a. Identify three sectors
   b. Source five companies per week within each sector
   c. Source contacts within companies
   d. Write pitch letters and phone scripts
   e. Mail pitch letters; follow up by phone
9. Write blog posts once a week in support of books; drive traffic to blog post using Twitter, LinkedIn and Facebook

Scheduling tasks

When you create your marketing plan, keep in mind that you can't do all the tasks in one day. You can write your "generate repeat business" pitch letter the day you are scheduled to sent it out; however, some tasks require considerable lead-time. For instance, if you want to run an ad in the March issue of a monthly magazine, you will probably have to submit that ad in December or January. And you will want to give yourself time to write and design it too. So, pulling your full marketing plan together may require some research so you can keep yourself as organized as possible.

In addition, as you complete some tasks you need to schedule follow-up tasks. For instance, when you send marketing material to prospects, you need to schedule follow-up calls. When making your follow-up calls, you may connect with people who ask for more information about your services, want to meet you, or even ask for a quote on a job. If so, you need to send requested information within a day or two or schedule a meeting. If you send information or a quote, you have to schedule a follow-up call or e-mail to see if the person has any additional questions. And so it goes.

When you are trying to generate repeat and referral business, your initial contact with clients could lead to additional tasks. If you write a document for ABC Marketing, you will want to schedule an "ask for repeat business" follow-up in your marketing calendar. If ABC replies to your follow-up inquiry with "there could be something coming down the pipes in a month or two," it is up to you to schedule the next follow-up. If you complete several jobs for ABC, you will want to schedule an "ask for referral" or "ask for testimonial" task in your calendar. Once again, the important thing here is that you plan and schedule your tasks.

And that, ladies and gentlemen, is the marketing plan—a series of scheduled tasks based on your business vision and business plan.It is also organic in that it grows and shifts with the work you do, the tasks you complete, the new tasks you have to schedule, and the new contacts you make.

When to do it

When do you create your business and marketing plans? I develop, review, and revise my business vision, business plan, and marketing plan in November or early December. There is no time like the present, however, if you don't have such plans in place. Also, there are times when situations might force you to review your plans. For instance, when the dot-com boom went bust, I revamped my plans not that long after I had created them. I was "the dot-com writer" so my reasons for reviewing my plans should be obvious.

If you are monitoring your revenue and see that you are falling behind projections, you may have to revamp your marketing plan. Don't do it as a knee-jerk response to a bad week or month; however, look at picking up the marketing pace, or implementing some unscheduled marketing tasks, if you have a poor quarter.

When I create my plans, I try to plan for the year. However, I review my marketing plan toward the end of the first quarter and make adjustments if I am not on track to meet my objectives. My main objective is to make a living doing what I want to do, based on my business vision. If I am earning more from one type of writing and less from another than planned, or if I am making less from my writing work but more from my training, I do not panic. I panic only if I am earning less, overall, than planned.

If I have put a lot of effort into one area of my plan and it has not paid off, I will take some time to review what I have done and evaluate reasons why it hasn't worked. If it's an important part of my business vision, such as writing and selling this book, I will look for new and additions ways of marketing.

So, as I said, the plan is organic. At the same time, do not delude yourself. Don't think you can hold it all in your head and make it happen. Make your thoughts concrete by getting them down on paper where you can see them. Adjust them as may be required, which means comparing results to projections on a monthly and quarterly basis.

The system works if you dedicate time to it in a disciplined manner. As you get busy working billable hours, pull back the marketing reins. As you land new clients, deliver stellar work, and generate repeat business and referrals, you can do less cold mailing and calling—unless you want to expand a particular part of your business where you have no or few clients.

To gauge the effectiveness of your marketing, ask people who e-mail or call you how they heard about you. If you find a particular marketing task is working well for you, review it to see if it makes sense to repeat it or to do more of it. In other words, place more effort on the marketing tasks that work; however, don't abandon a task after trying it just once or twice. Revise your message first and try again before discarding a task that doesn't seem to be working. In addition, be open to new ideas, as long as they are in line with your vision.

In short, you can daydream about working as a freelance writer, or you can do what it takes to become one. That involves dedicating time to marketing tasks that make sense according to your business vision and evaluating and revising your business and marketing plans based on business results.

Brief word about targeting the government

I contemplated devoting an entire chapter to targeting government ministries, departments, and agencies, but I don't think one chapter would suffice. Allow me to say that you can find work with targeting government ministries, departments, and agencies. Most government ministries, departments, and agencies have very formal methods for bidding on jobs. You have to learn how to meticulously follow a process that generally includes formally replying to a request for quote. Of course, the process is slightly different to very different depending on the government ministry, department, or agency that is issuing the request for quote. It is also different for federal, state or provincial, and municipal government ministries, departments, and agencies. And can be different for various departments within the same ministry or agency.

If you are interested in landing gigs with federal Canadian government ministries, departments, and agencies, start at www.merx.com, a website that lists many government contracts. Merx, however, is only one of a number of websites where you can find information on federal government contracts. With that in mind, I highly recommend *Getting Work with the Federal Government: A guide to figuring out the procurement puzzle*, by Marion Soublière (www.meseditingandwriting.com). It is a concise, comprehensive look at how to tackle government jobs and includes a wealth of information and many websites well worth visiting.

A couple of caveats before you go racing across the Web looking to find government links and resources: beware of websites that promise to help you find work with the government for one low fee. Nobody can promise to land government work for you. Also, keep your sectors in mind. For instance, if you know nothing about fisheries and oceans, why would you try to land a contract with the Ministry of Fisheries and Oceans? On the other hand, if you are an environmental expert, it would make sense to look for gigs with the Ministry of the Environment or with departments or agencies devoted to dealing with environmental issues.

Chapter 38: How Much to Charge?

We've talked a great deal about money in this book. Money is important. It's not the be all and end all, but it allows you to do other stuff, the stuff of your life vision. (Don't worry. I am not going to make you create a life vision.)

At some point, all this planning and marketing will begin to pay off. Potential clients will start to call or e-mail you. You will hear that little voice in your head, "Now you've done it." You will have to discuss dollars and cents. That might involve some back and forth negotiations, which is not unusual. It's your job to be prepared, be professional, and be flexible—to a point. In other words, do not sell yourself down the river for a pittance when setting your fee and issuing quotes.

Arriving at a quote

You can arrive at a quote for a project in several ways, depending on the needs of the client and the nature of the job. But before you submit a quote, it is a good idea to know what your corporate rates are (see section on "setting corporate rates" in this chapter) and approximately how much you would charge per project, such as for writing a media release, a website page, a direct response brochure, and so on. As you'll see, what you actually charge will vary, but you should know how much per hour you want to make and your minimum fee for a particular type of job.

To help you wrap your head around arriving at a quote, let's look at how clients might approach you—what they might need or want.

Here is exactly what we need

The client spells out the details of the assignment and asks for a firm quote. You clarify the details (more on how to do this in the next chapter) and quote on the job. The client says yes, no, or maybe (as in "maybe if you can come down to this price"). You may or may not mention your hourly or per word rate, but you need one on which to base your quote.

How much do you charge? How long will it take?

The client may want to know how much you charge per hour and how long you think it will take to complete a job. The client is looking for an estimate but expresses a willingness to be flexible because the scope of the job may not be clearly defined. Generally, with this method, you keep a detailed timesheet and let the client know when you are coming close to reaching your estimated number of hours. The client then authorizes additional hours.

We need you almost exclusively

The client may want you to be on call for a series of jobs and will pay you an hourly rate. Usually you do not have to generate a quote. But you have to agree to an hourly rate and you have to keep a detailed timesheet so the client knows exactly what you've done, when you did it, and how long it took you to do it.

How much per word?

Sometimes the client will want to know how much you charge per word and will ask for a document of x-number of words. You still want to define the scope of the project (again, more on this in the next chapter) before you issue a quote. For instance, will you have to go in for meetings? How many? Will you be making revisions based on feedback from the client? If so, you want to take all that under consideration before you present your per word fee (the more work you have to do, the higher your fee should be). Speaking of revisions, you will most often write several drafts. Get used to revisions and make sure your quotes take them into account

Beware of charging a per-word rate on advertising copy, video scripts, or promotional e-mail. You may write only a few words of finished copy, but you will do a great deal of research, synthesizing, processing, creative brainstorming, writing, and revising before the job is finished, and you should be paid for all that brain power, not just for the final word count.

Per-word proofreading or copy editing

The same thoughts as above apply to per-word proofreading or copy editing. If no meetings or research are required—you just receive the work and edit it—you can price the work based on the number of words of original document and the type of editing that is required.

For instance, you would charge less per word to proofread a relatively clean document (ask to see a sample of the work before you quote) that you would to copy edit a poorly written document because it's going to take you more time to do the copy editing. You would charge even more for a substantive copy edit, one that required major revisions.

Notice how I used three terms here: proofread, copy edit, substantive copy edit. In each instance, the client might ask you how much you charge to proofread. You ask to see a sample of the work you have to edit so you can clarify what is expected, and how much time it might take, before you quote on a job.

Some clients will ask you how much you charge for editing, and then ask you to turn a 2,500-word white paper into a 750-word flyer or brochure. That's not editing. That's writing. I would probably charge an hourly rate for such a job, but if the client wanted to know your per-word rate, you would have to clarify if they were paying you to edit 2,500 words or to produce 750 words.

In short, if you do not clarify situations like this up front, you could have a billing battle on your hands down the road. "I just assumed..." doesn't cut it when you are debating an invoice.

Per-page editing

This approach is appropriate for many editing projects. As above, base your quote on the number of pages you receive from the client and the type of editing you have to do. Look at a sample of the writing before you quote. Not only do you want to evaluate the writing, you also want to know whether the copy is single-spaced or double-spaced and whether the type size is 12 point or eight point. In other words, you can cram a lot more words on a page if it is single-spaced eight-point type rather than double-spaced, 12-point type.

Per-hour editing or writing

You will quote many jobs on a per-hour basis. You don't, however, always keep a time sheet. This may be a tad repetitive, but it's an important point: in many instances, you define the scope of the project (see next chapter) and issue a firm quote based on the number of hours you estimate it will take you do the job. The client doesn't need to know how much you charge per hour or how long you think the job will take.

On the other hand, as mentioned, you might quote an hourly rate and keep a timesheet if the work required seems vague or involves multiple meetings and/or interviews, or involves a great deal of research and minimal word count (ad copy, promotional e-mail, headlines for ads, slogans, video scripts, and so on), or involves you working on multiple jobs simultaneously. In other words, if the client doesn't know exactly what he wants, wants you to work on a complex job, or wants you to work on a number of documents, making it difficult for you to issue a firm quote, then you want to be charging by the hour.

But how much do you charge per hour?

Setting corporate rates

When it comes to setting rates for the corporate market, you have to know the following:

- How much you want to gross per year
- What your time is worth
- What skills, ability, experience you bring to the table
- At what level you are working

What do I mean by "at what level"? When it comes to corporate communications, there is a rate hierarchy. From top to bottom, it goes something like this: strategic planner, consultant, project manager, writer, researcher, editor, and proofreader. I'm sure editors and proofreaders would disagree. And I know we need them (or that I need them). But that rate hierarchy is there.

Strategic planners and consultants give high-level communications advice (and may do some writing or hire the writers). Project managers usually co-ordinate all aspects of large communication projects (a major corporate video or annual report, for instance) from start to finish. They may also do some writing or hire the writers, designers, printers, or video crews. And, yes, project managers may do some consulting and consultants may manage projects.

For the most part, writers write. It's possible that as a writer you will give advice, make suggestions, give the client options, help develop strategies, and move the project forward in some way. However, primarily you write and revise. That's what you charge for.

But if the client asks for more (part of your job when quoting is to define—in consultation with the client—your role), you also ask for more.

How much do you charge?

There is no one right answer. I know many writers. They charge anywhere from $35 to $250 an hour. They charge anywhere from $.50 to $5 per word. You determine what you are worth and/or what a job is worth, and set a rate. Of course, if you want to charge $250 per hour, then you have to find clients willing to pay that rate—which is not an impossible task.

Once you set your rate, you negotiate with prospects based on that rate. When negotiating, you choose whether there will be any give and take. But take before you give.

Still find yourself saying, "Yes, but... How much do I charge?" Let's review the math you did earlier.

How many billable hours do you think you can work per day? Billable hours do not include functions such as market research, marketing, invoicing, filing, or paying your taxes. That you do on your own nickel. With that in mind, let's say you work, on average, four billable hours per day, five days per week, 50 weeks per year.

Some days you may work more, far more, and some days you may work less, far less, but let's say you average five billable hours per day.

Here is the formula

Here is the billable hours formula:

Billable hours per day x 5 = billable hours per week
Billable hours per week x 50 = billable hours per year
Billable hours per year x hourly rate = gross income

Plug in an hourly rate and you know how much you can earn, gross (before expenses and taxes), per year. Let's say you plug in $50 per hour:

4 hours/day x 5 days/week x 50 weeks/year x $50/hour = $50,000/year.

Plug in $100 per hour, and you will earn $100,000 per year—as long as you work four billable hours per day, five days per week, 50 weeks per year. You could charge more and still work four billable hours per day, five days per week, 50 weeks per year. You could charge more (or less) and work more (or fewer) hours. That all depends on how well you market yourself and on the nature of the clients you acquire.

If you are just getting started, you might find it difficult to come up with $50 or $100 per hour gigs, especially if you are selling your services to small businesses or under-funded not-for-profit organizations. If you have been doing corporate work for a year or more, $50 per hour should be your absolute rock bottom rate. Take $50 per-hour clients only if you have no other work to do. In fact, you might be better off investing time looking for better-paying clients.

Some writers I know charge $100 or more per hour, but offer small businesses and non-profit organizations a discount, as I have done. However, when I invoice the client, I put my full rate on the invoice and then add the discount. It helps me demonstrate and maintain my value. It also helps me boost my rate after working with the client for a while.

Would it be nice if the corporate world paid one rate for writers so we wouldn't have to figure out what to charge? If that rate was set at $100 per hour, the writers who earn $250 per hour wouldn't think it was such a hot idea. So think about you, what you offer, and how much you want or need to earn. Set your hourly rate and look for clients who can pay it.

If you want more information to help you establish rates, go to *What to Pay a Writer* (www.writers.ca/whattopay.htm). Although it is a Canadian site, the rates listed would be of interest to writers anywhere in North America. Allow me to summarize the suggested corporate writing and editing rates on the site. I don't agree with all fees posted, and think there are many factors you should take under consideration before you quote (as I will explain). However, the list should give you a good ballpark as to where you want to position your fees.

From What to Pay a Writer

You can use these rates as guidelines. Assess each job, though, before you issue a quote.

Advertising material
Copy/Scripts/News Releases:
- $350 to $500 per page
- $750 to $1,000 per project for brochures
- $75 to $150 per hour

Advertorials (articles commissioned by advertisers)
- $0.40 to $2 per word
- $100 to $3,000 per article
- $40 to $100 per hour

Corporate/business writing
Reports/Marketing Plans/Technical Writing
- $1 to $2 per word
- $300 to $12,000 per project
- $50 to $125 per hour

Editing
Varies according to publication/project
- $30 to $60 per hour; $500 to $20,000 per project

Ghost writing
Articles: Generally 2-3 times the usual newspaper or magazine rates
Books: $10,000 to $50,000 flat fee; entire advance + 50% of royalties

Government writing
News Releases/Studies/Reports
- $1 to $3 per word
- $500 to $100,000 per project
- $50 to $125 per hour

Newsletters
Writing only; layout extra
- $0.30 to $1.50 per word
- $400 to $6,000 per issue
- $50 to $80 per hour

Website writing
Varies widely; "business" sites pay higher
- $1 to $3 per word
- $60 to $100 per hour

Scripts
Radio (highly variable): $40 to $80 per minute of script
Television (highly variable): $60 to $130 per minute of script

Speech writing
- $500 to $8,000 per speech; $60 to $130 per hour

Translation/adaptation
Literary: $0.10 to $0.20 per word
Other: $0.25 to $0.60 per word; $40 to $80 per hour

These rates can guide you. Ultimately, however, you have to decide what you are going to charge and you have to issue the quote. Conversely, if offered a particular amount of money for a gig, or if a prospect offers a lower fee than you've quoted, you have to decide if you are going to take the gig.

Knowing how much you want to earn per year, week, and hour will help you make informed decisions, decisions that are in sync with your business plan.

Chapter 39: Accurately Pricing Services

Although the formula I outlined should help you determine your per-hour rate, most clients are interested in the bottom line. "What's this document (media release, brochure, Web page, speech, script...) going to cost me? What is your quote for this job?"

Before you quote on a project, you need to define the scope of the project. To do this, you have to ask the client a number of questions:

1. When does the project start?
2. When is the project due?
3. What am I expected to produce (the deliverable)?
4. Who will I work with as the primary point person?
5. Will I need to attend meetings to discuss this project? If so, how many, how long, and where will they be held?
6. How many people will I have to interview? By phone or in person?
7. What kind of and volume of background research do you expect me to review? What other research is required?
8. What is the word count?
9. What is the approval process?
10. Who pushes documents through the approval process?
11. How many revisions do you expect?
12. Do you need soft copy (computer files) and/or hard copy (paper)?
13. What file format(s) do you need the files in?
14. Who takes it to the next step (design, printing, distribution, media contact, follow-up, video production...)?
15. Will I be working with that person?

All along, you take notes. (Get a headset or speakerphone so you can have your hands free to take notes while talking to clients and prospects.) Then the client asks you for a quote. Take a deep breath and say, "When do you need the quote?" In other words, don't quote during the conversation. Take an hour; take 24 hours before you issue your quote. If you have any additional questions (especially if it's a complex or somewhat nebulous job), ask them before you issue a quote. As you get better at it, you might feel comfortable quoting right away, but make sure you define the scope of the project first.

Then get back to the client with the quote, based on the complexity of the job. Generally speaking, look at how many hours you believe you will spend on the job and multiply that by your hourly rate. Use your minimum project rate (se chart below) as a foundation. In other words, don't quote less than the amount you think a particular job is worth.

There is one other somewhat nebulous factor to consider. An important marketing piece, one that will help your client generate revenue, is more valuable to your client than a price list with short product descriptions. Writing copy for a TV ad that has high production values (costs) is more valuable to your client than short biographies of corporate executives. Writing copy for a reply to a request for a quote is more valuable to your client than an internal document announcing new human resources policies and procedure. With that in mind, before you quote, consider the nature and scope of the job, your hourly rate, and the impact your work may have on the company's bottom line. Then issue your quote.

If you deliver your quote verbally, follow up with an e-mail message so all the details are in writing. The client may also want to send you a contract or purchase order that outlines the details of the project. Review it and make sure it conforms to what you understand to be the scope of the project.

Conclude any quotes with, "The quote is based on the details we discussed. Any additional writing, meetings, revisions, and interviews beyond what we discussed will be extra. I will advise you if the work has moved beyond the scope of the job as we have defined it." Use whatever words you are comfortable with, but make sure the client knows you are a professional who expects to be paid for the work you do, and that you will ask to be compensated for work that goes beyond the scope of the original project.

I did one revision on the article, which was part of an agreement, and the client asked for a second revision that was quite minor so I did it at no extra charge. Unfortunately, my client's boss decided he wanted several other revisions that moved the article in a different direction.

It sometimes happens when you are doing corporate work. Priorities or situations change. I have no problem with this. But I want to be compensated for such work.

I reminded the client that our agreement included one revision, and that I had already done two (even though the second one was minor). I also pointed out that I had delivered what I was asked for originally, on time and on budget, but that I was now being asked to make a substantive revision. The third revision was beyond the scope of the project as we had defined it. The client agreed and we negotiated additional payment for the work.

Estimating a writing job

Use the following chart to help you estimate a quote for a writing job. Notice that the chart has spots for minimum, maximum, and mid estimates. Before issuing your quote, determine the scope of the project and come up with three estimates. Then make a business decision about your rate, based on the factors we have discussed, and issue your quote. The more quotes you issue, the more you should trust your gut when it comes to coming up with a quote figure. At the same time, it doesn't hurt to be methodical in your approach to quoting. That helps your gut have an accurate instinctive reaction.

In short, be as accurate as you can be when estimating how much time it will take you to complete a writing job, but don't sweat the minutes. You will become more accurate over time, with practice.

Stages of Work	Estimated Hours		
	Min.	Max.	Mid.
1. Initial briefing/meeting			
2. Transcribe meeting notes, if required			
3. Read background material			
4. Interview sources			
5. Other research/meetings			
6. Organize research material			

7. Write document outline	
8. Consult with client and amend outline	
10. Write first draft	
11. Polish first draft	
12. Consult with client	
13. Revise, revise, revise	
14. Work with photographer/designer	
15. Write titles and/or picture cut lines	
16. Edit/proof	
Totals:	

Final quote

So, what is your final quote based on?

As you should be able to tell by now, there is no magic bullet. Your quote is based on how many of the elements in the above chart are appropriate to the job and how long you think it will take to complete each task, combined with your hourly rate, your minimum rate for the type of job you are being asked to do, and the value of the job to the company. Ultimately, it is up to you to put a figure on the job and up to the prospect to accept it, reject it, or negotiate.

Before you issue your quote, it might help to ask yourself several other questions:

1. How should you position your quote: per project, per hour, per word, per page?
2. How will the client view the high, mid, and minimum prices?
3. How many quotes is the client receiving? (You can ask the client if she is getting multiple quotes.)
4. How urgent is the deadline?
5. How valuable is the work to the client's bottom line?
6. How important is the job to you?
7. How in-sync is the quote with your business vision and business plan and what you hope to earn on an annual basis?
8. How would you feel if you landed the job at the high quote? At the low quote? At the mid quote?
9. All things considered, what is your best price scenario?

What if your minimum quote is $2,500, your maximum is $5,000 and your mid-range is $3,500? What do you quote?

Ask yourself this: if I land the gig for $5,000, how would I feel? Happy, I suspect. But what if you are you bidding against others? If so, what if you low-ball it and quote $2,500 and get the job. How do you feel? Not so good? If not so good, look at your mid-range quote. Would you feel okay if that's what you were paid? If so, maybe that's what you go with. At the same time, if you are busy like crazy with jobs paying you at the high end, why would you go with mid-range payment?

With all the above in mind, decide on how much should you quote. I know this might all sound a tad vague, but you are doing this work so you can charge your clients a fair rate and so that you will be paid a fair price. Again, the more you do this, the better (and faster) you will become at it. And then, if you land the gig at your quoted rate, you might find yourself thinking, I could have quoted a higher rate! Maybe. Maybe not. The fact is, if you go through the process outlined here, both you and your client should be happy with the rate. And if you are both happy with the rate and you do a great job, then you could find yourself in a long-term relationship with a client. And that is a good place to be.

What if...?

Here are a few other quote-related *What ifs*? for you to ponder.

What if you issue a firm quote based on 10 hours of work and it takes 15 (and the scope of the job has not changed)? Live and learn. Next time you will quote more accurately.

What if it only takes eight hours to complete the job? Treat yourself to lunch. (Do not offer the client a refund!)

What if the client and you agree that a job should take about 10 hours but you have not issued a firm quote because the job is a bit nebulous? Track your time. If, when you get about six or seven hours into it, you realize it will take longer to complete, notify the client, give a new estimate on the hours required to complete the job, and agree on a new final figure.

What if you've agreed to one revision and the client asks for a second one? If it's a major revision, especially if the scope of the project has changed, it's time to speak frankly. If it's a case of cleaning up a few minor details and you sense the possibility of repeat business, give the client a freebie.

Other fee considerations

Other fee considerations may come into play. One involves being paid up front or in advance. Another involves calculating your fee for a long-term project with steady hours, or working on retainer.

Think in advance

Ask for an advance of 50 percent of your quote the first time you work with a company. I confess that I break this rule on occasion. I don't always ask for advances from well-established companies. I do ask for advances if I have never heard of the company, or if the person I am dealing with offers me the moon for work that seems a bit odd or is particularly rushed.

To get the advance, issue an invoice. If the company sends you the advance, and doesn't pay the final invoice (it happens; more on this in the next chapter) at least you haven't lost your shirt. If the company balks at paying an advance, move on because this is a sign that you would probably have trouble getting paid for your work once you've completed the job.

Retain the client

If a company offers to put you on retainer, it can be pretty cool. A retainer means you agree to devote a minimum number of hours per week or month to one particular client. You get paid for the minimum number of hours even if you do not work them (i.e., the company doesn't send you enough work to keep you busy). At the same time, if your work exceeds the agreed-upon minimum, you bill for additional hours at an agreed-upon rate.

One of the drawbacks of retainers, I've found, is that you can get lazy. You have a certain amount of money coming in each week and you slack off on marketing or turn down other jobs because you are on retainer. Then the client changes direction and cancels the retainer. She usually has to give you a negotiated notice. Even so, you will find yourself scrambling for work.

How do I know this? Been there, done that, bought the t-shirt! I am not, however, suggesting that you turn down a decent retainer. Just make sure you keep this book handy for when the retainer ends and you have to go back into marketing mode.

Issuing estimates/quotes

Now you know how much to quote. How should you present your quote?

I prefer to issue quotes in writing, and by that, I mean e-mail. That way the client and I have a record of the quote. Even when I give a quote over the phone, I follow up with an e-mailed quote. I can't remember the last time I mailed or faxed a quote, but if a client wanted me to issue the quote that way, I would.

Below, you will find sample estimates based on actual estimates I have issued. Before you issue any estimates, ask clients what they need. Some want only the bottom-line figure, the price to do the job. Others want to know how many hours and how much. Some clients want a detailed breakdown of exactly what you will be charging for.

I prefer a detailed breakdown, without the hours. That way, if the client asks me to do anything that we have not discussed—anything that goes beyond the defined scope of the original project—I can start to talk dollars and cents again, within limits. Writers are not lawyers. We don't bill on a per-second basis. At the same time, we are not doormats or footbridges or braided rag rugs. We do not let clients walk all over us!

I am suggesting that you want to find a balance between nickel-and-diming a client to death and letting a client take advantage of you. The best way to cover your assets, so to speak, is by issuing a detailed estimate that defines the scope of the project, as you understand it, after discussing it with your client.

What you cover in a reply to an RFQ

A reply to a request for quote (RFQ) or request for proposal (RFP) can cover a myriad of topics. How informal, formal, or legalistic a person are you? How informal, formal, or legalistic is your client?

The more formal you are, or your client is, the more detailed your reply should be. The higher the stakes, the more formal the reply. If you are writing and coordinating the annual report for a publicly traded Fortune 1000 company, you may even want to have a lawyer create, or at least vet, a formal contract.

Unless the client has a purchasing office that puts all of that information into one document for you to sign in triplicate, it will be up to you to put your quote, and the details it's based on, into an e-mail message (or an attached Word or PDF file).

As you will see by my replies to RFQs on the next page, I am a fairly informal person, although I don't work on handshakes.

Here are the topics your replies to RFQs can cover:

1. **Project parameters**: Number of meetings, amount of background research, your role (consultant, writer, editor, all of the above), who co-ordinates what with whom.
2. **Project details or deliverables**: Number of pages, word count, tone, style, file type to send the client, number of revisions.
3. **Project schedule**: Deadlines for completing research, interviews, outlines, first draft, second draft, final draft.
4. **Fee**: The amount and what it covers (all or any of the following: meetings, research, interviews, deliverables, revisions, any other work under project details or deliverables).
5. **Expenses**: Any out-of-pocket expenses (long distance calls and faxes, meals, travel, accommodation, supplies and so on) you can charge for; the approval process for incurring such expenses.
6. **Invoicing**: When you invoice, who you invoice, how you invoice, when you get paid.
7. **Errors, omissions, and indemnity**: Who is responsible for final approval; any penalties if errors or omissions cost the company. (I suggest that the company should be responsible for the final approval, but if you are concerned, then spell it out.)
8. **Copyright**: Who owns it? Generally, the company does, but if your work is bylined, you should clarify the matter.

Sample replies to RFQs

Here is a sample reply to an RFQ issued after a phone discussion (to define the scope of a project) with a prospect:

> Thank you for the opportunity to bid on ABC Inc.'s Y2K white paper editing and writing project.
>
> My quote (below) is based on the following criteria, as discussed:
>
> 1. Meetings and phone interviews: four hours
> 2. Read document; make notes on document structure, consistency and editing requirements: two hours

3. Edit document, with emphasis on the FAQs and Glossary: eight to ten hours
4. Research and write two additional sections (approximately five hundred words each) as discussed: twelve to fifteen hours
5. Revise the document once, based on client feedback: two to four hours

Total estimated time: up to thirty-five hours

Quote: $2,750; an advance of $1,000 due upon acceptance of this quote.

Note: This quote does not include any approved out-of-pocket expenses or any work beyond the scope of the project, as defined above. For instance, should I be asked to research and write additional sections of the document or attend more than one meeting, I would bill you $90 per hour. Such work will not commence without prior approval from you. Should the project be terminated before it is completed, I would bill you $90 per hour for any work done.

If you have any questions or comments, feel free to e-mail or call me.

I put hours in my quotes if the client wants to know how long and how much. I prefer to answer "how much" but am prepared to answer both. I estimated the job should not take more than 30 hours but built in a contingency fee, something to think about when issuing quotes for large jobs. That way you can do a little extra and feel you are being paid for it. The client, on the other hand, feels you are going the extra mile at no charge. In addition, I wanted to come in under $3,000 because the client was getting three quotes. But I covered myself with my "note" in case the client requested unexpected additional work.

Here is a follow-up e-mail, on a more nebulous project, sent after the client has agreed to a quote. Notice how it reinforces the writer's defined scope of the project so there is no misunderstanding.

Thank you for agreeing to my quote today. This e-mail is to confirm the details of the assignment. As discussed, I will write a white paper of up to ten pages (maximum) concerning the importance of the Product Name to the life insurance industry.

The focus will be on the need for the life insurance industry in North America to improve customer service and productivity and meet competitive challenges by consolidating customer policy information on a variety of legacy systems that do not communicate with each other. The white paper will present the *Product Name* as the solution.

Product Name will be positioned as a solution that helps the insurance industry preserve and extend its IT investment, while serving as the logical next step in the migration path to next-generation systems.

The white paper will be aimed at a business audience, decision makers who will consult with IT on the feasibility of implementing a solution like the Product Name. Therefore, the white paper must build a solid business case, rather than a technology case, for implementation. However, the document can include a big-picture technology overview.

As discussed, I charge $95 per hour for research—meetings, interviews, background reading, third-party information gathering (contacting firms such as IDC for stats)—and writing. I estimate that the job will take approximately fifty hours to complete but I will timesheet all activities by item, date, and hours spent. If we approach thirty hours and the job is not close to completion, I will notify you.

Our first meeting is scheduled for September 15 at 11:00 a.m. at your office in Toronto. Before the meeting, you will send me soft copy of several documents you want me to read. At the meeting, you will give me the names of industry analysts you want me to interview.

The first draft is due October 30. I will present a formal outline of the white paper, including proposed title, by October 1.

An advance of $1,500 is due upon acceptance of this quote. I will issue a final invoice at the end of the job.

If you have any questions or comments, e-mail or call me.

This was an almost open-ended project. It was to involve a great deal of background reading and a number of meetings and interviews. I had to prepare an outline that had to be reviewed and approved. The first draft would be reviewed by several people, and I was told to expect multiple revisions. It's difficult to estimate hours for a project of this nature. Not impossible, but difficult.

If the company had been asking for three quotes, I might have estimated about 60 hours of work, and I would have spelled out in detail the number of meetings, interviews and revisions. However, the company wanted me to write the white paper and was content to let me keep a timesheet.

Here is an e-mail quote on a book-editing job:

> Thank you for the opportunity to submit a quote for copy editing <Book Title> by <Author's Name>.
>
> My quote is based on the following criteria:
>
> - **Project**: Non-technical, how-to book; estimated word count: twenty-five thousand
> - **Total estimated time**: Twenty-five hours. Quote: $1,750
> - **Service Provided**: Copy editing. This will include proofreading for spelling and grammatical errors, improper punctuation, and consistency of style, as well as editing to correct confusing or awkward language or sentence structure. Edited work to be provided in Word (.doc) format.
>
> As discussed, any work beyond the scope of the project as defined (twenty-five hours) would be invoiced at $75 per hour. No additional work would commence without your approval. Should the project be terminated before it is completed, I would invoice at $75 per hour for any work done.
>
> **Start Date**: November 1, 2009
>
> **Turn Around**: Approximately three weeks from receipt of manuscript
>
> **Terms of Contract**: $500 advance. Balance due upon delivery of completed work and invoice.

If you have any questions or would like to discuss this quote, e-mail info@paullima.com or call 416-628-6005.

Additional pricing questions

Finally, here are some answers to questions about pricing that people have asked me over the years.

Q: Should I charge different rates for writing, editing and proofreading?

A: Most editors charge $50 to $75 per hour for editing ($30 to $50 per hour for proofreading; know the difference!). Most writers charge $75 to $150 per hour for writing. Look at the work before you issue a quote. Sometimes a request for proofreading (correcting spelling and grammar) is actually a request for editing (making individual sentences stronger) and a request for editing is actually a request for rewriting (restructuring a document and making sentences stronger).

Q: Are there different rate structures for Toronto and Montreal, Toronto and New York or London, or large cities and smaller centers?

A: The rates clients are willing to pay are all over the map, no matter where they are located. Smaller businesses tend to pay lower rates. Companies in smaller towns may expect to pay lower rates. But some big companies are located in small towns. Your job is to know what you want to earn and then find clients who are willing to pay that rate.

Q: I charge small businesses $55 an hour and larger clients $60 to $70 an hour. Is that a good range?

A: Quote per job based on a set hourly rate. If you don't think a small business will accept it, offer a small-business discount of 15 percent so the client can see what you normally charge. If you land better-paying gigs, tell low-paying clients that you can no longer offer the discount. They either ante up or find another writer. Overall, consider boosting your rate to $75 per hour, or more.

Q: Many entrepreneurs cannot afford standard hourly rates. What is the best way to handle this?

A: See above. If you have no work, and the only way you can land a gig is by lowering your rates, use the discount method outlined above. But also invest more time looking for better-paying clients!

Q: When you are working on a long-term project, will you work for a lower hourly rate? How do you determine what this lower rate should be?

A: How do you define long term? A few hours per week for a month, or many hours per week for months? I would not consider several hours per week for a month a long-term project. However, if I am on retainer—say a guarantee of 10 hours per week for at least two or three months—I will offer a 15 percent to 20 percent discount. Remember, a retainer means you are guaranteed a minimum number of hours. If the client does not produce work for you, you still get paid. And if you work more than the minimum, you charge for the additional hours.

Q: When I work on a subcontract, what is the lowest rate I should accept?

A: What is the lowest rate you would accept on any job? Also, how many billable hours are you working? If none, taking $50 per hour on a sub-contract is better than nothing. But... What are you doing to find regular, steady, higher-paying work?

Q: What is a normal commission/finder's fee?

A: I generally do not pay finder's fees and generally do not accept them. I have accepted a few upon passing jobs on to other service sectors, to a Web designer, for instance. And I would pay one if a writer helped me land a media-training gig, as media training is something I want to develop. However, I know writers who ask for a 10 percent or 15 percent finder's fee for passing on work to other writers. Why would they forward work? They may be too busy, or the job is not something they want (vision!) to do.

Q: Right now, I bill by the hour. I'm considering moving to a flat fee. What do you recommend?

A: How do you define flat fee? Rather than issuing a flat fee, quote per job! I can see offering a flat fee for writing media releases, as they are now commodities. And a friend of mine charges a flat fee for white papers—$500 per page. That includes two meetings, phone calls, research, writing, and two revisions. See how carefully he has defined the scope of the project? I'd want to know what the client expects of me before issuing a flat fee quote. If I am expected to come in for six meetings to write a media release, forget about the flat fee if it is a low fee. So, with that in mind, flat fee is relative!

Q: I have trouble conceptualizing the time involved for larger projects, especially meeting time and revision time. Is there a good rule of thumb for estimating these?

A: Welcome to the most difficult part of freelancing—the quote. While there is no good *rule of thumb*, experience is a great teacher. Before issuing your quote or estimate, review the Estimating a Writing Job chart. Jot down the estimated hours per item, add them up, and go from there. If you come in low and land the gig, live and learn, and do better next time.

Chapter 40: Managing the Process

As I have said, before you quote on a project, you need to define the scope of the project. That is, in fact, the first stage of managing corporate clients. If you do not manage them in a professional, politely assertive manner (emphasis on professional and polite), jobs can get out of hand.

To help you manage the process, make sure you know the information listed below. If you do not know it, ask. It may seem like a lot to ask, but the more work you do up front, the less of a chance there is for chaos and confusion down the line. Also, the second time you work with a client, the less you will have to ask. The third time, the client will ask "how much" and you'll quote a price and get to work .So it gets easier as you do more work for a client.

Here's what to ask.

Is your first contact going to be your prime or project contact?

It could be that the person who contacts you for a quote is not the person who will co-ordinate the project, and hence is not the person with whom you will be working. Clarify that. Get the project manager's name and contact information. Find out whether you are to call the project manager or the project manager is to call you.

Has the scope of the job changed?

If you get the job and are handed off to a new contact, go over the project with the new contact and clarify the scope of the job. Be prepared for change. The scope might not change, but it's your job to find out. If you have given a firm quote and the scope has changed, be prepared to discuss the changes and renegotiate your quote.

What is your working relationship with the prime contact?

Is the prime contact the person who directs you, sets up interviews with others in the organization and forwards research material to you? Do you submit all material to the prime contact? You need to know this.

Who else do you talk to, and under what circumstances?

If the prime contact requests that you interview others (in the organization, customers or suppliers), ask:

- When and how you should contact others.
- Whether they will be expecting you.
- When you should report to your prime contact for further instructions if you are having trouble hooking up with a person or having trouble accessing background research.

Who signs off; who manages the approval process?

Many companies and government ministries or agencies have complex approval or sign-off procedures. The document does not leave the building until a number of senior managers have signed off.

You need to know what your role in the approval process is. Do you simply deliver the goods to your prime contact (who is then responsible for acquiring approvals), or do you usher the project through the approval process?

Project managers tend to usher projects through the system; writers tend to revise based on information delivered through the prime contact. You have to clarify your role.

What rights are being purchased?

When a corporate client contracts with you, it's generally done on a work-for-hire basis. The client owns all rights to your work.

The company buys all rights because the work you do is generally suitable only for the client and sometimes involves a degree of confidentiality. The client can post the work on the corporate website and in various publications. Company staff can edit the work any way they want. The exception would be (or should be) if your byline appears on the work. In other words, when a company wants to use your name as the author, you should not sell all rights.

If the work is generic and not confidential and is something you can resell, you might want to keep copyright, although most companies expect to buy copyright as part of the fee they pay. If your name is associated with the work, do not sell moral rights. That way, the client cannot dramatically change the work and use it under your byline. Bottom line for me: If the client is paying a decent rate and my name is not associated with the work, they can do whatever they want with it, because it's work for hire.

Contract or confirmation letter?

Part of managing the job involves knowing if the company you are working for will be issuing a contract or a confirmation letter, or if it's up to you to do so. Either way, contacts or confirmation letters should include the following information:

- Rate paid: project rate, hourly rate, or rate per word, etc.
- Advance: if so, how much.
- Expenses; expense approval process for long distance calls, travel, and other possible out-of-pocket expenses.
- When/who do you invoice and when do you get paid? If the job will be finished in a couple of days or a couple of weeks at most, you can invoice at the end of the job. However, if this is a long-term job, you don't want to work for months before you are paid. Negotiate a payment schedule.
- What happens if the project is cancelled?

I'm sure you don't want to think about that last point; however, occasionally, a project may be cancelled for reasons beyond your control. You should not lose money because of this.

Make sure you negotiate a project-cancellation fee or kill fee. This fee is usually based on your hourly rate multiplied by the number of hours you have worked on the project. If you were working on a per-word rate and submitted the article, you should be paid the full amount. Negotiate this up front to save problems down the road.

What of the writing of the project?

Although the client has come to you for your expertise as a writer or editor, you should ask a few questions about the writing and the project before you plunge in. The more you know up front, the better able you will be to deliver the right words that will help your client achieve his or her objective.

With that in mind, consider asking your client the following questions:

1. What is the deliverable: media release, case study, white paper, brochure, website page, etc.?
2. What file type should you deliver: Word, PowerPoint, PDF, Web page, Excel, etc.?

3. What is the objective/purpose of the writing? To inform, educate, sell, persuade, lobby, entertain, etc.
4. Who is the target market? Include consumer or business demographics and other pertinent information.
5. What overall tone/style of writing is wanted? What impression does the client want to make? Some clients want to be strictly business; others want to be perceived of as fun and funky. You need to know before you write.
6. What action, if any, does your client want the reader to take?
7. Revision process and due dates for the outline, first draft, second draft...

Hurry up and wait

Knowing all of the above will help you manage the project from your end. However, the company's end of the project may produce delays over which you have no control. If something does not arrive the day it is due, if an interviewee is suddenly unavailable, keep your prime contact informed. It's entirely possible that she does not know something has gone awry. A quick call or e-mail may be all that is required to get the project back on track.

Expect delays. In the corporate and government environment, it's hurry up... and then wait.

It has to do with internal politics, complex approval processes, sudden shifts in direction, and the fact that most organizations are run on the fly. If you know this beforehand, it can save you a great deal of aggravation. Just be sure you have your ducks lined up and that you are keeping your end of the deal.

Invoices and receivables

After all that work, I'm sure you want to be paid. That means you have to invoice the company. It also means you have to keep an eye on your receivables (the money owed to you).

You can easily create an invoice in Word. Some writers use Excel, especially if they keep a timesheet in Excel. I use Excel for timesheets and create my invoices in Word. For projects where I am paid per hour, I e-mail both my invoice and my timesheet.

The timesheet shows dates, items (what I worked on), hours spent and the total hours/fee for the work done each day. The items include research and background reading, writing, revisions, meetings and anything else related to the job, including phone calls and reading/replying to e-mails.

Invoices (see sample, next page) are relatively simple, but important, documents. They include:

1. Client's name and address (even if sent by e-mail).
2. Date issued.
3. Invoice number (for tracking).
4. PO# (purchase order number), if one was issued by the client.
5. A brief description of the job (commencement speech for CEO as assigned by prime contact's name).
6. Amount due (based on a quote, hours worked or number of words written).
7. Any applicable taxes and expenses (long distance calls, travel, copying).
8. If you work in Canada and do not have a GST number, register for one. (See www.cra-arc.gc.ca/bnfts/gsthst/menu-eng.html for more information.). Even if you are not required to have a GST number (you need one if you earn over $30,000 per year) you should have one because corporate clients in Canada expect businesses to have GST numbers. And you are in business, are you not?
9. Date invoice is due. I like to use "payable upon receipt" unless I've negotiated other terms. Some companies have a policy of paying in 30 days, although some larger corporations can take 60 to 90 days to pay. Whatever the case, remind the company in your invoice when the bill is due.
10. Who the cheque is payable to (along with your address, phone/fax number, e-mail address).

Here is a sample of an invoice that you might send a client. If you have accounting software that produces invoices, use it. However, if you do not, feel free to create an invoice based on this one.

The most important thing when invoicing a client is to clearly identify yourself, the client, the job, the fee, and, of course, your address. In other words, don't create confusion when you invoice a client. That only creates payment delays.

I've seen invoices that include little more than the writer's name, address, and an amount. Such invoice may get paid, eventually, after the client has sent it to accounting and accounting has sent it back, asking the client to ask the writer to send a clearer, more meaningful invoice that they can pay.

Sample e-mail Invoice

To:	<Contact Name>	**From**:	Paul Lima
Company:	<Company Name>	**Phone**:	(416) xxx-xxxx
E-mail:	<Contact e-mail>	**Pages**:	1
Re.:	Invoice #: PL###	**Date**:	<Date>

Item: PO # (if applicable)	Amount:
Research, write and edit 750-word case study on <topic> for <Company Name>; assigned by <Contact Name>	$1,000.00
Billable expenses	N/A
*GST/HST# R11010101	130.00
Total:	$1,130.00

Payment due upon receipt, unless otherwise negotiated. Send cheque to:

Paul Lima
<Address>

If you have any questions or comments, please e-mail me or feel free to call (416) 628-6005.

Regards,
Paul Lima

*****Note**: GST/HST is a tax charged on all services in Canada. Some provinces charge HST (GST combined with a provincial tax); others charge only GST. Make sure you talk to an accountant or tax expert to find out if you need to charge taxes on your services, and how much you need to charge.

Cheque is in the mail

Once you send your invoice, you need to track payment. You can use a spreadsheet program such as Excel, accounting software or Tasks in Outlook.

If you are not paid in the agreed-upon time (or within a week of the agreed-upon time), e-mail your contact and say something like, "I am following up on invoice X, sent on such-and-such date, for which I have not been paid." It may take your contact a few days to get back to you. Usually, you will hear "the cheque is in the mail" and it will arrive. Sometimes you will be asked to re-invoice. Do so. Companies lose invoices all the time. But sometimes there are problems and you will have to make business decisions around money, which most of us hate to do!

Will you take less?

I once did some sub-contract work for a company (call it Company A) that was co-coordinating a massive shareholders' meeting for Company B. By the time payment was due, Company B was under financial duress. Company A got only $0.75 on the dollar, which is what Company A then offered me.

I had two choices: insist on my full rate (and take the company to court) or settle. I chose to settle and move on. I didn't want the hassle of a court case, especially one I might lose. But I know other writers who would have gone to court. The decision, should this ever happen to you, is yours to make.

I based my decision on answers to the following:

1. What is my time worth?
2. How much time would a court battle take?
3. Would I win?
4. How much would I lose in billable hours by fighting the court case?

Ripped off?

You may run into occasions where the company you are working for has severe financial problems and cannot pay, or times when an unscrupulous business owner deliberately rips you off. I don't know what to say other than, sometimes you don't get paid. It happens to most businesses.

Your job is to minimize such losses. If you do due diligence—ask for an advance, ask for a purchase-order number and ask for references so you can speak to other sub-contractors who have done work for the company—you should be okay. But now and then, you might run into problems.

You can cry. You can rant. You can be a squeaky wheel (recommended). You might get some or all of your money. You can take a company to small claims court. At some point, you might have to cut your losses. It hurts. It happens. Move on. Find better clients!

Generate repeat business

Look, we're back to marketing!

If you generate fair quotes, if you clarify your working relationship with the client and manage the project well at your end, if you deliver clean, well-written copy, if you meet your word count, if you meet your deadlines... you will, in most cases, generate repeat business.

Why only in most cases? Sometimes the client has no more work. Sometimes the client likes to use a variety of writers for a variety of projects. Sometimes your contact leaves the company and the new person wants to establish his or her own stable of writers. Sometimes a company likes to make changes for no rational reason. Sometimes the client hires someone full time. Sometimes the client actually forgets you exist. If any of that happens, don't take it personally.

But remember, it's your job—part of your marketing effort—to actively generate repeat business.

Because we are talking $$$

Unless you love to do your taxes and handle financial matters like pension or retirement savings plans, find an accountant or tax expert who can do them for you (and advise you on how to handle HST/GST, if applicable). Discuss deductions, appropriate bookkeeping methods, registered retirement savings plan and pension plan contributions with your accountant. He can save you hundreds, or even thousands, of dollars.

Chapter 41: Cold Call Tips; Final Notes

Some people seem to be naturals at cold calling. Others need help. Either way, cold calling is an important way of developing your freelance writing business. The cold call tips below were originally presented by freelance writer Adrian Blake (www.adrianblake.com) and are reprinted with permission.

Here are eight tips to help boost your confidence when it comes to selling yourself, and your writing services, over the phone.

Loosen up!

Before you sit down at your desk and make that first call, it's important to limber up your brain and your tongue. It helps to reduce any nervousness you normally have before making calls.

Watch your posture

You may prefer to either sit or stand when making calls. Standing helps to dissipate nervous energy. If you're sitting, keep your back straight, your shoulders back and your head up, not cradling the phone on your shoulder. Proper posture helps project your voice and gives you a more confident-sounding tone.

Smile

A smile projects a friendly tone and makes an instant positive connection with your prospect. Place a mirror in front of you so you can check your smile when making calls.

Rehearse

Rehearse your script so it flows smoothly. Practice with a marketing buddy first. Tape your calls so that you can hear how you sound to a prospect.

Get into a routine

Make your calls at the same time every day, preferably in the morning. It's better to try to reach your prospects early to avoid gatekeepers. Don't do anything else when you make calls so that you're not distracted.

Target the decision maker

Make sure you target the highest person on the corporate ladder or the one who is in charge of the particular department you're interested in. They are the people who have the power to hire you. It's best to start at the top, i.e., president or CEO, and then be referred down.

Deliver your message assertively

When you get your prospect on the phone, use a strong, clear voice. Your message should be only 20 seconds. State your name, who you are and the main services you offer. Then, ask: "Do you work with freelance writers?" Yes or No are both opportunities. Voice-mail is an opportunity to leave a free 20-second commercial.

Follow up

Too many small-business owners fail to follow up on calls. Persistence pays.

Final notes

I hope you have found the information in this book practical and worthwhile. I know that what I have presented works for me. I hope it works for you as well. All the best with your business!

You can stop reading now, but if I may, I'd like to write a bit more—about my seminars, e-courses, and other books. Also, look for writers' organizations and associations in your area that offer professional development opportunities and check courses at local community colleges and universities. While the professional development is important, attending courses and workshops also gives you the opportunity to network with other writers.

About the Author

I was seven years old when I published my first magazine. Using a stubby pencil, I meticulously printed articles about members of my family and illustrated the articles with crayon art. I produced only one copy of the magazine, but my entire family read "The Lima News." I had great fun doing it and words have been an important part of my life ever since...

That's a lovely story, isn't it? However, when I want to sell myself as a writer, I strike a different tone.

Based in Toronto, Ontario, Paul Lima (www.paullima.com) has worked as a professional writer and business-writing instructor for over 25 years. He has run a successful freelance writing, copywriting, business writing, and media relations training business since 1988.

For corporate clients: Paul writes news releases, case studies, copy for direct-response brochures, sales letters, advertisements, and other material.

For newspapers and magazines: Paul writes about small business and technology issues. His articles have appeared in *The Globe and Mail, Toronto Star, National Post, Backbone, Profit, CBC.ca,* and many other publications.

Qualified educator: Paul presents in-person and online seminars on business writing, creative writing, search engine optimization, and the business of freelance writing.

Seminars, workshops, and e-courses: Paul offers various seminars, workshops, and e-courses on the business of freelance writing, writing for newspapers and magazines, and business writing. Read more about his seminars, workshops, and e-courses online at www.paullima.com/workshops and www.paullima.com/ecourses.

Education and other experience: An English major from York University and a member of the Professional Writers Association of

Canada, Paul has worked as an advertising copywriter, continuing education manager, and magazine editor.

Additional books by Paul Lima

Paul is the author of 10 books, all part of the Workshop in a Book series:

- *How To Write A Non-Fiction Book in 60 Days*
- *Harness the Business Writing Process*
- *Everything You Wanted to Know About Freelance Writing...*
- *The Six-Figure Freelancer: How to Find, Price and Manage Corporate Writing Assignments*
- *Business of Freelance Writing: How to Develop Article Ideas and Sell Them to Newspapers and Magazines*
- *Copywriting That Works: Bright ideas to Help You Inform, Persuade, Motivate and Sell!*
- *How to Write Media Releases to Promote Your Business, Organization or Event*
- *Do you Know Where Your website Ranks? How to Optimize Your website for the Best Possible Search Engine Results*
- *Build A Better Business Foundation: Create a Business Vision, Write a Business Plan, Produce a Marketing Plan.*
- *(re)Discover the Joy of Creative Writing*
- *If You Don't Know Where You are Going, How are You Going to Get There? Business Vision Short eReport*
- *Building Your Business Plan and Your Marketing Plan: A Step-By-Step Guide to Planning and Promoting Your Business Short eReport*
- *Put Time On Your Side: Time Management Short eReport.*

All books and short reports are available online in print and/or digital format, from www.paullima.com/books.